RENEWALS 458-4574

© Nathan Wiseman-Trowse 2008

All rights reserved. No reproduction, copy or transmission of this publication may be made without written permission.

No portion of this publication may be reproduced, copied or transmitted save with written permission or in accordance with the provisions of the Copyright, Designs and Patents Act 1988, or under the terms of any licence permitting limited copying issued by the Copyright Licensing Agency, Saffron House, 6-10 Kirby Street, London EC1N 8TS.

Any person who does any unauthorized act in relation to this publication may be liable to criminal prosecution and civil claims for damages.

The author has asserted his right to be identified as the author of this work in accordance with the Copyright, Designs and Patents Act 1988.

First published 2008 by
PALGRAVE MACMILLAN

Palgrave Macmillan in the UK is an imprint of Macmillan Publishers Limited, registered in England, company number 785998, of Houndmills, Basingstoke, Hampshire RG21 6XS.

Palgrave Macmillan in the US is a division of St Martin's Press LLC, 175 Fifth Avenue, New York, NY 10010.

Palgrave Macmillan is the global academic imprint of the above companies and has companies and representatives throughout the world.

Palgrave® and Macmillan® are registered trademarks in the United States, the United Kingdom, Europe and other countries.

ISBN-13: 978–0–230–21949–6 hardback
ISBN-10: 0–230–21949–7 hardback

This book is printed on paper suitable for recycling and made from fully managed and sustained forest sources. Logging, pulping and manufacturing processes are expected to conform to the environmental regulations of the country of origin.

A catalogue record for this book is available from the British Library.

Library of Congress Cataloging-in-Publication Data
Wiseman-Trowse, Nathan.
    Performing class in British popular music / Nathan Wiseman-Trowse.
       p.   cm.
    Includes bibliographical references, discography, and index.
    ISBN 978–0–230–21949–6
    1. Popular music—Social aspects—Great Britain.
    2. Popular music—Great Britain—History and criticism.   I. Title.
    ML3918.P67W57 2008
    781.64086'20941—dc22   2008021223

10   9   8   7   6   5   4   3   2   1
17   16   15   14   13   12   11   10   09   08

Printed and bound in Great Britain by
CPI Antony Rowe, Chippenham and Eastbourne

Library
University of Texas
at San Antonio

Performing Class in British Popular Music

Nathan Wiseman-Trowse

Senior Lecturer in Popular Culture, University of Northampton, UK

WITHDRAWN
UTSA LIBRARIES

palgrave
macmillan

Library
University of Texas
at San Antonio

Performing Class in British Popular Music

For Kelly

Contents

1
Introduction: A Class Act

On 14 August 1995 British popular music reached a significant point in its history. A fulcrum of tensions that had been prevalent for over a century came to a climax (albeit a temporary one) through the simple act of two bands releasing singles on the same day. Blur's release of 'Country House' alongside Oasis' 'Roll With It' was more than a simple story of two competing young British bands trying to outmanoeuvre each other. It was class war. The implications of Blur and Oasis both competing for the number one slot in the British singles chart were profound enough that the BBC evening news carried a story on the event alongside numerous accounts by the tabloid and broadsheet press. What caused a relatively simple account of rivalry between two guitar bands to be of such importance to the nation as a whole? Certainly the soap opera of British pop life rarely made any significant impact outside of the pages of *New Musical Express*, *Melody Maker*, *Q* or *Select* magazines, yet the country, for one week, was gripped by the race for the top slot.

The answer, at least to a significant extent, is class. Blur were from the suburban Essex town of Colchester, Oasis from Burnage, a somewhat rundown satellite of Manchester. Blur were art school students, Oasis were lads on the dole. Blur were knowing, playful and ironic, Oasis were straightforward, direct and hedonistic. Blur were southern and middle class, Oasis were anything but. When Blur beat Oasis to the number one position on Sunday, 20 August 1995, many assumed that some kind of battle had been won; however, Oasis were going to make it clear that they were going to win the war. By September Blur released their fourth album, *The Great Escape* (1995), to good reviews but disappointing sales while a month later Oasis' *(What's the Story) Morning Glory* (1995) would

1

commence a path to three Brit awards in 1996, global sales of over 19 million units and more than two years in the British album charts. While it is not the purpose of relating this event to understand why Blur were ultimately less popular, the contest between 'Country House' and 'Roll With It' illustrated in spectacular fashion two competing (and sometimes complicit) strands that stretch through British popular music: working-class grit and middle-class artistry. As *New Musical Express* journalist Anthony Thornton put it,

> The single theme of British music of the last decade has remained constant: no one likes a smart-arse ... But then of course it's Oasis' fault that we find ourselves at this juncture. They beat Blur so comprehensively – so completely – that, to be in a band and be smart, to challenge assumptions, or go out on a limb became unthinkable. The amazing lineage of British art-school bands simply fizzled out: The Beatles, The Who, The Stones, Roxy Music, Sex Pistols, Wire, Blur and nothing. Since then, all the new big and important bands have been salt-of-the-earth types (Stereophonics) or sweeping romantics (Coldplay).
>
> (2004)

Certainly the tensions between Blur and Oasis seemed to be oriented around issues of authenticity. Following the release of Blur's *Parklife* album in 1994, the band had not only had their most successful album to date, but they had also been highly criticized for being 'mockneys', wrapping the band up in the iconography of the East End of London and the Thames Estuary. Such an approach seemed at odds with their previous incarnations and their well-known roots in suburban Colchester. While both *Parklife* and *The Great Escape* tap into a particular theme of British popular music, an ironic engagement with the mundane, everyday life of little England (The Kinks, The Who, The Small Faces), they seemed too capable of slipping in and out of differing styles and identities to be truly authentic. Oasis, on the other hand, were a straightforward rock band singing songs firmly fixed (at least on their debut album *Definitely Maybe* (1994)) in the geography and vernacular of northern working-class culture (as it stood in the early 1990s) articulating the dreams of a gang of lads yearning for a life of fame and excess. While Blur were as praised in the British music press at the time as Oasis, the clash of idiomatic approaches to rock music highlighted a crisis that has haunted popular music for over a century.

The purpose of this work is to explore the ways in which representations of class in British popular music are used to articulate authenticity.

This will be achieved by looking at particular flashpoints around which issues of class have arisen through the history of British popular music. As such its remit is by no means exhaustive, yet it will provide a model to understand the use of class in other areas of popular music. Equally, class is very rarely the only issue at stake when listening to a piece of popular music (if at all). Issues such as gender, ethnicity, age and religion can all have an effect on the way in which one engages with a piece of popular music. However, this book deliberately sidelines such considerations (although gender and race are influencing factors that are discussed where they intersect with class), concentrating instead on class as a signifier of authenticity. As such the focus in this work on class should be understood only as part of a larger story. However, its role leads us to significant conclusions about the ways in which a listener identifies and uses a musical text. Particularly, the role that class has to play in authenticating a piece of music leads us to a number of conclusions relating to subjectivity and the listening experience (for a fuller example of the interrelations between musical texts and identity, see Hawkins, 2002. However, Hawkins' work tends not to deal with the issue of class in any direct sense).

One might wonder why popular music should require a concept such as authenticity, and further why should it be such a hotly contested issue? As Thornton's claims show, in the nine years between the Blur/Oasis battle and his review of Franz Ferdinand's eponymous debut album (2004), from which the above quotation is taken, the focus had been most definitely on bands who shunned experimentation in a musical sense and irony and subversion in a lyrical sense. Instead bands such as Stereophonics, working-class Welsh lads singing songs about life in a small town, fitted into a climate that fostered a visible link between the singer, the song and the 'real world'. This desire to ground popular music in everyday experience, an experience that is recognizable as being that of both the performer as well as the audience, is a desire that can be seen throughout the history of popular music not only in the United Kingdom but around the globe. Richard Middleton (1990) suggests that the academic study of popular music has brought with it a focus on the concept of authenticity, a focus that prioritizes it because 'honesty (truth to cultural experience) becomes the validating criterion of musical value' (197). In other words, 'authentic' popular music becomes valuable because it speaks of the people who create it and the cultural and social environment from which it comes. For academics, particularly those influenced by a critical theory interested in the individual's relation to capitalism and its alienating effects, authenticity is often a marker of resistance and subversion, voiced in a number of ways across differing temporal and spatial environments.

The role of class signification in popular music is often used as a means by which to articulate authenticity, and as the above chart battle shows, authenticity is not always open to all class positions. While Blur fit into a tradition of English songwriting that allows for musical experimentation and lyrical irony, their position as middle-class art school boys – a position most commonly articulated outside of the musical texts themselves in the music press and other ancillary media surrounding popular music – places them at a disadvantage. While any cursory investigation of popular music over the last century reveals its amorphous relationship to differing class positions, working-class experience has been consistently valorized, particularly in the United Kingdom. The focus of this work will be primarily upon British musical traditions, but it is worth noting that working-class experience acts as a provider of authenticity in other cultures. For example, Petersen (1997), Malone (2002), Cantwell (1996) and Fox (2004) illustrate the relationship between constructions and articulations of class identity and authenticity in country and folk music in the United States. While their work certainly lends itself to a broader discussion of class in popular music, the focus here will remain upon British forms primarily because working-class identity carries its own specific resonance in Britain, a resonance that connects to pop music culture in particular ways. To broaden such an account to American idioms, or more broadly global idioms that would take into account the specificities of class identities outside the United Kingdom, would be a monumental task. Equally, the role of class in British popular music carries with it its own very specific preoccupations that do not necessarily carry over easily into other cultural and social scenarios. Yet the focus on the representation of class in Britain tells us much about the way in which class operates in popular music on a more global scale.

If class representation, be it lyrical, musical or visual, operates as a reassurance of authenticity, why is authenticity needed? Popular music has often been seen as a highly disposable commodity, yet authenticity requires us to believe that it is something more, that the singer of the song is in some way making a claim about their relation to lived experience outside of popular music culture. This work understands authenticity as a necessary strategy to counter the seemingly paradoxical relationship between art and commerce displayed within popular music culture. If one is capable of identifying a piece of music as being in some way authentic, then there is some level of reassurance that what you are listening to is not merely another piece of mass-produced pop fluff that thousands of other people are enjoying. It has the capability to mean something to you, to be more than just entertainment, to not only connect you with the performer in a psychological way but also to commune with social groups who value the authenticity of performance in similar ways as yourself.

However, it is not enough to say that if class positions are articulated in popular music as a carrier of values of authenticity, that representation of class is merely a musical version of class positions as they exist in society. Rock music, in its variety of form and genre, constructs class representation to suit its own ends and in particular ways that are often at odds with the world outside. This is primarily achieved through connection with a *folk voice* within popular musical forms that has historically been attributed to working-class experience since the Industrial Revolution in Britain. This folk voice can be understood as a perception of popular music being *of the people*, or more specifically, the working classes. It is a voice that gets invoked throughout the history of British popular music following the urbanization of the agricultural population following the birth of the modern British industrial landscape. It shapes the way in which class is represented, and particularly valorizes working-class experience in popular music as an assurance of authenticity.

Chapter 2 interrogates the ways in which class has been understood in relation to subjectivity, an understanding that has traditionally been attributed to subcultural activity.[1] From the analyses of Marx and Weber and through Bourdieu's work on status, to more contemporary understandings of class, the emphasis will be removed from understanding cultural representations of class as being direct manifestations of class positions in a socio-economic sense. Instead class identity is understood as a relatively mobile form of subjectivity that can be invoked through cultural texts such as popular music. This distinction is significant because it allows for participation in class identities that may not be in accordance with an audience's actual social background. The ways in which popular music texts represent class will also be understood as particular manifestations of class identity that are specifically informed by 'rock discourse'.[2] This discourse – created around popular music texts by music journalism, marketing and promotion, music videos, performance practice and fan culture, as well as through popular music itself by the accumulation of textual values across time and space – shapes class representation in certain ways to reinforce and construct authenticity.

Chapter 3 goes on to explore the role of authenticity in popular music, and the ways in which authenticity has been understood to operate.

Authenticity here is understood not as a value in itself but rather as a value constructed in opposition to inauthentic forms (often mainstream pop music). As suggested above, authenticity works as a strategy to mask the commercial aspects of popular music. Almost all music that we hear is in some form shaped by commercial imperatives, and defining a piece of music as being in some way authentic (class representation is often a means by which to make such claims) allows the listener to reconcile, or rather deny, the commercial form that that music is part of. The implications of this are further explored in Chapter 4, which takes the idea of using authenticity as a strategy to counter commercialization to a subjective level. That rock music is clearly capable of meaning so much to those who listen to it suggests that authenticity is not only a strategy to confirm integrity over commercial imperatives for a piece of music. It is more significantly a strategy by which subjectivity is understood to be unmediated by capital, while the subject is at the same time taking part in a web of identification that exists within flows of capital. As such, the performance of class positions as an assurance of authenticity has implications for the subjectivity of the listener and his or her relationship to the music industry. By invoking the folk voice, rock music reinforces its own integrity in ways that are specific to rock music. Equally such invocations can be highly temporary, often used for as long as a song takes to be experienced. The work of Judith Butler, a writer usually associated with the performance of gendered identities, provides us with a model of identity that relies upon the performance of pre-existing subjectivities provided by a discursive field, in this case rock discourse. The implication of understanding class representation as a performative strategy afforded by rock discourse to mask its own industrialized and commercial nature is that the listening subjectivity is potentially forged by the text and appropriate ways of engaging with that text. Of course not all listeners will respond or engage with the proffered subjectivity in the same way, but regardless of the reaction to a piece of music, it is always in the last instance informed by rock discourse, even if it is resisted. It is in this resistance, or ambivalence, that rock discourse shapes class identities in its own reaction to more dominant social discourses of class outside of popular music. It is in this site of performative resistance that rock authenticity is forged.

Chapter 5 explores the evolution of the folk voice in British culture, from its roots in the archiving and construction of a folk tradition by collectors such as A L Lloyd and Cecil Sharp, through the incorporation of aspects of rock 'n' roll in the 1950s into the folk voice and on to contemporary rock discourse. This voice can be understood not as an organic strain that mysteriously articulates itself from the people, but rather as an idiom that is constructed, again in opposition to more commercial forms and the perceived encroachment of bourgeois values, through various forms of popular music and, more specifically, rock music.

Chapters 6, 7 and 8 consist of case studies that trace the development and articulation of the folk voice at different times through British popular music after the advent of rock 'n' roll in the late 1950s. These case studies not only utilize a performative approach to understanding class, but, by definition, also trace influential factors that help to shape the interpretation of class signification that may be outside of the boundaries of class at first glance. Equally, while the focus of this work is on British popular music, where appropriate I will look at non-British music (American hardcore, for example) to illustrate British conceptual developments.

The first case study looks at the conflation of folk and rock music at the end of the 1960s. Here the idea of folk music as a form that needs protecting to maintain its status as an organic, socially motivated musical form with links to tradition and heritage is supplanted by its integration with rock music. While many artists involved in the folk rock scenes understood their contemporary approach to folk as an updating of an increasingly ossified musical form, the effect of the engagement with rock music was largely to transform folk from being particularly a voice of the people into a catch-all term for (often) acoustic musics that connoted authenticity through a lack of mediation in performance (acousticity) and a romantic ideal of the pastoral that stood in opposition to industrialization and modernity (and by implication the commodification of music itself).

The commodification of rock music assumes particular significance in the second case study, concerned as it is with the British punk movement. While punk has often been caricatured as music belonging to working-class youth, such assertions have increasingly been difficult to maintain. However, the fact that it has consistently prioritized itself in this way says much about how it constructs its own values of authenticity in relation to rock discourse. The case study shows how the punk offshoot Oi!, and hardcore in America, have come to exist as musical strategies to deal with the internal contradictions of the first wave of British punk rock. Both genres affirm working-class solidarity, and particularly do so in a way that grants working-class subjectivity a primarily masculine character. In this way class within popular music can be understood as gendered. The implication of gendered class identities reveals much about how those class identities are granted specific values within rock discourse.

The final case study in Chapter 8, regarding the relationship between the 'shoegazing' or 'dream pop' scene and the emergent 'Madchester' phenomenon within British indie culture at the end of the 1980s, goes even further to demonstrate the ways in which class identity assumes a gendered subjectivity, particularly influenced by the role of the weekly British music press. The middle-class (southern, feminized) introspection of dream pop is set directly at odds with the working-class (northern, masculinized) hedonism of Madchester, a pattern that would later be replicated in the battle between Blur and Oasis during the height of the Britpop phenomenon.

It is worth noting at this point that the case studies are not so much an application of a specific theoretical model. Rather, they are examinations of the prevailing strains of discourse surrounding certain musical and cultural moments. What ties them together is an examination of authenticity that has class as its central theme. In the case of musical moments such as the shoegazing phenomenon, class is significant largely because of its absence in the musical text, at least in an explicit fashion. However, it plays a role in a network of associations that go to shape musical meaning and as such is relevant to this work. As noted above, issues of race and gender are equally complicit in the construction of authenticity in popular music, but they are only of concern here in the ways in which they intersect explicitly with class. In this way one might understand class positions to be gendered in certain ways, but gender itself, or indeed race, is not the focus of this work.[3]

Two moments from the Britpop documentary *Live Forever* (2003) go some way towards outlining the territory within which articulations of class in British popular music take place. Oasis' Noel Gallagher suggests to the interviewer, referring to Blur, that he 'worked on building sites, that fundamentally makes my soul a lot more purer than theirs'. Gallagher's assertion that his band is in some way more authentic than Blur because of his background may be ironic, and Albarn's sarcastic reaction to the issue of authenticity and class may be clear later in the documentary:

> Interviewer – 'The strange thing about it is that you were suddenly, Blur were the sort of inauthentic, middle class pop band and Oasis were the real, gritty working class heroes.'
> Damon Albarn – 'Hmmm'
> Interviewer – 'How did you feel about that?'
> Damon Albarn – 'That was a very intelligent observation by whoever made that wasn't it.'

(*Live Forever*, 2003)

But both Gallagher and Albarn are more than aware of the role that their class background has played in their careers. The important point here, though, is that their class is only as important as rock discourse makes it. The reality of Gallagher's or Albarn's social context is not the motivating factor that grants authenticity or not. Rather, class within British popular music works in a way that is particular to rock discourse. It is a method by which working-class identity can be prioritized as a carrier of a folk voice at odds with the obvious commercialization of popular music on a more general level. It is a masking of the conditions of production, conditions that from a performative standpoint have deep implications for the subject's relationship to commerce. As the comedian Robert Newman ironically points out, 'if this is not a remembered part of our history, what possible significance could that have in and of itself?' (Newman, 2006). While he is talking about his attempts to uncover hidden facets of Middle Eastern political history through his comedy routines, his point holds true in relation to the performance of class in British popular music. The reality of class is not as important as the way in which it is remembered and articulated. Remembrance and recognition are achieved in representation, and rock discourse represents class identity in specific ways that maintain its own concerns. To expect popular music to act in a documentary fashion in relation to class is perhaps asking the impossible. Popular music can only ever act as a prismatic lens through which lived relations are refracted in ways particular to its own discourse, as they are remembered or iterated across time.

Class representation then acts as a way to mask what popular music inherently is, by providing subjective identities through performance that position themselves (usually) in opposition to the very industrialized form that grants that identity. It is this contradiction that not only causes working-class subjectivity to become an icon of authenticity, but also positions that authenticity only ever as a performance, detached from social relations outside of that form. As such, contradiction is not only a problem for understanding class within popular music, it is the very fire from which it is born.

2
Class and Popular Music Theory

In 1996 Jan Pakulski and Malcolm Waters published *The Death of Class*, a pronouncement upon the demise of class as a useful method of social and cultural analysis. In the face of globalization and the collapse of any viable alternative to free market capitalism, they claimed that class had ceased to be a relevant social concept. Social inequalities had become centred around consumption rather than production. Whether this is so or not is largely irrelevant to this work; popular music has and continues to engage with the idea of class and it is the purpose of this research to understand why class has consistently maintained a presence in the worlds of pop and rock music. Equally, despite Pakulski and Waters' reservations, class has continued to play an important role within the disciplines of sociology and cultural studies, even if it is a rapidly evolving role.

There are a number of reasons for choosing to incorporate class into an analysis of popular music. Initially, it might be to examine potential audiences, particularly from an ethnographic point of view. Such an analysis might use the concept of class position, amongst other factors, to account for the uses and gratifications that popular music might provide for audience members. In this sense the class position of the listener/consumer could be said to act as a nexus (amongst others) around which meaning might be created and thus interpreted by the ethnographer. A second approach might be to look at the musical or lyrical text itself. Lyrical or even musical signifiers of class within a particular piece of music could suggest certain class positions being prioritized, derided, celebrated or lampooned. From this textual starting point one may be tempted to examine the listener/consumer's reaction, and again the researcher may well take the listener's own class position as a determinant factor in the music's reception and use. Another way of using class might be to explore the class positions of music practitioners and producers themselves, particularly at the local, cottage industry level of musical production. The forms of interaction and involvement, particularly in relation to musical communities, might then say something significant about pop music and class.

What the above approaches all share is a response to class, and perceptions of class, which focuses on objectively determined rationales of social positioning. While the very concept of class can be difficult to pin down, attempts to analyse it in relation to pop music, from within both the fields of sociology and cultural studies, have traditionally seen the determinant of class as a given. In other words, the listener is defined, at least to an extent, by his or her class position, and hence the listener's relationship to the musical text, productive community or critical commentary hinges upon this one determinant position.[1] At first glance this does not seem overly problematic. The researcher may be able to ascertain the listener's class position and extrapolate conclusions about musical taste, reception or consumption from that starting point, taking socio-economic stratification as a guide to patterns of leisure consumption. Even were we to factor in the differences between class as determined by economic, social or geographical determinants, or class as a category of self-perception, it might still be possible to perceive the subject as operating within a specific class category within a given period of study. Such an association would provide for a reading of punk, for example, as a primarily working-class music, produced by working-class practitioners and consumed by working-class youth.[2] Equally, one might be able to explain the popularity of progressive rock amongst suburban middle-class listeners in such terms.

Class and cultural studies

There are historical reasons for such an approach to class within academia having become predominant. In the first instance, it is imperative to understand that the evolution of the study of popular music has grown not only out of a textual approach to literary work, but also from the study of youth culture and subcultures, most notably forged in the United Kingdom by the Centre for Contemporary Cultural Studies at the University of Birmingham.[3] Here class is often seen as a determining factor in the relationship between youth groups and popular music (amongst other factors such as style, argot and territory). This approach has been equally informed (although its focus and aims are somewhat divergent) by the work of American sociologists such as Albert Cohen

(1955), and the Chicago School of sociologists, who initiated the study of subcultures by investigating urban delinquency during the 1940s and 1950s. For Cohen, subcultures allowed disenfranchised youths to form their own social hierarchies, defined in terms of shared characteristics within the subculture. Such a strategy had the effect of valorizing the nonconformist elements of subcultural interaction (delinquency, deviance), which in turn allowed the link to be made by the CCCS writers between oppositional style and ideological resistance. In other words, the social placing of subcultures became a locus around which analysis took place, a pivot that defined subcultural activity either in terms of working-class delinquency (in the first instance) or working-class agency and resistance (in the second). Hodkinson (2002) provides a succinct critique of both the Chicago and Birmingham approaches to subcultural theory when he suggests that,

> ... through their theoretical emphasis on the solving of status problems in one case, and on symbolic structural resistance in the other, both traditions present an overly simplistic opposition between subculture and dominant culture... While Albert Cohen assumes that subcultures solve the same status problems for all members, Birmingham theorists presuppose the existence of singular, subversive meanings of subcultural styles which, ultimately, reflected the shared class position of participants. (11)

This trajectory has had, in broad terms, the effect of equating youth with delinquency, and as the study of subcultures progressed into the late 1970s and early 1980s, the consequent effect was that class, particularly working-class experience (and dissatisfaction with working-class experience in the social realm), came to define any analysis of subcultural experience. As a result the study of popular music has been caught up with the preoccupation of class as a relatively static determining factor, precisely because the study of subcultures and popular music have been so intimately linked. Perhaps the most well-known example of such a link is Dick Hebdige's *Subculture: The Meaning of Style* (1979) which sees subcultural activity as a strategy amongst working-class youth to position themselves in relation to a parent culture that has become increasingly irrelevant, and to define a sense of self that does make sense in relation to like-minded individuals (echoed by Cohen, 1972). Class is at the heart of the motivations behind subcultural activity for Hebdige, and as such the music associated with glam rockers, teds and punks equally becomes a matter of class. In other words, such music acts as another tool to articulate a particular class-consciousness, albeit one refracted through subcultural idioms. As stated above, this might not be problematic if popular music worked in a simple, documentary fashion, that is to say that it responded to class in a way that replicated class in an unproblematic and unmediated form. However, as the following chapters will show, class is rarely treated in a straightforward manner by popular music.

Class and subculture

The focus on class within subcultural activity is understandable for a number of reasons. In the first instance, the approaches of both the Chicago and Birmingham Schools understood subcultures as an effect of class positions. Subcultural activity becomes a means by which disenfranchised working-class youth may exert some level of agency and control in the world. Hebdige saw class as the factor that defined a social group's ability to articulate ideological signification:

> If we pause to reflect for a moment, it should be obvious that access to the means by which ideas are disseminated in our society (i.e. principally the mass media) is *not* the same for all classes. Some groups have more say, more opportunity to make the rules, to organize meaning, while others are less favourably placed, have less power to produce and impose their definitions of the world on the world.
>
> (Hebdige, 14)

Hebdige's focus is on the amount of agency and power that social groups can exert, and given the perceived lack of counter-hegemonic power held by the working classes, subcultures represent an alternative form of ideological resistance. Such power is then inherently placed within class and because of class, performing a role that has a potential to escape conventional social stratification while being initially defined by it. When Hebdige talks of the incorporation of spectacular subcultures into mainstream society, he outlines a model that in the first instance demonizes subcultures in the mainstream media, and then situates that subculture into a repertoire of images and meanings dictated by the mainstream, 'those young people who chose to inhabit a spectacular youth culture are simultaneously *returned*, as they are represented on T.V. and in the newspapers, to the place where common sense would have them fit (as "animals" certainly, but also "in the family", "out of work", "up to date", etc.)' (94). Hebdige's work thus sets up a model of hegemonic resistance and incorporation that situates itself against actual class experience. The incorporation, or 'recuperation' (94) as Hebdige puts it, of spectacular youth cultures becomes a means of controlling deviant behaviour (as perceived by the dominant culture), and therefore troublesome class activity. However, what his analysis fails to account for is the way in which articulations of class in popular music do not just present lived relations, rather they have the ability to construct a vocabulary of class that defines texts that follow after, constructing a discourse of class values that provide a mythic lexicon from which to talk about class positions. As such the signification of class within popular music encourages a prismatic discourse that speaks of class in particular ways. It will be the purpose of later chapters to examine quite how such a discourse operates.

Hebdige does note that subcultures (and he notes punk as a particular example) move from a position of perceived authentic articulation to a cycle of semiotic stereotypes. While much of punk's power lies in its ability to appropriate and reorient cultural texts, it is of course open to incorporation and assimilation into the larger culture industry:

> Punk was forever condemned to act out alienation, to mime its imagined condition, to manufacture a whole series of subjective correlatives for the official archetypes of the 'crisis of modern life': the unemployment figures, the Depression, the Westway, Television, etc. Converted into icons (the safety pin, the rip, the mindless lean and hungry look) these paradigms of crisis could live a double life, at once fictional and real. (65)

In punk's case this cycle is almost an effect of the nihilistic attitude of the subculture (no future), an aspect Hebdige opposes against the utopian leanings of the Rastafarian subculture. One way out of this, from a musical perspective, were the possibilities afforded by post-punk, a shift most notably taken up by John Lydon's Public Image Limited, Siouxsie and the Banshees, Wire and many others. Post-punk allowed its parent form to become a starting point from which it could recreate popular music, benefiting from punk's minimal musical embryo (arguably the very point of punk was to point to new musical directions). However, it is notable that much post-punk music[4] veers away from the subject of class, placing more emphasis on musical form and experimentation. It seems appropriate to understand this as an effect of punk's preoccupation with class signification:

> It was at this point [1977] that punk's fragile unity between working class kids and arty, middle class bohemians began to fracture. On one

side, you had the populist 'real punks' (later to evolve into the Oi! movement) who believed that the music needed to stay accessible and unpretentious, the angry voice of the streets. On the other side was the vanguard that came to be known as 'post punk', who saw 1977 not as a return to raw rock 'n' roll but the chance to make a break with tradition, and who defined punk as an imperative to constant change.

(Reynolds, 2005, xvii)

While Hebdige sees the after effects of punk in terms of incorporation, he fails to acknowledge that the 'mime' of signification that he identifies actually goes on to provide a discourse within which class can be understood in particular ways. As such the development of punk into Oi! can be understood, not just as a process about working-class identity, but also about the class signification of musical form.[5]

Bennett (1999) goes some way to outlining the inherent problems with Hebdige's use of the relationship between subcultures and working-class youth. As he identifies, subcultural forms that come after punk do not fit as easily into a primarily working-class social strata, a problem particularly evident in the gothic subculture, for example. Similarly, Bennett quotes Clarke (1981) who suggests that 'most of the punk creations that are discussed [by Hebdige] were developed among the art-school avant-garde, rather than emanating from the dance halls and housing estates' (Clarke, 86). Certainly, it is not difficult to see a more fluid relationship between class and subcultures operating than that given by Hebdige. Indeed subsequent work (Thornton, 1995; Muggleton, 1997; Hodkinson and Deicke, 2007) has tended to review that relationship; however, models that use lived social relations as a starting point have still tended to dominate. In other words the temptation is still to look at the class position of a subcultural agent and understand their participation in those terms. Thornton (1995) does provide an interesting variation on this theme when she discusses the 'fantasy of classlessness' (101) perceived within rave culture, a level of communion that transcends class origins. Thornton claims that generational factors unite subcultural agents at a far deeper level than class, affording a level of fantasy around class affiliations articulated at a subcultural stratum. Yet rather than focussing on the mobility of class perception, Thornton sees the removal of class as a category by which subcultural agents understand themselves. Such a fantasy goes some way to suggesting a level of performativity that steps away from Hebdige's more deterministic model, yet it still places a heavy emphasis on the use of subcultures to operate in socially resistant ways. Class assumes importance as a way of both articulating socio-economic circumstances and subverting those very positions. Indeed it is clear that anti-hegemonic subversion is what is being primarily valued in much work on subculture (although more recent work has tended to be suspicious of this position). As Laughey (2006) suggests,

> The homogonous working class character of youth subcultures was thus romanticized as a lone oppositional voice against the hegemonic bloc successfully secured by the dominant with the consent of the subordinate parental culture. Subcultural youth was in this sense a class of its own . . . This isolation from the parental culture, however, was demanded because incongruous class positions problematized the assumed unity of youth subcultural resistance. (23)

This unity assumes significance for Hebdige and the CCCS given the importance of resistance placed upon subcultural activity in the face of the hegemonic bloc.[6] However, when attempting to understand the ways in which British popular music signifies class positions and meanings, the subcultural approach only goes so far. In the first instance it takes class as a purely 'real' element, in other words, class becomes a factor only in the way in which it is lived in a practical and physical sense. Secondly, the emphasis on resistance and agency prioritizes working-class or proletarian subcultural agents, marginalizing those who may be less easy to classify or incorporate into the 'resistance frame'. Finally, the subcultural approach actually tells us very little about how class operates *through* popular music. Music is seen as a means to create subcultural formations, amongst others; yet it is clear that class is not only just a factor experienced within music consumed by subcultures. Articulations of class abound throughout British popular music, and operate in more diffuse ways than just speaking the voice of the marginalized.

Thinking class

Whilst the study of subculture has tended to view class position as a determinant, a starting point (or at least a particular point of focus) from which to proceed, there has been a shift towards a more fluid conception of class in relation to identity, what Devine *et al.* (2005) call the 'cultural turn'. However, to understand why such a 'turn' should take place, indeed *needs* to take place, some understanding of the study of class must be undertaken. In sociological terms the study of class has primarily been motivated by either Marxist or Weberian conceptions of social stratification. While these two models have an influence over the determination of class stratification, they fail to provide the necessary mechanism by which images of class can become mobile in relation to participants.[7] However, to understand why class should be experienced as a mobile significatory category, both Marx's and Weber's conceptions of class need to be understood.

For Marx class stratification acts as an effect of the mode of production of any society. Such classes are inherently dynamic, powered by inter-strata struggle. As Edgell (1993) notes,

> In the case of the transition from feudalism to capitalism, the urban bourgeoisie or manufacturing middle class played the revolutionary role, pushing aside the monopolistic guild masters and eventually displacing by force the ruling landed aristocracy. Thus Marx argued that the bourgeoisie became the ruling class in the new type of society – capitalism – by combining together and engaging in revolutionary class conflict. (4)

The capitalist mode of production created a number of crises that it sought to resolve (particularly an excess of production) through the creation of new markets, an increase in the intensity of labour and the creation of a proletarian working class. As Edgell points out, the division between those in control of the mode of production (the bourgeoisie) and those alienated from their labour by a lack of control (the proletariat) produced a class system that held within it the potential for the very demise of such a system. Indeed Marx's concern for the coming to class-consciousness for the proletariat is at the heart of his work.

The proletariat themselves need to be understood in order to ascertain how contemporary readings of class have been formulated. For Marx the proletariat are defined as a class who have undergone a shift from self-employment to employee status. As capitalism progresses the working classes become employees concentrated in large urban areas (a process that Marx suggests is an effect of the increased efficacy of big capital against small scale capital), creating a cheap work force who will be instrumental in the demise of self-owned businesses and industries, resulting in a subsumed middle class who will join the proletariat in their impoverished status. Artisanship becomes increasingly irrelevant in a market driven by low production costs and mass-industrialized output. In this way Marx understands class as an effect of a particular economic set-up, but one that is capable of dynamic movement over history.

Such a formulation has been integral to both the disciplines of sociology and cultural studies. Marx's model provides in the first instance a proletarian *mass* who are seen as either a threat to the cultural and social order (Arnold, 1869; Leavis, 1933), or as a pacified group de-radicalized by the industrialization of cultural forms (Marcuse, 1968; Benjamin, 1973; Adorno, 1991). This model has historically suited the implicit aims of intellectual study from both left and right wing perspectives. Even a brief examination of the work of the CCCS, for example, shows subcultural identity as an attempt by a primarily pro-letarian youth to organize social relations on their own terms, a form of agency that has at its heart revolutionary potential. Weber's work on the other hand has different aims. Weber's focus on class is less integral to his overall schema than Marx, and there are significant divergences in their understanding of the concept. In the first instance Weber's analysis of social stratification does not condemn capitalism (although he is cautious of its de-humanizing potential via bureaucracy). Weber understands social stratification to be determined not just by class as an economic category, a marker or effect of one's position in the market, but also by a measure of status (as it is experienced by others) and affiliations to the political domain. Some participants have privileged positions in the market whilst others are limited in their socio-economic power, but such power has as much to do with social status as it does with an economic determinist understanding of class. In contrast to Marx, Weber moves away from the idea that class is merely understood in terms of a participant's relationship to the means of production. He suggests that identification with any particular class is complicated by other fac-tors (education, for example) that produce other status positions, often within overarching economic class positions. As Edgell suggests, 'this essentially hierarchical and highly pluralistic account of class (and sta-tus) recognized that the expression of class interests was problematic, not least because of the variable connections between class and status' (14). Status has subsequently been used to understand the complexities of social relations that are not accounted for by Marx's account of economic stratification, yet it still fails to account for the highly complex ways in which class can be experienced, both at an psychic and a cultural level.

Interestingly, the concept of status appears as a new social cate-gory in Aitken's account of *The New Meteors* (1967), a survey of the social and cultural changes sweeping Britain through the sixties. While Aitken talks of a new meritocracy that many understand to signal the death of class, class is still the basis upon which such a meritocracy is built. Aitken quotes the actor Michael Caine, freshly successful from a string of box office hits (*Alfie* (1966), *The Ipcress File* (1965) and *Zulu* (1964) amongst others):

> Now, a few years ago if I'd been a successful actor I'd have still been thought of as a cockney, and all the nobs would have turned up their noses at me socially, even though they might have turned out their pockets to see me act. But now it's all very different. This new aristocracy business is true, and I'm received in some places as though I was the Duke of Cockney. I suppose it's because we've now seen that Britain has no natural resources beyond the creative power of our young people. (268)

However, Aitken understands the new aristocracy to still sit within a stratified class structure in the United Kingdom, even if it is one that allows a certain level of class mobility that was significantly more difficult previously. Particularly, he identifies those who adopt working-class identity to connote authenticity, 'there are the class tobogganers, announcing their intended descent by uttering four-letter words at pseudo-smart parties in pseudo-Lancashire accents...To a detached observer it is all a laugh a minute' (262–3). Status (achieved for someone like Caine through his abilities as an actor and as a box office draw) may open new doors, yet it fails to replace class stratification in any significant sense. The meritocracy only goes so far. Indeed Aitken's account suggests that class mobility (down as well as up) might be more available to some than others (an idea explored in greater depth in Chapter 4).

While the study of class has evolved through numerous subsequent permutations (Wright, 1985; Goldthorpe *et al.*, 1987), it has tended to continue to concern itself with class in a deterministic relationship. In other words, classes are understood as social phenomena that provide their own relations (or have their relations imposed upon them), rather than as *ideas*. Particularly, the academic focus on working-class culture has meant that in the face of a perceived demise in a culturally distinct form of that class (Abrams *et al.*, 1960; Zweig, 1961), it has become increasingly difficult to analyse exactly what makes up particular social strata for the purposes of analysis. As Devine and Savage (Devine *et al.*, 2005) illustrate, numerous studies, particularly throughout the 1970s and 1980s, found that,

> Class imagery was often incoherent, contradictory and fragmentary, ambiguous and uncertain. The prevailing view was that there was no tidy relationship between class structure and position and cultural

beliefs and practices...Culture could not simply be made reducible to structure for it appeared that cultural meanings were much more indeterminate than...had [been] allowed. (7)

Class-consciousness[8] then starts to unknit analyses of class that see cultural and social formations as *effects* of particular class positions. Studies such as Moore's work on Durham miners (1975) and Bell and Newby's analysis of farm workers (1975) suggest that one's self-perception in relation to class is often diffuse, contradictory and problematic. Devine and Savage suggest that such an analytical impasse results in the late 1970s in a turning away from the study of individuals in relation to their class towards an analysis of collective organizations and class practices (Marshall, 1988), particularly within sociology. The individual's relationship to society and culture through class position was rejected as sociological inquiry found it too diffuse to analyse in any meaningful empirical or ethnographic fashion.

Such an impasse would suggest that within the discipline of sociology, the study of perceptions of class had largely reached a dead end. However, as Devine and Savage suggest, a cultural turn in sociological inquiry (Chaney, 1994; Abbott, 2001) has subsequently led to a shift in emphasis in the study of class. This shift has been a move away from stratification analysis towards an engagement with the uses of class and perceptions of self in relation to class largely influenced by the work of Pierre Bourdieu. Devine *et al.* suggest that 'Criticisms have been made that much stratification research ultimately prioritized employment as the key axis of inequality...leading to the marginalization of other axes of inequality such as gender, race, ethnicity and age, and that it relied on discredited, "enlightenment" theoretical foundations' (1). In response to this suggestion that stratification analysis relies too heavily on empirical data regarding employment status to talk about class, a number of writers have turned to an alternative position that does not position class-consciousness as an effect of class position, rather class-consciousness becomes a state, an imagined subjectivity. Such analyses (Alexander, 1994; Skeggs, 1997; Reay, 1998) provide an account of class that is not so much a label of position but rather a 'claim of recognition' (Devine *et al.*, 12).

Re-thinking class

Following Bourdieu (1984), and increasingly influenced by post-structuralist theory, Devine *et al.* outline a model of understanding class identity which focuses on perception and value over economic stratification. Utilizing the concepts of habitus, capitals (economic, social and cultural) and fields, class-consciousness becomes a matter of participants staking relational claims to other participants. In other words, perceptions of self in class terms become fluid and often oppositional and contradictory. The perception of one's relationship to class ceases to be merely an expression of one's own stratified position, as in work influenced by Marx and Weber, both of whom place a stress on the recognition of one's class position and the economic inequalities underlying it. Instead, class-consciousness becomes a contextual and mobile series of strategies to place oneself in relation to one's own perceptions of class within a field. In relation to popular music, such a field becomes the way in which class is articulated through the music media, and as such participants relate to class as it is presented by those media (amongst other factors).[9]

Skeggs[10] (2004b) provides a particularly useful model of analysis that focuses on the symbolic production of class (over an account that relies on identifying participants' stratified economic positioning). Skeggs uses Bourdieu's work (particularly *Distinction: A Social Critique of the Judgement of Taste* (1984)) to understand the ways in which class signification and representation are accrued by bodies over temporal and spatial variations. Skeggs reverses Marx's emphasis on production over generalized exchange, and instead analyses exchanges that make up the symbolic economy, within which the category of class can reside. Skeggs suggests that such a reversal is needed due to the '*de-materialisation* of commercial production and therefore the predominance of symbolic exchange in post-industrialisation' (47). Given the dual roles of hypercommodification and the industrialization of culture, new markets have to become identified through the commodification of culture. Caught up in this commodification is the category of class that becomes another economic resource that can either be deployed or consumed in a variety of ways.

Central to Skeggs' argument is the idea that class can be understood as a cultural property. Particular classes (especially the middle class) have an enhanced ability to appropriate working-class signification to authenticate themselves. As such representations of class have to be understood as constitutive rather than as reproductions of economic stratification. Such representations for Skeggs assume a moral aspect, one that associates working-class culture 'as excess, as waste, as entertainment, as authenticating, lacking in taste, as un-modern, backward, as escapist, as dangerous, unruly and without shame' (49). To support these claims Skeggs points to a survey in *The Daily Mirror* newspaper

(9 February 1997) that presents a number of claims, agreed or disagreed with by the querent, to determine whether Britain is a classless society. As Skeggs points out, the survey is actually asking whether participants are working class or middle class through a series of statements that rely on moral judgements ('I believe the death penalty is sometimes justified', 'I know someone who has taken crack cocaine') and the ability to apply the *right knowledge*, 'Knowing to go to Tuscany [on holiday], how to appreciate the theatre and eating out' (50). The survey shows a perception of class position that is based less on economic terms and more on cultural practices. Further, while the survey seems to suggest a level of class mobility, Skeggs is keen to see this as *rebranding*,[11] a form of appropriation of class identity based on practice over socio-economic stratification.

The inclusion of 'authenticating' in the above quotation certainly seems appropriate when it comes to a discussion of the signification of class within British popular music. Skeggs analyses this idea of authentication through the appropriation of aspects of black working-class masculinity in Hollywood cinema and blues music. Using the work of Diawara (1998), Skeggs shows how black working-class masculinity becomes 'a mobile cultural style that can be used by different characters in film, be they black or white' (Skeggs, 2004b, 58). Indeed such a resource is often only appropriated by white bodies, as they are capable of achieving these qualities in a temporary and mobile manner whilst black bodies are tied to such values with little recourse to plundering from white identities, working class or otherwise. Skeggs understands this mechanism as rebranding brought about by the privileged place inhabited by middle-class white bodies, which allows them to accrue cultural capital in a way that black working-class counterparts cannot. Further, this immobility within class signification is part of what makes black working-class identity desirable, as a perceived lack of ability to rebrand oneself in class and racial terms connotes a level of authenticity that can then be appropriated by white middle-class practitioners:

> In fact this process is so well established that the majority of the music industry could be seen to be fuelled by it, as could the tradition of crime movies... The movies made by Guy Ritchie (Mr Madonna) – *Lock, Stock and Two Smoking Barrels,* and *Snatch* are a perfect example of a cultural intermediary (Featherstone, 1991), in which an upper-class British man generates his career and money by using others to reproduce and generate a fascination with low-life danger and criminality. (59–60)

Crucially, the ability to accrue cultural capital from others is seen as a marker of increased capital in and of itself. In other words, Skeggs is suggesting that the ability to appropriate is a desirable cultural strategy that confirms and improves one's status. For those not in a position to accrue such value, such as working-class black males in Skeggs' analysis, a further level of capital is lost due to an inability to rebrand without loss of identity.

The concept of rebranding, the ability to accrue capital through the adoption of class signification (usually working class in origin) by (often middle class) practitioners, provides a model of class analysis that escapes the strictures of stratification analysis, whilst still being informed by it. While it may be appropriate to decipher class positions in relation to economic or social determinants, such a formulation fails to take into account the ways in which class positions may be made to live mythically through cultural texts. The films of Guy Ritchie and the music of urban hip hop have significant audiences amongst young white middle-class males, and as such cannot be simply read as *effects* of a particular stratum of society. Rather the signification of class within such texts exhibits a more fluid and mobile mechanism by which it operates. Class-consciousness then assumes a mythical level of significance, mythical precisely because it speaks a myth of class that is often removed from lived experience.[12] As Skeggs points out, 'the middle class comes to "know" its inner city other through an imposed system of infinitely repeatable substitutions and proxies; census tracts, crime statistics, tabloid newspapers and television programmes' (65). *The Daily Mirror* questionnaire mentioned above works exactly to define a notion of the middle class self against moral judgements made about material practices defined as working class in a mythical way. No account is made for the possibility that going to the theatre or having a holiday in Tuscany might be working-class pursuits, rather the paper sets such practices up as indicators of a class sensibility, defined by its other.

Working-class heroes

Where Skeggs' analysis of class rebranding becomes problematic in relation to British popular music is in the primacy of a middle-class position from which to accrue working-class capital. For Skeggs, 'it is the middle class that is doing the re-branding because they have access to the circuits of symbolic power and distribution, they are the cultural intermediaries. The middle class are the ones who are positioned as always/already belonging to the nation' (61). As the subsequent case studies will show, working-class lived experience is situated within the field or discourse of British popular music as a privileged significator of authenticity, a category within which class sits. While the *Daily Mirror* questionnaire assumes a desire for a middle-class sensibility, utilizing negative moral judgements in relation to perceived (in terms of tabloid newspapers) working-class bugbears (aggressive dogs, drug abuse, petty crime), it is equally possible to see a desirable working-class (and therefore more *authentic*) identity transmuted through popular music culture. As such the signification of working-class identity is not always painted in a negative light. As Rubin (2005) suggests, 'a trope of early rock and roll . . . is the doomed (or at least threatened) love relationship between a poor boy and a rich girl or, somewhat less often, a poor girl and a rich boy ("Leader of the Pack," "Down at the Boondocks," "Dawn," "Rag Doll," "Hang on Sloopy," "Uptight," and many others)' (174). For rock 'n' roll the class inequalities exemplified by these examples serve both to reinforce the commitment of desire between the boy and the girl (despite the social divisions that would otherwise separate them) and to grant the protagonists of the songs a level of authenticity and truth that is usually constituted against a parental culture. That such values are painted in a positive light suggests that the adoption of working-class signification is not uniformly a bad thing.

The values associated with working-class culture mentioned above by Skeggs assume a different perspective in relation to popular music as issues of community, authenticity, or a perceived lack of artifice are often privileged. Indeed, if we were to apply Skeggs' model uncritically to British popular music, we would undoubtedly expect to see a privileging of middle-class mythic imagery over a denigrated working-class identity, and this is obviously not the case. While Skeggs uses Pulp's 'Common People' (1995) to illustrate the 'impossibility of being and becoming working class' (2004b, 61) and the concurrent resentment towards cultural tourism, the song also paints a picture of working-class culture that has its own attractions despite the attack on those that wish to appropriate it. This dichotomy is illustrated particularly in the extended edit of the song where Jarvis Cocker sings what would appear to be the lynchpin of the song (interestingly edited out of the radio version). Here Cocker draws parallels between the working classes and dogs, threatening to bite and eviscerate the unwary class-tourist, before he sets up a vision of working-class existence that is characterized both by a lack of social control or agency and a depth of cultural and social life that seems to be denied to the middle classes despite their privilege. While this passage and the song in general is keen to point out the supposedly futile and mundane nature of working-class culture, it equally situates itself against the rich girl who wants to appropriate it by prioritizing that very working-class culture over her own. While the equation between the 'common people' and dogs seems unflattering in the extreme, the final line of the extra verse suggests an immediacy and vibrancy that the cultural tourist will never be able to experience. As such the animalistic nature of the working classes is redrawn as a positive attribute, a 'natural' characteristic that is situated against the artifice of the girl in the song. The ambivalence of the lack of control is countered by a suggestion of authenticity strongly situated within class and mundane everyday experience (the flat, the chip shop, the club, the dead-end job). Such a moral prioritization of working-class culture *over* middle-class culture seems to step outside of Skeggs' model, yet it is seen again and again within British popular music culture. It might be even more pertinent when one considers Cocker's own background (a comfortable middle-class upbringing in the primarily working-class neighbourhood of Intake in Sheffield and further education at St Martin's College in London), a factor that suggests not only a continued ambivalence within and without the song, but also a display of a discourse (field) that prioritizes both the identification of a working-class identity in a negative light while situating that class position as redeemable, and preferable, in the face of other class positions. As such the song itself becomes a paradox in that it encourages rebranding, asking the listener to identify with the working-class protagonist of the song, whilst rejecting the middle-class positioning of the girl. Of course both positions are operated mythically here, shaped by a discourse within popular music that equates working-class positions as natural, authentic and unmediated (no matter how artificial such characteristics may be).[13]

The signification of class then has to be understood in ways that do not merely rely on the social positioning of subcultural agents. The musical text itself is made to appropriate class signification and make it its own, articulating it in terms of popular music culture (or specific pop music cultures). As the following discussion will identify, class signification within popular music is often more concerned with articulating authenticity *per se* rather than actual lived experiences or social relations. Such articulations then have the possibility of informing actual social relations as they are lived through the audience. Reynolds' identification of 'working class kids and arty, middle class bohemians' (2005, xvii) partaking in the punk phenomenon suggests that working-class signification failed to alienate middle-class youth, and as such a performative class identity, lived in relation to the music, accounts for such a relationship.

Hearing class

The purpose of this chapter has been to interrogate the role of class in the study of popular music, from the determinist models used by the CCCS, through to a more fluid model that allows for a broader range of interaction, interpretation and engagement with class signifiers. Given the historical shift away from a primarily Marxist reading of popular culture that might view pop music in an ideological light (from Adorno's 'On Popular Music' (1941) onwards), the very category of class has become somewhat marginalized, particularly from the point of view of cultural studies. However, it cannot be denied that signs of class proliferate throughout British popular music, from Lonnie Donegan to Arctic Monkeys, and given its panoramic reach it would seem that what is not said by analysis might allow us to identify the processes by which class might be understood. Relationships between music, media and listener might be understood as a set of discourses that allow symbolic polysemy and mythical fluidity at all levels, a potentially immense process that removes determinism from an understanding of all three categories.

The one area where class has failed to appear significantly in any analysis of popular music is within the text itself. By this I mean that representations of class within the pop song text have rarely been treated with any kind of insightful investigation. While it is entirely appropriate to understand how listeners' class position or activity might draw them to certain genres or types of music as part of wider (sub)cultural activity, the actual exhibition of class signifiers in pop lyrics and performance has rarely been dealt with. The use of the term 'signifier' here is advisable as it becomes increasingly clear that when class is addressed within popular music, it is never easily reconcilable as a musical performance of material or objective class positions, however they may be identified. Instead such manifestations rely on a lexicon of class within the discourse of popular music. They are, that is to say, 'performed'. Even more problematically, it is impossible to understand the importance of such signifiers simply as utterances that mean something transparently in relation to the artist or group from whence they come. It is vital (and particularly so in the light of any communal/social aspect that the music may have) to understand how the listener might engage with such signification. As Hawkins (2002) suggests, 'as an amalgam of sonic references, pop texts, as I see them, are a consequence of the complex set of connections between the body and countless modes of thought patterns' (15), a set of connections that may be unpicked by an engagement between musicological decoding and cultural analysis. Such an approach would attempt to place the listener and his or her experience of such music in the centre of analysis on a phenomenological level (albeit one constrained by the possibilities of the musical text), seeking to understand how the listener interacts with class signification within popular music.

This strategy is necessarily fraught with difficulties, primarily because of the sheer number of variables that might influence interpretation. The researcher might take the class signification within the song and the listener as two starting points. Within the song, factors such as lyrical content that do not deal with class, musical style, generic categorization, gender of performer and many others might well shape and influence interpretation. On the listener's side matters become even more difficult. Aside from the standard categories of class, race, gender and age, one might have to factor in the environment within which the song is heard, the familiarity the listener has with the song, the artist, the genre, the listener's family life, social background, any subcultural affiliation and so much more. This brief list of variables does not even begin to scratch the surface of potential problems when attempting to understand how class signification might work. However, it might be suggested that the pop music text often provides us with a model of an *implied listener* (to adapt Iser's concept (1974)), who might be identifiable as a figure constructed or interpellated in the lyric text and performance, and as such it is the purpose of this work to understand the potential relationships between a textually implied listener, and actual listeners in the real world.

The implied listener

The work of David Brackett gives us some insight into the ways in which a listener might be implied by the musical text. In *Interpreting Popular Music* (1995) Brackett moves from structural models of meaning (Stefani, 1987; Middleton, 1990) that relate musical moments to extra-musical factors that may shape meaning to a more context-oriented model that acknowledges the role of discourse (or musical code as Brackett puts it) in forming meaning and interpretation. Brackett does not outline an implied listener, indeed he warns that,

> There are no ideal 'addressers' or 'addressees'; 'context' functions not only in the Jakobsonian sense of providing a context for a specific

message, but also in telling us about the larger social and cultural context, about the individual backgrounds of the senders and receivers of the message, and about the background of the message itself. (13)

In this sense meaning becomes a mutable factor, and it is impossible to expect that any song should be received in a uniform manner by everyone who listens to it. Writers such as Brackett (1995), McClary and Walser (1988), and Walser (1993) amongst others have particularly shown how the unitary textual meanings of traditional musicology have been exploded by the invitation to a heterogeneity of meaning in popular music. Yet the context of popular music and further the context of a particular song can often provide a means of identifying certain characteristics that imply a certain type of listener. The very basic form of this can be seen in love songs that address a gendered object. It is possible for myself as a man to listen to Avril Lavigne's 'Girlfriend' (2007), a song written from a feminine perspective aimed towards a masculine object, and still potentially adopt the role of the protagonist. That I might have to make some leap of identification to achieve this only goes to show the potentialities of interpretation available to any listener at any time. However, it is clear that 'Girlfriend' implies identification with the protagonist of the song, and it would be incorrect to suggest that a male listener would be unable to place himself within the nexus of meaning in any real fashion.[14] As such the role of the implied listener seems to add to the network of associations that are open to the listener of any piece of popular music where such an element is present.

The idea of an implied listener might still be problematic, not least because one might assume that the implied class position is going to create a resistance in certain quarters of the potential audience, for whom such signification is not socially or culturally relevant. Certainly, it is possible to see such resistance in operation within British popular music, but the concept of the implied listener allows a certain amount of interpretive fluidity, precisely because popular music deals with class in a mythical fashion. By this I would suggest that the format the text is presented in, a popular song delivered via a mass-entertainment medium, generates a level of relational distance that allows the listener to interpret the song in ways other than a traditional determinist model. That is to say, in rather general terms, that you do not have to be working class to find relevance in a working-class motif within a pop song. Rather the very nature of popular music, albeit at differing inter- and cross-generic levels, allows mythical identification. The term 'mythical' is significant here because it displays class (and other categories such as age, gender and race) as a representation, detached but related to socially lived experience. Popular music deals with reality as a prism deals with light, engaging with social and cultural reality but refracting it through a discourse that is particular to popular music itself. As such, the *documentary* aspect of popular music, what one might call the 'folk voice'[15] becomes open to different identifications as soon as performance historically reaches a mass audience.[16] For while it is problematic, even in a full scale ethnographic study, for the researcher to account for the multiplicity of potential interpretive responses in an audience, it is equally difficult for the band or artist to relate to that same multiplicity. As such the very notion of class becomes dislocated from the 'real life' social and cultural experience of the performers and audience, and is instead presented as something that makes sense when understood as a mythical depiction, a depiction that allows the listener to suspend those very social and cultural experiences as the determining factor[17] of interpretation and instead adopt a performative approach to class personae.

The above account might immediately suggest that the listener can simply don a mask to relate to all music, and its class signification, equally. This is obviously not the case. If it were so, taste might become an obsolete factor in critical judgement, as other categories could equally become mythologized. Listeners clearly make judgements based upon certain criteria to determine which forms of popular music they might choose to interact with, which particular instances they prefer or discard, which songs they like and do not like. There has to be some accumulation of criteria that makes a listener gravitate towards Oasis rather than Sophie Ellis Bextor, and one of the criteria that might influence that choice might be one's understanding of self in class terms. However, each musical text has to be seen in relation to an overarching set of discourses that influence the interpretation of signification. We need only look at the example of the girl group Spice Girls to see a number of signifiers based around particular group members that make sense in a pop context (or discourse) but are rather more troublesome when seen as relating to the social and cultural sphere in a way that might be perceived as truthful or authentic. The most obvious example is Victoria Beckham, or 'Posh Spice'. Her adopted nickname suggests upper-middle class or even aristocratic leanings, yet she can only be understood as 'posh' in relation to the other band members ('Ginger', 'Sporty', 'Scary' and 'Baby') who are situated by her name as lower class leisure consumers. In particular, each name works when placed against the same framework of leisure activity from whence the band and its music come, in other words, mainstream pop/club culture. It does not take a great amount of semiotic excavation to realize that Victoria is no different in terms of class position to her fellow band members. However, she does represent a mythologized form of class image that equates her dress style (Gucci and Prada) with something clearly different to that of her band mates (track suits, leopard print, baby-doll dresses). This difference may be influenced by actual class structures in British culture, but it only makes true sense when experienced against a pop discourse that represents class in mythological ways. Such myths place any signification presented by the band in the context of not only British society at the end of the twentieth century but also female (and male) pop artists who have preceded them, contemporary acts against which they might be judged, and the variety of music and mainstream media through which such images might be presented. These elements all provide a prismatic discourse through which Beckham's image is understood in relation to pop music in the first instance and wider society in the second. As such her signification matters as an example of social relations refracted through cultural representation, a refraction that makes meaning in its own image rather than that of 'lived experience'.

The role of the implied listener or audience, then, is to provide a framework that the actual listener or audience can inhabit to interpret the presentation of class signification within pop music. To take the example of Oasis, one might suggest that the implied listener is working class, male, heterosexual, young, ambitious, extroverted and countercultural to a limited degree. However, the band's success cannot be understood as being the result of a large number of like-minded individuals alone. What Oasis present is a version of working-class experience that is informed for the listener by previous rock acts; the songwriting craft of The Beatles, the male bravado of The Rolling Stones, the British vernacular psychedelia of The Small Faces, the mod styling of The Who and the particular ongoing tradition of British pop music[18] represented by such acts. The listener is not required to be particularly familiar with such archetypes (indeed close familiarity can encourage accusations of musical thievery on the part of Oasis, as has often happened regarding The Beatles' musical influence on the band). However, so pervasive are such archetypes within British rock discourse that the success of Oasis could be accounted for by their very familiarity. Fifty years of rock history potentially provides the listener, even at the most casual level, with the requisite interpretive tools to allow them to adopt the position of the implied listener. Equally, such a position operates at a remove from the listener's social and cultural background, precisely because it is constructed through rock discourse rather than through lived experience, and as such it becomes mythologized. A rather flippant example, but relevant nonetheless, might be the celebration of 'Cigarettes and Alcohol' (1994), understood not in the light of real social concerns regarding alcoholism and lung disease (as one would see in the discourse of government health warnings), but rather as emblems of a rock lifestyle, an image made familiar through figures such as Keith Richards, Keith Moon and Sid Vicious. Very real social and personal consequences are subsumed and appropriated into an alternate value system, that of rock music, which refigures meaning in a mythological manner.

When understanding the role of myth in relation to popular music, the initial step has traditionally been to examine subcultural experience. As suggested above, this particular focus is attractive because the transfiguration of meaning exemplified by subcultural participation, communication and spectacle, is often seen as a means of social problem solving. Hebdige particularly sees working-class subcultures as a means of placing youth disaffected from their parent cultures into some form of context that is meaningful for them. The role of music in this formulation is seen more as an effect of the process rather than a motivating factor. This approach does potentially explain why mods might listen to The Small Faces, or why Rastafarians might listen to Burning Spear, but what it fails to do is to explain why anyone else might want to. Subcultures are not the only environment within which the listener can experience meaning or identification in relation to a piece of rock music. In fact, increasingly it becomes difficult to disentangle the borders of contemporary rock subculture in the United Kingdom, since musical forms previously seen as subcultural (nu metal, emo and goth, for example) have increasingly been promoted through mass-entertainment networks such as MTV2 and BBC Radio One. As subcultures become more diffuse, and indeed overlap, it seems that the mainstream audience have to be factored into exactly how meaning is constructed and experienced in the pop music text, and the ways in which the re-branding of class identity occurs.

3
The Problem of Authenticity

The study of popular music, even in the diversified stage that it currently inhabits at the start of the twenty-first century, continues to wrestle with pop's engagement with authenticity. In fact, it seems difficult to point to another area of cultural inquiry that has such an intense yet problematic relationship with the issue. Looking at the development of popular music over the last century it is not difficult to see that authenticity is a significant factor not only for artists and producers, but also for audiences, listeners and critics. As Philip Auslander (1999) points out,

> Taken on its own terms, rock authenticity is an essentialist concept, in the sense that rock fans treat authenticity as an essence that is either present or absent in the music itself, and they may well debate particular musical works in those terms. (70)

However, Auslander is quick to point out that authenticity is far from being an essential category, rather it is 'an ideological concept and...a discursive effect' (ibid.) that is both culturally and industrially motivated. At the level of reception particularly, authenticity seems to be a mutable value often at odds with the commercial nature of the production and distribution of musical texts, a network of meaning that seems to exist outside of the artefact itself in its more tangible forms (the physical product of the CD, its marketing and promotion) and the ways in which it is distributed or experienced (the music retail industry, radio and television). Authenticity, however it is experienced or felt, is often seen to reside in a space outside of these forms, either in the music itself, in the perception of the artist(s) responsible for its production or in the experience of perceiving it (the live arena, for example).

This prioritization of authenticity within popular music has historically served a variety of functions that will be explored within this
chapter in greater detail. Yet it must also be recognized that the study
of the cultural evaluation of popular music by academia brings with
it its own set of values that prioritize authenticity. This chapter will
explore the problem of authenticity in popular music from a number of
angles; the articulation of authenticity within popular music, its reception and interpretation at audience level, and also the problems that
academia, through the exploration of cultural forms, has encountered
when engaging with pop authenticity. Authenticity will be understood
as a judgement, made relationally to the inauthentic, defined in turn in
relation to an overarching set of discourses amongst which rock discourse
might be the most influential. Above all, such judgements can be seen as
strategies to deal with the ongoing antagonistic relationship between art
and commerce at the heart of the popular music industries (Dyer, 1979;
Frith, 1990). As such class becomes a means by which listeners reconcile
the commodification of popular music. However, authenticity is understood here as a strategy that is offered up by the surrounding discourse
of rock music to be performed by the auditor or listener. Chapter 4 will
more fully explore the performative nature of class experience and it is in
this performance that authenticity is engineered. Several strains inform
notions of authenticity, and these will be examined through this chapter,
but the centrality of class to British rock discourse creates a number of
tensions that in the first instance make authenticity problematic, whilst
also providing a strategy to reconcile the relationship between the music
and its industrialized origins.[1] As such authenticity has to be understood
as residing within the discourse of rock music, seeded within its own
mass-produced (and therefore inauthentic?) creation and dissemination.

Jeff Nuttall's distinction between pop, protest and art goes some way
towards outlining the distinctions between pop and rock discourse.
Nuttall (1968) sees a stratified model of youth culture split along three
lines: pop consumed primarily by working-class teenagers, the protest
movement motivated primarily by middle-class students and an artistic
vanguard. Tensions between these groups proliferate as 'the pop fans
despised protest as being naïve and art as being posh, the protesting
students despised pop as being commercial and art as being preten-
tious, and the artists despised pop for being tasteless and protest for
being drab' (138). Nuttall notes that such distinctions start to crossover
in the late 1960s originating from a number of cultural bridges. One
of these conduits focused upon by Nuttall is *The Goon Show*, a product of
National Service that united all three strands in a highly visible form in

the United Kingdom through the 1950s, '*The Goon Show* was protest [primarily against the class system that supported the officer classes in the armed services]. *The Goon Show* was surrealist and therefore art, and *The Goon Show* was every National Servicemen's defence mechanism, and therefore pop' (140). While such a radio programme illustrates a fusion of differing strata, roughly organized along class lines, it also illustrates enduring tensions throughout British popular music that exist up to the present day. The suggestion here is not that an enduring fusion of these strata failed to happen, rather that despite such crossover moments, these discourses continue to motivate patterns of consumption and difference to this day. Furthermore, it is through the fusion of the art, pop and protest movements that the very concept of rock arises. By 1969 Jonathan Eisen was suggesting that 'Richard Farina, Bob Dylan, The Beatles and drugs are testimony to the fact that rock now must be seen as an art form like any other that arises from and talks to the people in direct, charged and organic ways' (xii). While many have sought to integrate popular music into an artistic or high cultural frame, and in effect to delimit the effects of industry on pop music's status as art, the continued separation at a mythical level between *industry* and *music*, between pop and rock continues to hold sway. It is this distinction that provides the terrain of rock discourse that is the focus of this work, and the site for contestations surrounding authenticity and class.

The purpose of this chapter is to place articulations of class in popular music within a larger framework, that of authenticity. That is not to say that the articulation of class signification is uniquely the preserve of attempts to impart authenticity on musical practice, however. It would certainly seem shortsighted to suggest that the articulation of class is only ever an attempt to place a piece of pop music in a specific sociocultural context that grants it some form of truth of experience. However, the use of class signification within British popular music appears primarily to attempt to connect with an audience through a sense of common experience. Richard Middleton (1990) suggests that authenticity is experienced as the level of appropriation a listener may choose to exert on a particular song, in other words how much listeners are able to make it their own. As such authenticity is a way of engaging with a musical text. In this sense signs of authenticity speak of relevance between artist and audience, a level of communication and communion that relies on shared social experience. However, to suggest that authenticity is a direct representation of lived experience, something that a listener may be able to relate to, is a problematic notion at best. Middleton is quick to acknowledge that authenticity is often constructed mythically, primarily connected to romantic ideas of the artist as a mouthpiece for experience.[2] Yet he suggests that within such mythical processes, ideas such as active use and continuity may be at work that have an applicable function for the listener in relation to their lived experience. However, Middleton's analysis seems to relegate the importance of the discourse within which authenticity is presented, that is, the discourse within which any given piece of popular music can be understood. It is this discourse that provides a shape and context for any signification to take place, and signs of authenticity and class must be understood as parts of a larger stratified discourse that gives them meaning.

Stuart Hall's work on encoding/decoding (1980) provides us with a model that allows for not only the articulation of signs of class and authenticity, but also the specific forms in which these significations occur within British popular music. As Fiske (1990) explains, 'Hall argues that there is a hidden but determining relationship between the structures of thought and feeling in the audience, the encoded structure of the broadcast message, and the structures of the broadcasting institutions. All are interdependent, interdeterminate' (75). Further, rock discourse allows for the performative way in which these signs are experienced. As the later case studies will show, class signification within British popular music does not necessarily perform an exclusive function. Rather its nature is also inclusive, allowing audiences to adopt or perform a realignment of reception within rock discourse. As such it must be understood that both listeners and artists are not fixed within their own social circumstances, rock discourse provides a space within which both parties can *perform* other roles, even if such a performance may be deemed problematic. If such performativity is at the heart of the articulation of authenticity, and within that category, class, then the very concept of authenticity is at stake. Certainly, one is inevitably drawn to a maelstrom of postmodern simulation; however, it is important to acknowledge that popular music has its own formal characteristics that problematize representation, the ultimate goal of authenticity. This chapter will describe some of the elements that make up rock discourse and show the ways in which these elements articulate and shape both the signification and reception of authenticity and class.

Defining the (in)authentic

While it may be difficult to ascribe particular qualities to the authentic within popular music, it may in fact be easier to identify what is inauthentic. R J Warren Zanes (1999) provides a spatial model that not only displays the articulation of authenticity on the part of the performer (rather than the construction of authenticity by the auditor), but also an inherent paradox at the heart of such an approach. Zanes is attempting to bridge what he sees as a gap between academic preoccupations with the authentic, based on a relationship between cultural expression and lived experience (itself a problematic concept), and an engagement with authenticity on the part of the pop music listener that may be motivated by other needs. Zanes commences his examination with an explication of a song by Paul Westerberg, 'World Class Fad' (1993). Westerberg's track exhibits relatively conventional concerns about the commercialization of underground music, in other words, selling out. Zanes shows how the song articulates authenticity through a negative dialectic that first identifies the inauthentic and how far away the subject of the song may have gone to achieve perceived inauthenticity. However, as Zanes points out, the inauthentic is identified (in the terms of the song, becoming primarily commercial and spatially removed from one's roots) and then made to frame what authenticity was in the first place. There is no starting point as such; rather authenticity becomes an effect of what the song (and usually by implication the performer) deems to be artificial. Certainly, such a paradox exhibits what highly unstable categories the authentic and inauthentic are. Yet Zanes is quick to suggest that this semiotic instability is not the death of either concept, neither is he tempted to turn to irony to explain the use of authenticity, given the profundity of the use of such values to listeners, particularly teenage audiences, 'popular music, particularly in relation to the experiences of youth but certainly not restricted to them, is not engaged with at a distance; instead, it is a thing of intimacy and surprising faith. And the ironic investment simply does not do for the individual what such faith does' (40). Zanes suggests that rather than presenting authenticity in a postmodern trope of ironic detachment, popular music engages with authenticity in a fluid way precisely because the listening self is in an equally fluid state, engaging in a constant process of becoming. As such any instability in the values of the authentic or inauthentic are to be expected as each phenomenological listening experience will articulate authenticity differently (although there may be direction given by musical and textual codes that evoke similar social responses) in any given set of circumstances and to any given listener.

Of course, presenting authenticity within popular music is not simply a question of reading a particular song as a strong articulation of the songwriter's experiences and social positioning. As Zanes points out, not all popular music is autobiographical,[3] and one is faced with an enormous range of varieties of authenticity across the span of the history of popular music. While it may be a paradoxical relationship, determining what is deemed to be inauthentic in any given circumstance can often lead us to appreciate the way in which authenticity is being presented. For example, contemporary popular music in Britain still seems interested in the authority that supposedly more authentic artists carry (or are made to carry). For example, it is possible to look at certain oppositional relationships within mainstream pop music[4] in the United Kingdom to see certain values being utilized to various effects. While Will Young may have won the television talent show *Pop Idol* in 2003, his early career ran closely alongside the runner up, Gareth Gates. Both are young male pop singers, yet Young's later move into a more adult-oriented light soul sound has moved him semiotically away from the mainstream pop sound of Gates, who continued to aim his music at a significantly younger market. Young's appropriation of a more sophisticated soul sound came at a time (2003) when acts such as Norah Jones, Joss Stone, Katie Melua and Amy Winehouse were releasing albums heavily indebted to soul and jazz idioms that had been absent from mainstream pop since the mid-1980s, aimed primarily at the 25–40 age bracket.[5] It is this very engagement with musical forms and artists that already have associations of authenticity, often because of their historical distance, that go some way towards granting authenticity to an artist like Will Young.[6] Yet, it only takes a simple substitution of comparative examples to see a change in value. Place Will Young next to Ray Charles, or The Sugababes next to The Supremes, or Katie Melua next to Joni Mitchell, or Joss Stone against Angie Stone and arguably authenticity assumes a new set of values (a set of values that may have much to do with race as a framework of authenticity). In this case, Young's authenticity is partially forged by his relationship to Gates, a more overtly pop performer aimed at early teens rather than young adults.

Certainly, such a relationship supports Zanes' suggestion of authenticity being forged through its other, yet the above claims are highly contingent on a range of factors that are specifically relevant to one particular value position, in other words, mine at the time of writing. Zanes is stressing the part that I as listener play in conjuring up any notion of authenticity, in whatever fashion I see fit. Yet this is not to say that the listener is wholly responsible, as authenticity can be suggested by a number of strategies at the producer's end.

Authenticity and liveness

While this work seeks to understand authenticity in relation to a variety of engagements with British popular music, one area that seems to particularly relate to the concept of authenticity is in the realm of live performance. On stage the performer has the opportunity to engage with an authenticity that oscillates between the construction of the recording process and the immediacy of the live experience. Philip Auslander (1999) points out that the record a fan may hear might sound like a unique performance in many respects, one supposedly performed in the studio; however, it is of course the result of a process of recording, rerecording, overdubbing, mixing, mastering and so on that exceeds the possibilities of live performance. That is not to say that the listener is necessarily fooled by the constructed nature of recorded music, rather Auslander suggests that the recording is a representation rather than a reproduction of a musical moment. One might be tempted then to ask where the original form is that the recording is a representation of, and again one might be tempted to think of the live performance as an expression of that original (even if it is only a version of an idealized original). However, as Auslander points out, often the live performance is as much an attempt to recreate the studio recording in a live setting:

> It makes little sense, in fact, to speak of live performance of rock apart from recording, since rock is made to be recorded: it is constructed along principles derived from recording practices, inspired by earlier music heard primarily on recordings, etc. Even if a group is unlucky enough not to have recorded, epistemologically their music is still recorded music. (84)[7]

As such it is impossible to talk about an originating point, the live and the recorded are facets of each other. Authenticity then lies as a relational concept forged between recording and live performance, one that is mutable as it is applied through judgement on the part of the spectator or listener.

However, the performance of popular music in a live setting continues to hold a level of significance in the adjudication of authenticity. That such a search for authenticity in the live performance may seem fruitless fails to recognize the very concrete associations that can still be plotted to give form to judgements about a piece of music's authentic worth. Auslander recognizes that certain genres of popular music carry with them their own markers of authenticity that may be very specific to that genre. Rock performers, for instance, are often judged on their performance history (did they 'pay their dues'?) and their ability to perform music in a situation where its *liveness* can be assessed as an indicator of authenticity (can they cut it live?). What is crucial to Auslander's analysis is a recognition that the performer is in a position to perform authenticity through the tropes associated with their style of music, in other words the rules of rock authenticity will delineate what forms of authentic representation are available to the performer and the audience alike.

One example of how choices regarding authentic live performance are shaped by generic conventions regards the use of keyboards and synthesizers. In 1998, the Welsh rock band Manic Street Preachers toured the United Kingdom. As usual the three main members, James Dean Bradfield, Nicky Wire and Sean Moore took centre stage on vocals and guitar, bass guitar and drums, respectively. However, perched at the side of the stage was a keyboard player, almost hidden from the audience and in a position where one would most likely find a monitor engineer. The gothic rock band Fields of the Nephilim went to similar lengths to disguise the incorporation of a keyboard player in their line-up as they toured the United Kingdom in the early 1990s, and more recently a reformed Smashing Pumpkins placed their newly acquired keyboard player behind their better-known drummer Jimmy Chamberlain at the rear of the stage. In these instances, the sounds generated by the synthesizers and keyboards were recognizable and related to sounds that could be heard in the recorded versions of the songs being played. Equally, in such instances the keyboard players were not invisible as such, but merely relegated to less visible areas of the stage and to some extent purposefully obscured from view. If the audience in such circumstances accepts that the sounds that they are hearing represent an accurate representation of the recorded performance why then should these players be obscured? Certainly, the answer is as much to do with rockist notions of authenticity as it is about the keyboard players not being regular members of the band. Such strategies suggest that unless a regular band member plays the keyboards, they then signify a level of inauthenticity that needs to be in some respects occluded. Even where the recorded version of a song has keyboards played by a session musician, the implication is that the band in question needs to either delegate responsibility for keyboard duties or to play them in a separate time frame to the rest of the instruments (this is the case where a band member plays the keyboards but does so as well as playing their more closely associated instrument). In the case of the Manic Street Preachers, both options are available. Some songs from their set list at the time contain musical moments played on keyboards by Bradfield in the studio, and hence given that he is playing guitar and singing, this would prove impossible to replicate live on stage. Equally, there are keyboard parts that are not played by him on the recordings and these too would need to be played by someone else. To complicate matters even further, string parts recorded on the album would need to be replicated by the keyboards in a live context adding another layer of artifice to proceedings.

Why then would a session musician playing keyboards need to be relegated to the side of the stage? Rock music relies on a number of conventions that go to make this situation so. First, the session musician is marked out (or rather obscured) as not being a member of the band, merely an auxiliary member who needs to be at least nominally excluded to preserve the gang image of the band (particularly important to a band like Manic Street Preachers as they place themselves within a lineage of *gang-bands* such as The Clash and Guns 'n' Roses). The specific issue relating to synthesizers is perhaps more a question of what instrumentation is appropriate to rock performance. The Manic Street Preachers, Fields of the Nephilim and Smashing Pumpkins all feature vocals, guitars, bass guitars and drums as their primary instrumentation (in other words the core members of the band play these instruments). Although there are plenty of examples of keyboards and synthesized sounds in their collected recorded output, they must both be recognized in a live performance as representing the recorded performance, yet they equally point to the inauthentic nature of the recorded performance through the doubling up of musical roles leading to delegation. As such they are a reminder of the fact that the recorded performance is in no way immediate and is in fact highly constructed. Therefore the live performance constrains these potential attacks on its authenticity by both reiterating the recorded performance and by sidelining its constructed nature. Equally the standard rock band instrumentation exemplified by these bands still carries hallmarks of a suspicion that synthesizers are in some way capable of faking a musical performance. As Auslander notes,

> In the 1970s, some rock groups (Queen, for instance) wrote in the liner notes to their albums that they did not use synthesizers, thus stressing their connection to the traditional instrumentation of roots rock ('real' electric guitars, drums etc.). (71)[8]

If synthesizers are used to replicate the playing of stringed or brass instruments, for example, they are complicit in a further level of duplicity that potentially undermines the authenticity of the live experience. As such they need to be marginalized even as they are evident in the sound of performance.

Authenticity is to be found somewhere between the live and the recorded, and the criteria that shapes one's experience is often in transition. Auslander acknowledges that the influential discourses that shape our notion of the authentic are subject to change over time (the inclusion of analogue synthesizers in rock discourse after the 1980s to denote historicity or a retro aesthetic, for example). Equally not all rock bands will be subject to these specific limitations, certain more symphonic forms of heavy metal may be very explicit about the use of keyboards in a live context despite the prioritization of the guitars, bass and drums. Equally rock bands have been more forgiving of the nature of the synthesizer or digital instrumentation and utilized it as part of their primary performance strategy (The Killers, Comets on Fire and Keane amongst many others have successfully incorporated non-traditional rock instrumentation into their line-up with no significant problems relating to authenticity becoming manifest).

While live performance may be one arena where the relationships to the recorded take and the audience can be measured in terms of authenticity (albeit on a sliding scale), authenticity is not merely a measure of whether the artist can 'cut it live'. Authenticity has the capability to articulate concerns not only around performance, but also around perceptions of life as it is lived. Textual moments, both musical and lyrical, can suggest relations of authenticity, and these moments are usually configured through the artists themselves in relation to the listener. As such the role of the authentic artists requires further examination.

The liberal artist

Theodore Gracyk (1996), in one of the most sustained analyses of pop authenticity so far, sees it as an effect and a strategy connected to an ideology of liberalism that runs throughout rock music. This liberal strain places the artist at the centre of meanings and values associated with authenticity:

> The unifying thread ... is an assumption that the unique individual is basic to authenticity. In a word, liberalism: there is no essential, common good beyond whatever autonomous individuals seek and choose as most worthy for themselves. I am ... talking about liberalism ... in

the classical sense that underlies notions of artistic freedom…If not outright libertarian, liberalism promotes attitudes and political structures that favour independent, self-determining, rational, unique persons. It minimizes constraints on what they think, do, and *feel*. (220)[9]

Gracyk sees rock as 'a bastion of Enlightenment assumptions about the self' (226), assumptions deliberately at odds with the postmodern tendency to see authenticity as a shallow category that tends towards pastiche (Jameson's formulation of the cultural logic of late capitalism (1991) is particularly singled out). Instead 'rock authenticity posits an absolute dichotomy between the inner and the outer, between true self and the socially constructed mask. If rock sets itself an impossible task, the resulting tensions supply a large part of rock's power' (226). As such Gracyk relies on the distinction between music as a conduit for self-expression and the forms of delivery that allow such expression to reach any kind of audience. While his identification of liberal strains within rock music seems broadly accurate (with the implicit reactionary political tendencies attendant, if not fully explored), Gracyk fails to fully explicate the role that those methods of delivery have in creating any sense of authenticity. Again the dichotomy he identifies remains just that, a paradox that artists and listeners have to negotiate. As this chapter will explore later, it is the very centrality of this perceived dichotomy that necessarily produces authenticity; one side is not an inhibitor of the other in this regard.

Gracyk concludes his study by suggesting that authenticity within rock is not necessarily a rejection of bourgeois values, indeed it is a continued commitment to an expression of those very values. One is tempted to suggest that his explication relies too heavily on specifically American strands of artistic expression (Kurt Cobain, Lou Reed, Sonic Youth, Paul Westerberg again), yet when these values are overlaid onto their British counterparts, it is not too difficult to see a correlation. Yet the spectre of class within authenticity does provide a unique problem, as the notion of the artist is often the very thing that British rock authenticity seeks to overrule. At the heart of representations of authenticity within British rock music is a commitment to class identification, particularly allied to working-class values. As the later case study on punk shows, the Oi! sub-genre distanced itself from the perceived artistic pretensions of punk and post-punk. Such a removal may at first sight be understood as a strategy to conform to a back-to-basics ideology that prioritizes the experience of urban working-class life over bourgeois experimental trends. Yet it also relies on the notion of the autonomous individual articulating expressions concerned with dominant power factors in the real world. As such Gracyk's assertion that authenticity in rock arises out of the struggle between the musician as artist and the music industry as mediator still holds true. In fact, the identification of resistance between working-class factions and the processes of the music and entertainment industry still rely on the liberalism that Gracyk identifies. However, this is often cloaked in a class rhetoric that seems at odds with the idea of artistry (a term that assumes connotations of pretension, introversion and disavowal of the 'real world', at least in the United Kingdom). In other words, I as a musician have the power to articulate my lived experience (for Gracyk's American examples these are often internal drives that need to be expressed as opposed to engagement with the social sphere) in a way that is not compromised *either* by the perceived corrupting power of a music industry allied to profit creation *or* by more cerebral approaches to music making that potentially alienate me from that lived experience. At the heart of such apparently proletarian values lies Gracyk's stream of liberalism that places the individual in opposition to institutions that seek to determine his or her behaviour and expression. Precisely what allows this convergence of working-class identification and artistic freedom of expression within British rock music is the network of associations that make up British rock music itself. It is here that we find a tangle of influences that allow the performer as artist and as *non-artist* to exist through performance. Equally it is also at this point that the listener is allowed a space to adopt specific listening positions that allow appropriate readings of such articulations without any sense of contradiction. Only in the performativity of class relations are such problems resolved, even if only temporarily.

Romantic and modern authenticity

While Gracyk's analysis of authenticity in rock prioritizes liberal trends that place the individual artist against the corporate sphere, Keir Keightley (2001) identifies two concurrent conceptual strands within rock music, Romanticism and Modernism, which account for the primacy of the artist (and all its attendant baggage) on the one hand, and the socially positioned musician in touch with the voice of the people, on the other. Both Gracyk and Keightley agree on the perception of an oppositional relationship between art and industry in popular music:

One of the great ironies of the second half of the twentieth century is that while rock has involved millions of people buying a mass-marketed, standardized commodity (CD, cassette, LP) that is available virtually everywhere, these purchases have produced intense feelings of freedom, rebellion, marginality, oppositionality, uniqueness and authenticity. It is precisely this predicament that defines rock, since negotiating the relationship between the 'mass' and the 'art' in mass art has been the distinguishing ideological project of rock culture since the 1960s.

(Keightley, 109)

However, Keightley departs from Gracyk's suggestion of liberalism to focus on the influence of both Romanticism and Modernism in the ongoing struggle for rock authenticity.

For Keightley, the authentic is both an aesthetic and ethical judgement, a piece of music is judged to be 'good' if it is 'just' or 'true' (133), and such judgements are formed around the potential influence of Romantic or Modernist imperatives. On the one hand, the legacy of Romanticism has allowed the industrial practices of popular music to be critiqued by a perceived 'return' to values associated with the pre-industrial age;[10] roots, community, populism, sincerity, directness, organic traditions and working-class sensibilities. Examples of this position can be seen in the work of Billy Bragg, New Model Army, The Levellers, Squeeze, The Streets, Plan B, Arctic Monkeys and many others. It is not difficult to see the majority of these values being worked out in much British rock music, and indeed the following case studies will come back to these ideas. However, for Keightley, Romantic influences are not enough to account for the multiple ways in which authenticity can be articulated within rock music. Modernism also provides a framework from which a critique of the industrialized nature of the music industry can be sustained. However, authenticity here is characterized through the status of the artist as an experimentalist, someone able to make a textual and performative shift away from the norms of the pop mainstream. As such the sense of community offered by Romanticism is set against an elitism fostered by Modernism, while sincerity and directness are countered by irony and obliqueness (137). Such strands not only position rock against the pop mainstream, but also allow for differentiation within rock culture. Keightley is at pains to point out that such strands can often coincide[11] and are by no means exclusive, yet they also only operate, to return to Zanes, in opposition to mainstream pop, to the industrialized mechanisms of music production and dissemination, and to other forms of rock music. It is through these two strains that one is able to allow for Gracyk's assertion of the liberal artist, whilst also maintaining the 'folk' musician as a scion of authenticity. Both models assert their authenticity as a critique of the industrially mediated pop mainstream, but in ways that are sometimes mutually exclusive, sometimes highly inter-dependent, but also highly organized, at least in the United Kingdom, around class positions. The avant-garde rock pioneer becomes associated with intellectualism and artistry associated with economic and educational advantages afforded by a middle-class upbringing[12] while the working-class rock musician speaks the voice of the people through traditional rock forms untainted by the music industry. Of course, such distinctions are never so clearly cut, yet Keightley, although never relating to class so specifically, does provide motives and imperatives that inform the relationship between authenticity and class.

One example that bears out a romanticized level of authenticity that utilizes class and class-based identity is New Model Army's 'Green and Grey'.[13] New Model Army, formed in 1980 in Bradford, West Yorkshire, have continually developed a blend of punk and roots music styles, allied to a distinctly anti-Thatcherite stance, and a commitment to left wing politics and working-class identity. Such a stance resulted in considerable criticism when the band signed to EMI in 1985, as the following passage suggests:

> Bands initially didn't change the music industry but called into question the 'politics' of some of the bands signed to identified major labels, making the naive assumption that to be punk meant some kind of deal to be politicized in favour of anarchism. Conflict were the most hilarious, simultaneously holding down the title of raw and raucous anarchist punk heroes while crusading against EMI – particularly memorable was their hostile battle with major label 'cult' punk band New Model Army who had switched to EMI at the first chance. EMI guaranteed New Model Army chart success and New Model Army didn't break the punk tradition of appearing on Top of the Pops without being as angry, daring and dangerous as possible – their singer sported an official New Model Army 'Only stupid bastards use heroin' tee-shirt, only to be bettered by the official Conflict 'Only stupid bastards use EMI' tee-shirt.
>
> ('White Punks on Bordiga', 1995)

New Model Army is a band that surrounds itself with signifiers of class origin and conflict. In the early 1980s singer Justin Sullivan went under the stage name of Slade the Leveller, a reference to an ideological offshoot of Oliver Cromwell's own New Model Army during the seventeenth century[14] (the name change reportedly was also necessary so that Sullivan could continue to claim the dole while in the band). The wearing of wooden clogs (usually from the Walkley factory in Hebden Bridge in West Yorkshire) by both the band and the band's following, the Militia, resurrected images of northern heavy industry at the turn of the century, and the strong levels of commitment shown by the Militia in their following and support of the band and themselves provided a level of communion that was articulated in many of the band's songs.

'Green and Grey' particularly tells the story of a young man (depicted in the song through native American imagery as a *brave*) who leaves his northern town to make a new life in the city, a place both of opportunity and moral and physical pollution (the song insinuates that this is London but this is never made clear). Sullivan relies heavily on romantic notions of place that situate the song's narrator in both an impoverished social position (the town where nothing ever seems to happen, the Friday night pub fight that results in a trip to the casualty department) and also a privileged position of authenticity. The use of landscape to set up definitions of place in relation to class becomes a primary motivator of authenticity in the song. The valley and the rain-sodden hills and dismal weather of the bus ride are offset against the inauthentic fantasy of the posters of holiday destinations in the hospital. Landscape stands in for temperament and belonging. While the climate is deliberately set up as unforgiving, it is configured as authentic in relation to the artificiality of the poster, and by inference the dream of the young man leaving his town. While the word 'betrayal' is never used, the song suggests that the young man leaving is turning his back particularly on familial ties and obligations that the narrator has chosen to honour, despite the temptations of a new life in the metropolis. As such the migration of the young braves is seen both in terms of familial refusal and also as a social wrong that robs the provincial north to the benefit of the urban south. This is further compounded by the apparent forgetting of the origins of the man who has moved away, highlighted by the ambiguous note at the end of the song where the narrator wonders whether his letters (of which the song seems to be a part) have ever been read.

The song integrates elements of folk instrumentation that are developed throughout the parent album *Thunder and Consolation* (1989). 'Vagabonds' particularly incorporates fiddle playing to great effect, and this is seen in the break of 'Green and Grey'. Part of New Model Army's mythos develops ideas not only of northern working-class identity (the song conflates *northern-ness* with *working class-ness*), but also of traditional forms of British identity, particularly through the use of Celtic knot work on albums and artwork, as well as tattoos worn by both band members and their Militia following. While there may not be much in the way of an inherent connection between Celtic artistry and a post-punk band orientated around northern working-class culture, the conflation of the two provides a signifier of tradition, stability, history, roots, communion, tribe and responsibility. As such the increased use of instruments associated with folk forms in itself lends authenticity to the lyrical concerns of the song. As the above quote suggests, it might be pertinent to raise questions about the status of such music if it is released through a major record label such as EMI, yet 'Green and Grey' assumes a significance that is based on issues of class and place that lend it an aura of authenticity situated in opposition to the southern metropolis, and reinforced by the close relationship to the biography of the band, and in particular, Justin Sullivan. While, it may be possible to read 'Green and Grey' as an authentic articulation of Sullivan as artist, it is equally possible that the authority of working-class experience might translate to followers of the band who do not occupy that class position.[15] Issues of organic community (amongst followers of the band) situated by the song assume a level of importance set up by a discourse that prioritizes working-class authenticity over the economic advantages of a supposedly morally impoverished middle-class existence. What forms such associations is an intensely complex discourse that requires further investigation.

Authenticity and class in rock discourse

Even if one is to take a phenomenological stance regarding authenticity and the articulation of class, it is still vital to recognize the network of potential influences that may inform any response to the musical experience. For the purposes of clarity it will be appropriate to refer to this range of influences as *rock discourse*. The use of the term 'rock' specifically is appropriate more to the concerns of this work, given its concentration on popular music forms that fall under the banner of rock music (folk rock, punk, indie rock etc.).[16] However, while it is the purpose of this chapter to highlight certain influential practices that inform rock music, it is equally clear that there will be other factors that inform pop discourse, or soul discourse, or jazz discourse but the model will still be applicable. Equally it is important to recognize that rock discourse does not exist in a vacuum, for those who are in a position to model such discourse, or for those who partake in it at the point of reception. Agency is at the heart of rock discourse and in this sense discourse as a term should be understood as a set of mutable values that may inform and influence but never determine. Indeed, discourse in this sense is a vocabulary of signifying positions offered up to the auditor. Popular music is, at least on the surface, not fond of orthodoxy, and much of its power lies in its heterogeneity, as perceived in reception. People make of music what they will, and many arguments stem from this very problem. Yet rock discourse does provide a set of values that potentially shape experience and subjectivity, not only for the listener, but also as a prism through which lived experience can be channelled into forms that make sense within popular music. Class will only ever be a part of that discourse (race and gender are also important factors) yet it is a significant one within British popular music, and it requires some explanation as to its importance.

To understand why class is a recurrent theme in the articulation of authenticity within British popular music, one needs to understand the practices that create a discourse that places working-class experience as a token of that authenticity. Any listener at any time may be immersed in a web of associations that are supported by a variety of agencies that make up rock discourse. Initially one may make some suggestions as to who or what these agencies might be. One's listening experience will inevitably be informed by values incorporated from the music press, broadcast media such as radio and television, advertising, performance, staging, interaction with other listeners both within a subcultural forum and without, interaction with immediate friends and family, the list goes on. Such interactions will inevitably form a context that is specifically aligned, either positively or negatively, with the values one encounters in the production of authenticity in the listening experience. As we shall see with the articulation of class surrounding the early 1990s dream pop scene, the music press played a significant role in placing that scene within a category of bourgeois introspection, and further within a significant lineage of art rock. Such an association, despite the lack of specific class engagement by the musicians themselves, ultimately led to a series of negative associations with middle-class music in Britain. Of course that is not to say that everyone's listening experience of a young, southern, middle-class band such as The Kooks will be affected by what the weekly music press might say, indeed there may not even be an awareness of such pronouncements. Of the categories outlined above it is usual that only some if any might have a direct influence on the listener's reception. However, to a listener who reads the music press in a sympathetic manner, it may be the case that they will make value judgements on the music based on such class affiliation. Whether they choose to accept or reject such assertions, or accept or reject the music because of those assertions, will be influenced by a wider variety of factors that exist in the social realm outside of rock discourse. While such an approach fails to provide us with a deterministic model that might predict how class is received within popular music, it does highlight the highly complex network of associations involved. Similarly, it provides us with an understanding of the values supported by rock discourse that engage with class as a signifier of authenticity. The level to which the listener is immersed within rock discourse will be highly varied, indeed the concentration on authenticity within academic circles might be understood as the preoccupation of researchers who are very highly immersed within such values, no matter how critical they may be of them. But whatever the level of engagement may be for the listener, we can make some observations about the way in which they are invited to engage with authenticity. Popular music has continually walked a fine line between its status as the people's music and its existence as a mass entertainment medium. This has obviously led to a prioritization, particularly in the United Kingdom, of small scale production being in some way more authentic. It is precisely because of such judgements that the independent music sector in Britain has often been understood to be the home of creative freedom and agency in a way that the larger corporations are not. Clearly, economies of scale suggest that the product needs to be more overtly 'commercial' if it is aimed at a larger audience. There is a suggestion here that the further away from the heart of a supposedly monolithic music industry an artist may be, the less their artistic integrity and therefore their authenticity will be compromised by commercial imperatives. While this may or may not be the case (again such a judgement may inform one's reception of authenticity within rock discourse), we are left with a chasm between producer and receiver that can never be bridged. The articulation of authenticity, and class within that category, can only ever be an unstable representation, a signification of values that provide no assurance of their veracity. However, discourse does provide a space within which it is possible to fulfil the role of an auditor who accepts significations as 'authentic'. It is unfortunately at the heart of the problem of representation that the mechanics of authenticity reside.

Phenomenological authenticity

It is clear that any form of phenomenological experience is never free of a contextualizing discourse. Within music, one of the most significant examples of phenomenological listening is Pierre Schaeffer's acousmatics, a practice linked to musique concrète. Schaeffer (1966) attempted to present sound in an unmediated form, to '*hear* with another ear' (81) through the montage and cut-up techniques of musique concrète. Both musical and non-musical sounds would sit against each other, manipulated and distorted in such a way that the listener would (hopefully) distance themselves from the idea that the sound had an originating source, be it a guitar, flute, train or street. This immediacy of sound Schaeffer termed 'acousmatics', prioritizing the phenomenological immanence of the experience of the sound itself. We can situate Schaeffer's strategy within a larger modernist project that sought to focus on significant form at the expense of representation. Clear analogies can be made with the abstract expressionism of Mondrian and Rothko in the visual arts. Barthes (1985) extends this idea with his formulation of 'modern' listening, hearing sounds on their own terms rather than as effects of physical processes:

> 'Listening' to a piece of classical music, the listener is called upon to 'decipher' this piece, i.e., to recognize (by his culture, his application, his sensibility) its construction, quite as coded (predetermined) as that of a palace at a certain period; but 'listening' to a composition (taking the word here in its etymological sense) by John Cage, it is each sound one after the next that I listen to, not in its syntagmatic extension, but in its raw and as though vertical *signifying*. (259)

However, to suggest that one is able as a listener to perceive sound in a non-mediated way seems rather ambitious. Even at the most basic level the practice of listening as an aesthetic experience relies upon a variety of value judgements made by the listener that are the result of a lifetime's experience. The very act of listening corrupts the sound into a representation of value, either positive, negative or anywhere in between. Maurice Merleau-Ponty's *The Phenomenology of Perception* (1945) shows how the listening subject might indeed not be able to wrest the listening experience from the discourse that presents it and the listener itself. Merleau-Ponty's work shows how experience is not something that exists in separation from the outside world, rather it is a way of being-in-the-world that is irreducible to a private or discrete subjective consciousness. In this way, the listener is as much a part of the listening experience as the text itself, both constituted by discourses in the world. The subject of these discourses will be more specifically examined in Chapter 4.

The significance of this for the study of authenticity is that all experience of any signification, itself already highly charged as a representation of lived experience, is further charged by the discourses that surround that listening experience. It is impossible to locate authenticity within a listening experience primarily because it is so highly mediated and overdetermined. The recorded piece of popular music is notable amongst contemporary media forms for the sheer scale of affiliated ancillary texts that accompany it. For an instant let us ignore the multiplicity of listening positions that the listener may already possess prior to exposure to rock discourse. Were such a blank listener possible, they would quickly be caught up in a network of significatory practices that would hold some form of power over their listening experience. Thus discourse proffers ways of hearing, communing and being that allow for specific engagements that may or may not be taken up by the auditor. One example of this is the prioritization of the youth audience for one of Britain's leading radio stations, BBC Radio One. Since 1993 Radio One has practised a policy of orienting playlists away from music recorded prior to the 1980s during the 1990s, and music recorded prior to 1990 at the present time during the majority of its daytime schedules. This policy was part of Radio One's self-proclaimed commitment to 'new music', and while such an approach has admirable motives, it creates an environment where anything recorded prior to 1990 is understood as belonging to an older generation, at once alienating it from the majority of its listeners who are positioned by the station as a youth audience. In the rare instances when older music has to be addressed it must be seen as relevant to newer music, as one can see in the lionization of British rhythm and blues in relation to Britpop in the mid-1990s. As such the audience is already presented with a set of value judgements that they may choose to adopt as part of their listening strategy.

The outcome of such a strategy is a form of collective amnesia that resides in the suggestion of popular music as inherently disposable. Particularly within the mainstream pop idiom, disposability has been a significant factor in the reception of music, an approach reinforced by industry practice and patterns of consumption. The single format, in its variety of forms, has continued to be a transient pleasure, a text that can be potentially replaced at a weeks notice by the next new release. This is further reinforced by the rapid rate at which singles are deleted from a record company's roster after their release, usually within a month of a successful record's disappearance from the charts. Of course, were one to look at the growth of back catalogue album sales since the late 1980s and the rise in nostalgia radio stations in the United Kingdom such as Classic Gold it would be apparent that the industry has been able to incorporate an older market, one that perhaps viewed their music consumption as

transient and disposable in their teens, who have an historical awareness of popular music. At the present time this has resulted in a polarity
between primarily teenage target audiences who may not be easily able
to engage with the historical depth and breadth of popular music, and
an older market, primarily disengaged from the contemporary idiom,
but who are familiar with the back stories of popular music to some
extent. While these markets are to be understood as just that, simply
markets (there is no reason why a 17-year old in 2008 would not be able
to or want to listen to Japan or Parliament or The Yardbirds), they do
illustrate the mechanism by which sign systems within popular music
can be replayed over and over again. Indeed if one were to experience
popular music through BBC Radio One, daytime television music shows
and the mainstream music press, it would be easy to bypass a wide variety of music that might problematize notions of authenticity exhibited
through contemporary artists. British rock band Towers of London, for
example, are able to commit themselves to the usual displays of rock
rebellion (smashing equipment, stage invasions etc.), all highly contingent on an authenticity that is constituted through class amongst
other factors, primarily because they engage with an audience ostensibly younger than that which might deem their performance inauthentic
in relation to The Clash or The Who. That is not to say that a younger
audience are fooled due to a lack of requisite knowledge, such an assertion would be somewhat elitist and highly arguable, but that an older
audience familiar with the band's predecessors is able to experience the
authenticity of such a performance through a network of meaning that
renders their antagonism within a particular context.

Rebellion, recollection and amnesia

The connection between rebellion and authenticity here is pertinent,
particularly within the field of rock music. That rebellion is so often
signified within popular music through the supposed immanence of
performance, and within a vocabulary forged by rock discourse itself
(i.e. precursors), suggests both an immediacy and a historicity at work.
The role of class here is in the 'organic' nature of performance, the
immediacy of the folk voice at work through the performer in a supposedly unmediated fashion. While a 2004 concert by Towers of London
at Anglia Polytechnic University in Cambridge ended in the arrest of
their lead singer Donny Tourette (for damage to the venue) two possible
readings are at work simultaneously. The first sees the antagonism of
performance leading to a 'bursting out' of the aggression of the music

into physical violence, a suggestion that the content of the music is reinforced by an actual act. As such the content of the music and the band's semiotic presence is made manifest in a form that exceeds simply the performance of recorded output and the notion of performance as entertainment. However, it is equally possible to nullify such a manifestation by reading this violent act as a performance of applicable rock idioms passed down through rock discourse. Therefore we are left with an act that both relies on a historically based vocabulary of action dependent on precursors, while at the same time situating itself as immediate and outside history. How might one account for such a paradox? The most sensible way to understand this conundrum is to see this act as a performative strategy that suggests authenticity (through the breach in the performance of the music to incorporate extra-musical violence), constructed through a discourse that allows such acts, in other words rock discourse.

Such an approach creates a significant problem if we look at authenticity as being a rupture in mediating agencies such as the music industry or the rock press. Yet this is a problem that has continually haunted popular music. To return to The Who, Pete Townshend's trademark demolition of his equipment both allowed a locus of authenticity that stretched the boundaries of acceptable pop practice during the 1960s, yet it also quickly became an accepted part of the band's performance. Such is the nature of the semiotic articulation of rebellion within rock music. Yet this is not to say that for the audience such an expression is rendered inert through incorporation and repetition. Again the immediacy of the event becomes significant in allowing the audience to participate in such an expression as being inherently meaningful even if it does become a routine staple of performance. The same can be said of seeing the same band on two consecutive nights and experiencing the same 'ad-libs' between songs. The way in which authenticity in the live arena works is by foregrounding immediacy over historicity, indeed the value of much live music, certainly in the United Kingdom, is based around the experience of the *now*, rather than the contextualizing of the *then*. As such Towers of London's violent stage act contains both a perceived honesty in performance and a debt to precursors that can be experienced in a detached manner that is perhaps at odds with what the performance itself is trying to produce. In this way performance relies upon a certain level of immediate amnesia conjoined with recollection of the idioms of rock practice to give it meaning, particularly in relation to the articulation of the drives behind the music itself.

It is within this contradictory double bind that authenticity has to situate itself for popular music. Few artists escape the vocabulary of authenticity that in itself renders authenticity elusive. That authenticity in popular music is understood as a representation of the value of authenticity, rather than as an articulation of events, social situations, social relations or even class positions in the world outside of popular music renders it inert in anything more than an evocative sense. While the need for authenticity to be an issue for both fan and critic may have socio-political motives, this need is undermined in the last instance by the very performativity of such articulations. In this way, we are left with a curious situation where, on ITV's *The South Bank Show* ('The Darkness', 2004) lead singer of UK rock band The Darkness, Justin Hawkins, can present his group as both authentic (i.e. a traditional rock band responsible largely for their own musical output) and as entertainers (i.e. performers within a global entertainment network). Hawkins' comments cut to the heart of the performativity of authenticity within rock music. He is only capable of being authentic through the vocabulary that suggests authenticity within rock discourse. One is tempted to ask what playing rock music and trashing a music venue ultimately say in any real socio-political sense. Yet within the discourse of British rock music they say an awful lot, albeit in words hewn from a paradigm that exists within an entertainment medium. As such it is vital to understand articulations of authenticity (and class within that category) as articulations specific to a unique and often hybrid form, primarily erected in opposition to equally fluid and hybrid articulations of inauthenticity.

As such we return back to Zanes' spatial notion of identifying the authentic though a *moving away from*, an identification of the inauthentic to make claims about the authentic. Towers of London regain authenticity through performance rites that place them in opposition to the dominant idioms of highly produced and choreographed mainstream pop performance and leftfield indie rock, and in so doing claim a place within rock authenticity and discourse. Equally The Darkness claim their authenticity through opposition to both of these forms while claiming a more sophisticated relationship between authenticity and entertainment. In other words, it is possible to 'mean it, man' (to paraphrase John Lydon) while at the same time be an entity highly involved in the mainstream global music industry (something that Towers of London currently are not). However, such positions are not without their problems. The entertainment aspect of The Darkness' music might actually alienate fans who look to rock discourse as an assurance of authenticity.

The 'problem' of authenticity

If authenticity is then defined by its other, it is vital to understand the myriad practices that rock discourse potentially imposes upon any reading of a piece of music, a video, a performance or an artist. Ultimately, each individual experience is made up of web of meanings in constant flux that will shape the way in which we engage with a musical text, not all of which are defined simply by rock discourse (or whichever musical discourse is pertinent). However, the following chapters on folk rock, punk and dream pop attempt to unpick some of the contingent factors that shape authentic depictions of class at given moments. Certainly, no examination can ever be exhaustive, and, as suggested above, a variety of other contingent factors will shape any potential meaning at any given reading. Yet below the resonance that rock discourse seeks to impose upon signification is a deeper problem relating to the very articulation of authenticity, veracity and truth. That is to say that any textual articulation of class (as one example) can only ever be so as a representation. Popular music has historically made this more explicit by its situation within an entertainment medium. One reads a pop song not as documentary first and foremost but as an aesthetic experience related to pleasure and desire. A pop song will not hold up any notion of veracity with the same authority as a newspaper, or a documentary, it is forever tightly bound to notions of leisure, consumption and pleasure that often seem at odds with possible social agendas. That is not to say that popular music cannot connect with lived experience, the subsequent case studies show how such texts approach the problem. Yet given that the majority of popular music since the advent of rock 'n' roll has dealt with romanticized desire as its primary focus, a representation of an elusive and transient goal, all popular music is left with a gap between what it represents and that which is being referred to. The music of The Smiths provides us with a useful example here. Morrissey's lyrics notoriously take the accepted idiom of the love song and explicate desire through a lens that is almost socially realist in its focus. As such songs such as 'Hand in Glove' (1983) and 'How Soon is Now?' (1985) give the suggestion of desire being dealt with in an authentic way, in a way that the audience will recognize and deem authentic in relation to depictions of desire in mainstream pop music. Yet such depictions become equally fantastical through their very status as representation. The reality that such lyrics may aspire to slips ever further away into a new idiom of desire, one that may be at odds with traditional accounts, but one that is equally removed from its focus through its placing within the context of a popular song. Yet it becomes authentic through its opposition to contemporary depictions of desire that are explicitly escapist.

The suggestion that all representation demands a removal from the real is not new; indeed it is at the heart of post-Saussurian semiotics. Yet it is vital to understand that when the term 'authenticity' is used in relation to a piece of music, it is only ever an authentic experience in relation to other representations. Therefore acoustic Dylan becomes more 'authentic' in relation to electric Dylan through folk discourse, Oasis become more 'authentic' in relation to Blur through rock discourse and the use of class, McFly become more 'authentic' in relation to Blue through the intersection of pop and rock discourse. That they are authentic in and of themselves, that is to say that they articulate social concerns outside of popular music, is arguable and virtually irrelevant. The problem is compounded if the position is taken that the orientation of authenticity is actually constructed against an equally elusive set of values, in other words inauthenticity. To formulate notions of the authentic and inauthentic by juxtaposing two particular pieces of music becomes next to useless when no originating position is taken by the piece of music deemed inauthentic. As the later case study suggests, dream pop may be understood as inauthentic so as to affirm the authenticity of the Madchester scene, yet dream pop specifically fails to engage with any notion of authenticity. It is its very failure to do so that marks it out, through rock discourse, as inauthentic in any social or political sense. As such either value ceases to be based on any fixed set of determinants.

At this point one may be inclined to suggest that authenticity is not then an issue at all, merely a phantasm that haunts popular music historically and for no real purpose. However, as Goodwin (1991) points out, many consumers of popular music do insist on a distinction between serious and trivial forms within popular music, indeed such distinctions act through a highly charged set of value judgements. That these value judgements may be in some way related to socio-political trends outside of popular music, and almost certainly refracted by popular music discourse in all its forms, is almost certainly the case. Yet the very performativity of authenticity and its tighter relationship to rock discourse suggests that such articulations are radically decentred at best. So how is one to understand the highly charged role that these articulations have? After the deconstruction of authenticity one is left with only one clear conclusion, that articulations of authenticity within popular music are not so much about representing something outside of the discourse, but rather as an examination and affirmation of the insecurities that the subject may feel as a consumer, individual, social particle and national subject. Deleuze and Guattari's notion of the *concept* resisting representation is of use here. In *What is Philosophy?* (1994) 'concepts' are identified not as labels or names attached to things, but rather as orientations or directions of thinking. If we are to recognize that articulations of authenticity within popular music are made inherently problematic from a representational standpoint due to the prismatic nature of pop discourse, then such representations can only be seen as sites for the individual to explore the notion of authenticity. This would explain precisely *why* people invest so much importance in the notion, as pointed out by Goodwin. The problem of authenticity is a necessary effect of the nexus between commercial culture as a profit-making enterprise, and art as an expressive form.

As the later case studies suggest, the notion of the authentic becomes highly prioritized, is indeed even given birth by, perceived outside 'threats' closely linked to commercial imperatives. Folk music becomes homogenized and imbued with veracity in the face of the mass production of music and urbanization. Punk reacts in a range of highly charged forms to commercialization, particularly in its later styles. Madchester assumes class 'superiority' over dream pop through the music press due to the perceived emasculation of British indie music driven by middle-class affluence. The impact of commercial imperatives on popular music leads to a clash between its status as product and its status as expressive form. As previous studies have suggested (Frith, 1988 and Dyer 1979, particularly) it is not difficult to understand the two impulses as symbiotic, indeed it is the very nature of popular music. Yet the schism is still perceived as a real one, particularly in relation to groups who progress from local music scenes (as with Madchester) up to national and global exposure through signing contracts with media organizations. The very anxiety that commercial culture in some way bastardizes organic expression provides a site of contestation over the nature of authenticity. It is an effect of the perceived differing drives that shape what popular music is. That is not to say that popular music is in any way schizophrenic, rather that its whole arises out of two seemingly oppositional drives, profit and artistic expression. Were this not the case, mainstream pop music would assume a higher degree of authentic kudos, due to its highly commodified nature of expression. In not seeking to engage with social concerns in any real form it most accurately represents itself as a product of pleasure and consumption. Yet other musical forms continue to use mainstream pop music as a scion of inauthenticity to bolster their own veracity. Given then that such claims are inherently alienated from that which they seek to represent, one is left with no alternative other than to see the articulation of authenticity as a Deleuzian *concept* that performs the inherent anxieties about authenticity that popular music as a form produces. Such an understanding accounts for the often-contradictory messages that abound when dealing with authenticity, and also explains the ongoing negotiation of authenticity within a variety of discourses throughout popular music in all its forms.

To say that articulations of the authentic are reinforcing is however misleading. Rock discourse has stepped in the way of social veracity in such a way as to provide a mythical and fantastical field within which authenticity (and class again as a subset within that category) is perceived in mythical ways. Indeed it is that very mythical aspect that allows such problems to be dealt with in a non-threatening manner. Historically, whenever the notions of politics and pop music have crossed over, be it U2, Public Enemy or Wings, the main site of contestation has been over the issue of the form's ability to represent truthfully. Yet popular music is still capable of displaying anxiety over authenticity away from such considerations, through the value systems set up by rock discourse. As such it is vital to understand some of the forms this anxiety may take, and the mechanisms that prioritize such anxieties.

Rock discourse and authenticity

Rock discourse is a term used throughout this chapter and it necessarily requires some explanation. As already suggested the term here is used to suggest a network of factors that form value systems in any number of settings to allow potential readings of texts, images and representations within rock music. Although the term does not immediately suggest this, here it is taken as a system that is in this incarnation inherently British; however, that is not to say that it may not be informed by contributing factors from outside the United Kingdom (indeed it invariably is). It is also pertinent to suggest that an exhaustive examination of exactly what British rock discourse is would take up a whole other study, so it is only my intention to outline the way in which it might operate. Take a look at any singular experience of an individual musical text and the network of values exerted upon its interpretation will be myriad. Equally, as suggested above, the individual experiencing the text will exert their own value systems at the time of interpretation that may embrace or resist the forces of rock discourse. Pattie (1999) shows the performative nature of rock authenticity through his analysis of an encounter between Richey James (Edwards), guitarist and songwriter with Manic Street Preachers[17] and NME journalist Steve Lamacq. After Lamacq's questioning of the authenticity of James' band in the press, the guitarist approached him following a gig at Norwich Arts Centre, produced a razorblade and carved '4 REAL' into his own arm. Pattie understands James' visceral act as both a private moment that reinforces his commitment to what his band represent, and as an act informed by the public sphere of rock discourse (in particular Pattie points out the use of '4' instead of 'for', an idiosyncrasy often connected to the work of Prince; 'I Would Die 4 U', 'Money Don't Matter 2 Night'; 'I Feel 4 U').

> The act is private but has public consequences; the sign is authentic but archly so, calling attention to itself as an artificial statement as it declares its reality. In other words, James' act is both declaration and performance; it is manifestly constructed, but in a way that does not automatically invalidate it as a statement of real intent.
>
> (1999)

In the act of carving authenticity into his arm, James is connecting with a performative vocabulary that speaks of his authenticity as he performs it; 'Ritchie (*sic*) James' act was, and remains, extreme, but it can be read (and James undoubtedly wished it to be read) as a sign of his investment in the central myth of rock as an authentic, and authenticating language' (ibid.). It is through rock discourse that authenticity is constructed, articulated and understood, for both performer and audience. Pattie specifically points to the role of the music press in providing a forum within which authenticity can be understood in ways specific to rock music, particularly through reviews of live performances. His analysis of a concert by The Verve shows how an icon of authenticity (such as lead singer Richard Ashcroft taking off his shoes as he approaches the stage, both an articulation of readiness for battle and openness and vulnerability) constructs authentic value as it is performed, and is understood by the audience as both a performance and an authentically imminent phenomenon. However, the language of authenticity is not going to be overarching for the entire audience, rock discourse acts through a variety of outlets, shaping experience to a variety of degrees. As such it is important to understand this discourse only as a set of forms that potentially exert power over interpretation, they are never wholly determinant. To explain the forces at work, it is more useful to concentrate on an instance of interpretation and from that point examine the role of value systems, such as class identity, that may be present in an engagement with rock discourse.

In 1994 London four-piece Elastica released their third single 'Connection' on the Deceptive label. At first sight their place within the rock format is cemented by both their traditional guitar-oriented instrumentation and indie punk sound. The primarily female line-up (Justine Frischmann, Donna Matthews, Annie Holland alongside the one male member Justin Welch) is not uncommon within the category of British indie music at the time but places certain stresses on gender that are equally complicated by the band's tomboyish image. The single itself is a lurching punk pop song heavily indebted to Wire, indeed the band conceded royalties to Wire over the similarity between 'Connection' and the latter's 'Three Girl Rhumba' (1977). At the time Frischmann was widely known to be dating Blur's Damon Albarn, and had been previously romantically involved with Brett Anderson from Suede (of whom she had been an early member). Another contingent factor was Frischmann's parentage; her father was a wealthy engineering consultant, contributing to some of London's most eye-catching contemporary architecture including the Centrepoint building on Charing Cross Road and the National Westminster Tower. These factors jarred uncomfortably with the British music press particularly, who singled out Frischmann as an upper-middle class brat dabbling in rock music.[18] Her gender and relationships immediately placed her in the role of Blur's very own Yoko Ono (a name that has secured its very own blinkered gravitas within rock discourse as a curse), her class suggested an inability to relate to rock music in any authentic way, and her band's musical borrowings equally suggested nothing more than a conscious attempt to jump on to the emergent bandwagon of Britpop. While Elastica went on to be highly successful in their own way they never recovered any kind of critical kudos from the *New Musical Express* or *Melody Maker* and continued to be regarded as hangers-on. Their status was assured by values imposed by rock discourse that value originality and authenticity, certainly within indie culture in the United Kingdom. These values, as we will see, place notions of authenticity within class strictures. Indeed Blur at this time were reinventing their own image with the *Parklife* album (1994), moving away from their middle-class art school roots and engaging, albeit often ironically, with Thames Estuary working-class culture (something their Essex roots allowed them to achieve without too many problems, early reports often cite the band as originally from London, rather than the more suburban Essex town of Colchester). That Elastica failed to pull off a similar smokescreen relegated them to a perceived artificial version of what Blur and Suede were attempting to do. Equally Elastica's musical touchstones (Wire, The Fall, Magazine, The Stranglers) benefited from historical revaluation that turned them in to sacrosanct scions of post-punk (even despite the highly ambivalent attitude from the music press to The Stranglers at the height of their success). In other words the music press portrayed Elastica as a pastiche of an indie band, articulated primarily along economic, class, gender and historical lines.

While such a portrayal within the music press only serves to outline the notion of authenticity that the music press wishes to deal with, it does provide a significant amount of resonance when papers such as the *NME* and *Melody Maker* hold (or held) an enormous amount of power in getting indie and alternative artists into the mainstream, as they did in the early 1990s. Place Elastica on *Top of the Pops* in front of an audience unversed in such value systems and one is left with a whole new set of concepts, that might speak much more highly of authenticity when compared to the mainstream pop that appears alongside the band. Equally seeing Elastica play live adds automatically through the immanence of performance to throw the argument in new directions.

To summarize, one might understand rock discourse as a value system that works horizontally through history (and that history's representation) and vertically through the variety of media that any musical text may utilize. Its importance here is in its capacity to represent authenticity, and class within that category, on its own terms while appearing to engage with a lived experience outside of the music industry. However, it is only ever able to do so as a site of contestation and anxiety about the individual's place in relation to the industry. While the *NME* may berate Frischmann's origins, it does so in a context that allows its own status as a magazine owned by a multinational publisher, in close connection to the mainstream music industry (a relationship that has become significantly closer since the mid-1990s). Perhaps Elastica's role was vital to Britpop in that it provided an example of what not to be that was still situated within the scene itself, creating a whipping boy that conferred authenticity on other artists. Certainly, Suede's Brett Anderson and Blur's Damon Albarn gained in their relationship with Frischmann as mediated through the weekly music press. That such gains held little or no validity outside of the discourse of British rock music is largely irrelevant to the argument.

4
Performing Class

Chapters 2 and 3 have outlined the ways in which the categories of class and authenticity have been understood, and the potential problems with applying such understandings to readings taken from the canon of British popular music. Class itself becomes a category that is not so much an effect of economic, political or social determinants (although they undoubtedly play a role) but rather a category of self-perception that can be used in a variety of ways for differing ends at differing times. If we are to understand authenticity as the primary motivator behind articulations of class in British popular music, equally we must see it as a fluid category, a value associated with certain textual moments or performances that undermine its very status as truly 'authentic' in its more commonly understood definition. Throughout the above discussion I have come to use the words 'performance' and 'performative' to suggest the way in which the categories of class and authenticity may be used. It is the role of this chapter to explore exactly what is meant by these terms in this context.

Performativity theory has increasingly become a hotly contested area within a variety of disciplines, from the study of the philosophy of science (Pickering, 1994) to economic sociology (Callon, 1998) and, of course, performance studies (Phelan, 1993; Schechner, 1994; Diamond, 1996; Conquergood, 2002; Schechner, 2002). In relation to popular music, performativity and performance theory have enjoyed a limited usage, although it is currently a developing area of critical inquiry. This is primarily because essentialist ideas of authenticity, amongst other areas, have largely been rejected in favour of processual means of understanding popular music. Simon Frith (1996) acknowledges the performative relationship between artist and audience when he says,

The performance artist depends on an audience which can interpret her work *through its own experience of performance*, its own understanding of seduction and pose, gesture and body language; an audience which understands, however 'instinctively' (without theorizing), the constant dialogue of inner and outer projected by the body in movement. For performance art to work it needs an audience of performers; it depends on the performance of the everyday. (205–6)[1]

In this way Frith understands performance not as a one way method of expression that is clearly definable against 'realness', rather it is a set of tropes that are recognizable to an audience, and which the audience interpret through their own performance in a dialogic manner. This relationship is culturally based for Frith, an effect of 'urbanization and the decline of intimacy . . ., as an effect of industrial capitalism . . ., as an effect of commodity fetishism' (206). Performance is understood through the conventions of performance and the audience are complicit with the performance, even if they are inclined to see it as naturalized for whatever reason and that naturalization is significant in that it assures the veracity of a performance even as it is *performed*. Indeed Frith shows how performance is key to the process of making a piece of popular music significant to the listener:

We don't, after all, consume the stars but their performances. If the singer's voice makes public (makes manifest, makes available) the supposed sounds of private (personal, individual) feeling, then these public gestures are consumed privately, fitted into our own narratives, our own expressive repertories. Similarly, if all songs are narratives, if they work as mini-musicals, then their plots are a matter of interpretation both by performers attaching them to their own star stories *and* by listeners, putting ourselves in the picture, or, rather, placing their emotions – or expressions of emotion – in our own stories, whether directly (in this situation, in this relationship, now) or, more commonly, indirectly, laying the performance over our memories of situations and relationships: nostalgia, as a human condition, is defined by our use of popular song. (211)

Other writers studying popular music have similarly sought to integrate performativity and performance theory into their theoretical framework. Walser (1993), Fast (2001), Waksman (1999), Warwick (2007) and Malbon (1999) have all integrated elements of performance theory into their work. Malbon sees the clubbing experience as a site of performative actions that shape identity and subjectivity through the learning and performing of bodily actions, styles and forms of spectatorship. In this way clubbers perform consumption to mark themselves out from others and to include themselves within a culture. This accounts for the way in which cultural agents become so through learned performance, and Frith's work shows how performance is not merely the artificial but a means of connecting an audience and performer through a dialogue. However, the conflation of *performance* and *performativity* is to be treated with care. Certainly, performance studies has adopted the notion of performativity, yet performativity is not merely the aspect of performance in a staged setting (indeed Schechner's work has gone some way to show how the staging of theatre potentially fails to contain the limits of performance). Performativity has particular relations to language, discourse and subjectivity, relations that initially have very little to say on the subject of class and authenticity, let alone popular music.

Herbert Marcuse (1955) uses the concept of the 'performance principle' as a form of Freud's reality principle to account for levels of instinctual repression under capitalism. Marcuse suggests that given the overabundance of wealth generated by capitalism, libidinous drives need to be checked by something other than scarcity. Instead capitalism modifies our sense of self into a consuming narcissistic subject that seeks to acquire (goods and capital), providing momentum for capitalism's ongoing existence. Later, and perhaps most significantly, performativity is analysed in the conjunction between philosophy and language, from its origins in the work of John Langshaw Austin, particularly *How to Do Things with Words* (1962), to the influential work of Judith Butler. Between Austin and Butler there is a transition in the use of the concept of performativity, from speech act to cultural and subjective performance through the work of Searle (1969) and Derrida (1988). As Loxley (2007) illustrates, Derrida's contribution brings the element of deconstruction that allows an understanding of subjectivity shaped through the process of doing (it also broadens the scope of what performativity refers to beyond conscious performance types), and as such performativity becomes a 'carry-home concept' (Loxley, 2) that finds applicability in a number of realms of theory.

Butler's work particularly assumes importance for the application of class signification in British popular music for a number of reasons. In the first instance her analysis of sexuality, gender and desire provides a performative model that accounts for the way in which articulations of class and authenticity constitute symbolic subjects, or implied listeners within popular music. Such an approach connects with a more general post-structuralist trend that understands subjectivity as a fluid and constituted entity in flux (Weedon, 1987; Zweig, 1995). Secondly, Butler's model of performative gender relations is predicated on a discursive model, influenced primarily by Michel Foucault, Jacques Derrida and Pierre Bourdieu, which relates subjectivity not just to performance but also to relations to discourse. As such class articulations become an effect of a discourse (what I have hitherto called 'rock discourse') that interpellates listeners to perform class positions in relation to textual moments. Even where some level of resistance, or to use Butler's phrase 'ambivalence', is encountered in relation to such interpellations, class still becomes a performative act in negation. As such the act of listening to a piece of popular music, and consequent identification with it in whatever form, amounts to a performative act, regulated by a discourse of values and associations that constitute the listener in the act of listening. Of course it must be recognized that Butler's work on performativity has rarely been equated with British popular music. In its application to the study of class in British popular music, a whole new terrain needs to be mapped, but Butler's work does provide a theoretical model that allows a shift away from Marxist and Weberian determinant models of class and class-consciousness, towards an understanding of class as constituting signification.

Butler's work can be understood as a continuation of Austin's concept of *Performative Utterances* (1962). Performative utterances are language moments that do not describe the act of doing something, but constitute acts in themselves. Common examples are the 'I do' of the wedding ceremony, 'I claim this land in the name of the Empire' or 'I name this dog Rover'. Such utterances are not merely representational, they are performative in that they enact the act as it is uttered. Butler utilizes Austin's concept to question assumptions regarding sexuality, gender and desire, particularly the *naturalized* status of sexuality in relation to the body. Through *Gender Trouble* (1990a), *Bodies That Matter* (1993) and *Excitable Speech* (1997), Butler seeks to attack the regulative discourse that gives ontological priority to sex over gender and desire. Such a discourse positions sex as fixed and immutable while gender and desire are constructed in relation to it. The naturalization of sex is highly problematic for Butler, and her work illustrates the ways in which people *perform* their sexual identities in a myriad of forms. This performance is influenced by a discourse of sexual identity that not only provides the vocabulary of the performative act, but also seeks to hide its performative nature, ensuring its naturalization. In other words, sexual identity is not a biological determination, but a sequence of open-ended but discursively limited practices.

The discourses of sexuality itself are particularly the focus of Butler's later works. Discourse is understood by Butler to operate through repetitive signifying processes[2] that provide a certain vocabulary of performance through which to enact sexual identities. As such 'male' and 'female', categories seen as primarily natural, are revealed as performative identities provided for us by the iteration of sexual identities across time and space. Indeed such discursive influences go to formulate the subject through their performance. By 2005, Butler, in *Giving an Account of Oneself*, had called for a whole new ethical framework that centred upon the very fluidity of subjectivity, positioning the self as an effect of relations to the social sphere. Such a subjectivity then has no power to constitute itself, rather it is called into being by its recognition. In effect discourse, however it is constituted itself, iterates the subject into being.

Parker and Kosofsky Sedgwick (1995) provide an interesting example of the relationship between speech and act when they focus upon the policy adopted by the Pentagon in 1993 to police lesbians and gay men in the American military. Instead of homosexuality perceived as a state of being, in the terms of the policy homosexuality becomes defined by 'homosexual conduct, defined as a homosexual act, a *statement* that the member is homosexual or bisexual, or a marriage or attempted marriage to someone of the same gender' (5).[3] As such the Pentagon is enforcing a policy that refuses to acknowledge one's homosexuality unless one is seen to perform it in recognizable ways. In such an instance, the US military and their policy makers act as a discursive power that is willing to compel a recognition of homosexuality in response to the performance of acts prescribed as such. That formative policy is at the heart of such a document enforces the legitimacy of such recognition, and provides not only a legitimated model of identity (the serviceman who does not perform any acts perceived to be homosexual is perceived as heterosexual), but also a delegitimated one (the serviceman who does perform an act perceived to be homosexual gets expelled from service). While such guidance may be expedient in the face of an increasingly visible gay population in the United States (and one suspects that such attitudes are being redressed) it illustrates the ways in which a discursive power attempts to provide performative roles that exist prior to the subject. Butler addresses the potentially vertiginous effect of a mechanism that constitutes subjectivity through performances inscribed prior to that subjectivity:

To claim that there is no performer prior to the performed, that the performance is performative, that the performance constitutes the appearance of a 'subject' as its effect is difficult to accept. This difficulty is the result of a predisposition to think of sexuality and gender as 'expressing' in some indirect or direct way a psychic reality that precedes it. The denial of the *priority* of the subject, however, is not the denial of the subject; in fact the refusal to conflate the subject with the psyche marks the psychic as that which exceeds the domain of the conscious subject.

(1990b, 263–4)

It is in such excess that ambivalence can occur. It is by no means impossible that a US military serviceman may perform acts that constitute homosexuality, yet in the discursive field, such ambivalent acts are also defined by the vocabulary of the Pentagon and the US military and legislative framework. In other words, even if one does not conform, one's subjectivity assumes a dimension provided for, if only in a negative form, by a discursive field. In *Excitable Speech* (1997) Butler elaborates:

Thus, to be addressed is not merely to be recognized for what one already is, but to have the very term conferred by which the recognition of existence becomes possible. One comes to 'exist' by virtue of this fundamental dependency on the address of the Other. One 'exists' not only by virtue of being recognized, but, in a prior sense, by being recognizable. (5)

In *Excitable Speech* subjectivity becomes an effect of censorship, the limitation of performable identities by discursive fields. To relate this to popular music and class identity, rock discourse provides a legitimate form of ambivalence in relation to dominant discourses in a wider society that marginalize working-class experience.[4] That is not to say that rock discourse is independent of a broader discourse of class, rather it is an ambivalent effect of it, providing a means of articulating class subjectivities that may be at odds with dominant modes, but which are in the last instance still informed in relation to them. From Butler's work the role of excess related to ambivalent relations to discourse has to be understood as an excess of unconscious desire, that which is not accounted for by a wider social discourse of class. In other words, rock discourse is the excess of working-class subjectivity finding its own form. Yet the role of class articulation as an assurance of (supposed) authenticity goes so far as to reconfigure psychic excess as a mechanism by which commodification is made invisible. That is not to say that psychic excess related to class identity is not catered for by rock discourse, but it serves a dual role in confirming the subject's status as consumer while at the same time valuing agency, social communion and marginal identities.

Towards a performative theory of class

While Butler's focus is primarily gender oriented, it is not difficult to see how this can be applied to class signification. Having said that, the application of performance theory to the category of class has so far been relatively underdeveloped.[5] Rojek (2000) understands leisure as an activity that tells others who we are, suggesting the primacy of performativity, and one can situate popular music as a sphere within which leisure activities (listening, going to a concert, reading the music press) reside. Rojek suggests that leisure has departed from its role as a ritual to a new role as a performance, one that constructs subjectivity as it is engaged in. However, the roles of popular music and class are not fully explored within Rojek's analysis, leaving the specific mechanics of performance in relation to this aspect of popular culture unexplored. Ross (2001) addresses the absence of any coherent relationship between class and performativity with some incredulity:

> This critical neglect is especially perplexing in part because of the central importance of discursive construction and cultural performativity as analytic heuristics in gender and race studies. In these areas of inquiry, sophisticated conceptions of discursivity and performativity are employed to interrogate ideological constructions. Inexplicably, class is left out of such explorations, despite the fact that it is even more constructed and performed than gender and race. (3)

His point is well made, the connection between working-class subjectivities and discursive cultural spaces remains distinctly unexplored.

Fraser (1999) does attempt to provide an account of class performativity in relation to queer identity, an underdeveloped area of inquiry due to the lack of significant contribution to Queer theory by Marxism in the States. Fraser seeks to reconcile the lack of historicizing processes at work in Butler's performance theory, suggesting the need for a recognition of narrative as form, which historicizes performativity and discursive relations. Butler's focus on sexual status is deliberate, given her concerns regarding the shaping of gendered subjectivities in the face of cultural politics. However, Fraser provides an account of difference that sees subjectivity informed by (race), gender *and* class. Fraser points out the invisibility of class in queer identities, but that is not to say that class is not an important factor in the performance of queer identity. Using the work of Lawler (1999a) and Hennessey (1995), Fraser shows how the aestheticization of self that allows for queer identity is itself a quality of middle-class subjectivities, particularly the 'new bourgeois professional class' (Hennessey, 150). As such the aesthetic *theatricalization* of the body in queer identities is only possible because of implicit and naturalized discursive limits informed by class identities. Such limits not only position middle-class subjectivity as inherently 'right', but also grant the ability to aestheticize the body as a site of difference and mimesis that reverses the discursive conventions that stake 'queer' as unallowable. However, the very ability to reappropriate and recontextualize such an identity relies on the performativity of a particular class identity. Again, Skeggs' assertion that middle-class practitioners have increased forms of capital that allow for other forms of discursive ambivalence (the ability to recontextualize 'queerness' on the body, the ability to 'perform' working-class authenticity) is at odds with the ways in which class identities are performed within popular music. It is clear that working-class youth are capable of recontextualizing performative identities (mods, rockers, teddy boys), yet it is equally clear that the discourse of class continues to shape recontextualized selfhood, and it is in this relationship between an interpellated class identity and the limits of discursive potential that popular music signifies class in multiple ways.

It may seem straightforward to assert that working-class identity can be understood as a performative operation within rock discourse. However, it is imperative that the characteristics of Butler's understanding of performativity are isolated to understand the ways in which those elements allow for an understanding of class signification (or performance). In the first instance we must decide the level of performativity provided for by class articulations, however they appear in British popular music. Secondly we must address the nature of the discursive field that iterates these performative identities. Finally, we need to consider the role of ambivalence in relation to these proffered performative identities, an issue that will become significant through the following case studies, particularly when class identity is inferred by the negation of performance (thereby allowing for a new performative identity).

Class and performativity

How are class identities performed by popular music? One of Butler's motivations in providing a performative account of sexuality and gender is the perception that feminism has traditionally understood women as a group with shared, common characteristics. As such, feminism as a discourse equally provides *a priori* roles and performative actions that constitute womanhood. For Butler such assumptions undermine more radical alternatives for the construction of a gendered subjectivity. Equally, as discussed in Chapter 2, socio-economic stratifying models of class analysis have tended to focus on the shared characteristics of class participants in *real* terms; economic acumen, social practices, employment status and mobility to give just four examples. As suggested above, such formulations in relation to popular music have tended to treat class as an originating factor or influence: working-class kids make working-class music.[6] However, as Skeggs illustrates, the issue of the perception of one's class position is often very complex and fluid, a process that is capable not only of significant shifts but also of limitation against other class positions at any number of given moments. As such, an expression of cultural texts in a deterministic relationship with socio-economic circumstances very quickly becomes unhinged in the realm of popular music (as it does in other textual realms). Instead, popular music, when it utilizes class articulation, provides a range of performative class positions that are proffered through the textual moment. Returning to Pulp's 'Common People', a very clear invitation is made to the listener to identify with an unambiguous class position, that of the narrator[7] who is confronted with the class-tourist who wants to sleep with him. While the song is certainly not uncritical of working-class identity, the lyrics make it perfectly clear that the narrator is indeed working class (he identifies himself as one of the 'common people' that the narrative object might want to sleep with) and that the subsequent scorn heaped on to the girl in question is in response to her willingness and (in)ability to perform a class identity that is perceived to not be her own. Interestingly, the very idea of performance is both explicitly rejected and implicitly embraced when Cocker identifies certain icons of working-class existence that the girl can appropriate (the bed-sit lifestyle, the suppression of individuality through low grade employment, limited social opportunities) alongside the safety net of her family's wealth and privilege. However, Cocker's use of the idea of getting working-class identity 'right' suggests not merely the object's inability to perform a role adequately but also the subject's own adequacy at such a performance. On the one hand Cocker (if we accept Cocker as the protagonist of the song) limits the girl's adequacy through socio-economic determinants, her lack of working-class lived experience without the safety net of her own class position. Yet Cocker is also suggesting that he is capable of performing the role correctly, again due to his socio-economic position. As such we are left with a paradox, one that foregrounds the adequacy of performance in relation to socio-economic determinism and lived experience. Indeed it is such a paradox that allows for the song's perceived authentic qualities, prioritizing material and social determinants over the explicit performance of the girl in the song, and masking the implicit performance of the narrator.

Such paradoxes, however, do not end at a textual reading of the song. To take one instance of the way in which performance becomes the overarching criteria for class expression, Pulp's performance of 'Common People' at the Glastonbury festival in 1995 (standing in for an absent Stone Roses) provides some important clues. One of the elements that made their performance so memorable[8] was the audience singing along to 'Common People' at the climax of their set, approximately 50,000 people, performing the working-class identity of the song's protagonist despite the fact that tickets for the event cost £65 each (although prior to 2002 fence jumping was a significant problem for the festival organizers and contributed significantly to crowd numbers), a luxury that the song seems to suggest is outside the limits of such a class identity. While it may be overly simplistic to assert that because the tickets to the event were expensive, working-class festival goers would have been excluded, it would be safe to suggest that not all of the audience watching, dancing and singing along to Pulp that night perceived themselves to be working class in their everyday lives. Indeed many people in the audience (although perhaps a minority) might have more easily equated themselves with the upper-middle class girl who is the target of Cocker's disdain. It can only be appropriate to suggest that the audience, rather than rejecting a class position that was not relevant to their lived experience, performed an act of class identification set up by not only the textual limits of the song, but also by a wider discursive field that provided for a mechanism by which they were interpellated.

The mechanism by which such a relational event occurs is usefully outlined by Abercrombie and Longhurst (1998). The Glastonbury audience might be said to conform to Abercrombie and Longhurst's identification of a simple audience, an audience at some remove from, and with little control over the performance taking place on stage. However, Abercrombie and Longhurst suggest another form of audience, the diffuse audience, who are most often associated with mediatized forms of performance, but critically, an audience that utilizes the performance to construct their own identity. While the Pulp performance was not taking place through any electronic media, it is apparent that, even for a short time, the audience (or at least portions of the audience) were utilizing 'Common People' to construct a form of identity. Abercrombie utilizes concepts of spectacle and narcissism to account for the ways in which audiences make use of performance practice. In the case of Pulp's performance at Glastonbury, the stage frames Pulp's performance as something to be watched (a spectacle) while the audience are invited to make the performance their own through the show's status as a commodity. For Abercrombie and Longhurst commodity culture offers the audience the expectation that the spectacle they are watching can be, in some way, owned. As such the diffuse audience is capable of absorbing icons of class and authenticity to shape their own subjectivity. However, it is precisely the show's status as a commodity (and the song's status as a purchasable single prior to the performance) that allows the audience to make their own role a performative one through the spectacle that they are watching. Further it is the status and influence of rock discourse that invites the audience to make such relational claims.

Such an invitation is complex given the delineation of working-class experience against and because of middle-class presumptions and identities forged by the lyrics, a factor that should explicitly alienate a middle-class audience. Equally, but less inhibiting, is Cocker's own middle-class upbringing, albeit in a relatively working-class area of Sheffield. One could easily make the claim that Cocker is faking it and the Glastonbury audience are faking it too. That the subject of their deception is a song precisely about the inability to deceive makes matters all the worse. Yet there is no indication, which this author is aware of, that Pulp's performance is ever seen in such terms. Rather it is seen as one of a number of defining moments in the story of Britpop. All of these factors make problematic any notion of an authentic voice,[9] or even an authentic listener if such a figure could be identified, yet the song's lyrical focus is specifically about authenticity articulated through class, and as such the discourse that provides for class as the arbiter of authenticity needs to be excavated.

The discursive field (rock discourse)

In Simon Frith's 1991 article 'The Good, the Bad and the Indifferent', three discourses are identified that inform cultural judgements: art discourse, folk discourse and pop discourse:

an *art* discourse – the ideal of cultural experience is *transcendence*; art provides a means of rising above the everyday, leaving the body, denying the significance of historical time and geographical place;

a *folk* discourse – the ideal of cultural experience is *integration*; folk forms provide a means of placement – in a space, a season, a community;

a *pop* discourse – the ideal of cultural experience is *fun*; pop provides routinized pleasures, more intense than the everyday but bound to its rhythms, and legitimized emotional gratification, a play of desire and discipline. (591)

Frith is at pains not to associate these discursive fields with particular class positions or particular categories such as high, mass or popular culture. Rather he shows how they operate through all of the above categories, 'all at play across all cultural practices and indeed [they] produce each other' (ibid.). Certainly, it is appropriate to suggest that within popular music all of these discourses can come into play together at any given time. While the folk discourse informs authenticity in certain ways, as shown in the previous chapter, both art and pop are capable of informing authenticity in the pop text. One might choose to identify folk discourse in the work of Bob Dylan or Billy Bragg, art discourse in the music of Bardo Pond or Pink Floyd and pop discourse in The Pussycat Dolls or The Sugababes. However, it is not enough to suggest that any discursive example is in any way exclusively influenced. All of the above examples perform their own articulations of authenticity; however, they are often constructed in opposition to other forms. Frith suggests that within popular music, tensions can exist between the artist(s) who will prioritize their own work as art, and the audience who will perceive it as pop. Frith suggests that such a rupture is bridged by the role of the producer, whose job it is to make art commercially palatable and successful:

The commodification of culture, in short, in constituting a tripartite structure of communication – creator / producer / consumer – also constructed a series of evaluative oppositions (art vs. commerce, art vs. craft, the amateur vs. the professional) and a series of evaluative processes that are common to all contemporary cultural forms, that play across high and low cultural practices alike.

(ibid.)

The role of the producer in British popular music is not simply limited to the record producer in the studio, one must understand the role of the producer as a mediator of meaning, and as such the influence of the music press (both professional and amateur), television and radio are integral to forming the vocabulary of discourse within British popular music (as elsewhere). As the later case studies will show, the folk discourse articulates the folk voice to confirm authenticity in class-based terms, yet it does so through a vocabulary of authenticity created over time, often through associations from ancillary media outside of the musical text itself. However, it is not difficult to see the influence of art and pop in the music of a band such as Pulp, even though they may be articulating authenticity through engagement with the folk voice. What is significant however is the way in which rock discourse places emphasis on the folk or the pop or the art at given textual moments.

Butler's discursive field, highly influenced by the writing of Michel Foucault, provides a vocabulary of performative acts that regulate and constitute subjectivity. Throughout this work I have used the term 'rock discourse' to describe the discursive field that informs the articulation of class (amongst many other factors) in British popular music. Such a simple term masks the vast multiplicity of the concept, if indeed it can be seen as a unified whole, as it shifts and mutates through time. The Latin origin of discourse, 'discursus', suggests running between two different positions, and indeed the back-and-forth movement implied lends itself easily to the idea of discourse as being in a constant state of evolutionary flux.

Butler's use of discourse as a motivator of performed subjectivities points to the power relationships that are at the heart of gendered identities. Discourse in this light is understood as a vocabulary or language that talks about gender and sexuality in certain ways, ways that are useful in policing subjectivities and deviant sexuality (in other words performative identities that are ambivalent or resistant to the dominant discourse). The application of discourse will occur at the *inter-discourse* (Morley, 1980), the moment that subjects bring to bear their personal experiences and histories onto a text.[10] It is in the space of listening to a piece of popular music, the inter-discursive space, that discourse offers up potential performative identities. The listener is interpellated by the text, asked if he or she is the listener that the song is intended for. As we have already seen, it is not vital that one is actually the listener implied by the song, rather one must be prepared to perform that identity. If class signification is at play, then within the inter-discursive space one is asked to perform a form of class affiliation that may or not be relevant to one's lived social experience. However, such a connection with and recognition of the dominance of certain class positions is going to provide a strategy whereby one may prioritize class as a harbinger of authenticity. The effect of this is to not only associate a piece of popular music with the authentic, but to also perform an identity that is itself granted authenticity by *correct engagement* with the music, lyrics and performance. Foucault's extrapolation of the discursive field in *Discipline and Punish* (1977) and *The History of Sexuality* (1981) shows how discourse produces and acts upon the body, acting in a 'carceral' (Wilson, 1990) sense to discipline the body and make it more appropriate to the world around it (itself constituted by discourse). While the kind of discursive performativity we have discussed so far tends towards the interiorized psychic world, it is not difficult to understand subcultural spectacle as another strategy to engage with discourse, albeit often in ambivalent ways. Wilson uses Foucault to account for the uses of fashion to discipline the body in certain directions, and of course subcultural style works in a similar way. However, it may be that, at least in the early days of any subculture, spectacle is utilized in reaction to dominant discursive powers, producing new discourses of style that are always inherently tied to the dominant despite their opposition. As such it is not difficult to see why the UK heavy metal magazine *Kerrang!* ran a series of letters from readers through 2003 that complained about 'townies', people who conformed to mainstream popular music and style. Not only were townies safely pilloried in the pages of *Kerrang!* but the magazine also advertised a range of T-shirts that made that disdain more visible:

'Townies suck, innit' [T-shirt logo] The English language is just a vague concept to most of our inbreeding enemies and, with this great design, you can take the piss out of them and they probably won't even get it. I can almost hear the conversation: 'Oi, your shirt. It says townies suck, innit, innit? You better take it off, innit, or I'll cap ya, innit' et cetera.

('Townies suck, innit', 2006)

'WARNING Townies Give You AIDS' [T-shirt logo] Must be true. The dirty, greasy monkeys. They're always doing revolting things with each other, their friends, their cousins, their brothers and sisters, their parents. Explains why they all look the fucking same and dress the same and think the same. The retards. A friend of mine only fucks townie girls because he is 'guaranteed to get a shag' – guaranteed to get a disease, more like. And they obviously know bugger all about safe sex, judging by the amount of breeding they do. Do you think the spawn pop out with a gold earring in?!

('WARNING Townies Give You AIDS', 2006)

Regardless of the sexual and racial aspects of the above pronouncements, such spectacular displays as wearing T-shirts stating that 'Townies suck, innit' and 'WARNING Townies Give You AIDS' provide a performed subjectivity upon the surface of the body that operates as much in relation to dominant discourses of spectacular identities as the 'townies' do. Indeed the identification of 'townies' and 'chavs' (particularly the former) by subcultural groups has the double effect of creating a performative identity for the 'townies' in relation to a particular subcultural discourse (one oriented around the consumption of heavy metal in this instance), and also to define subcultural subjectivity in relation to a dominant or mainstream discourse of fashion, behaviour and consumption. As such, performed identities are never stable but constantly articulating and reinventing themselves in a flux of influence and power, difference and *différance*.

Wilson's assertion that fashion operates its discursive power in a regulatory way upon the body seems particularly appropriate to the discussion around subcultural display; yet of course many people who listen to popular music may not choose to articulate their performed commitment to certain rock idioms through dress. However, attendance at any rock festival, or a brief walk down Camden High Street,[11] will show that often such performance is attended by spectacular fashion strategies that reinforce and display identity. While the counter-cultural aspect of such display is prioritized, Foucault's work allows us to understand how such display is always an effect of dominant discourses that are reacted against, forming new discursive fields that are never wholly free of their relationship to mainstream culture. As such the very idea of *counter*-culture assumes importance, not as a stand-alone form of culture outside of the mainstream, but as an effect of the mainstream. A large part of such spectacular subcultural identities is predicated upon notions of authenticity that are set up in relation to mainstream popular music and fashion; however, that is not to say that to articulate authenticity in the inter-discursive moment requires subcultural allegiance; other forms of performativity are available that tend more towards the interiorized and the psychic, and it is these forms of performativity that are more complex to understand.

Discourse in performance

To focus on what we might mean when we talk about rock discourse, Pulp's Glastonbury performance will continue to provide at least an example of some of the forms that come into play to suggest performance identities and prioritize certain values and ideas. In the first instance it seems clear that we can apply the term 'rock discourse' to Pulp's performance for a number of reasons.[12] While Pulp have many of the hallmarks of what might be constituted a 'pop' act (they play short, radio friendly songs that tend towards the structurally traditional, and have enjoyed a certain amount of chart success[13]), they sit easily within a definition of rock music that prioritizes the immediacy of performance, a clarity of connection between the performer and text and a level of communion between the artist and audience. Having asserted Pulp's position as a rock act, and therefore subject to rock discourse, there are a number of other considerations that are going to influence the performative nature of the engagement between the band onstage performing 'Common People', and the audience. While the following list is by no means exhaustive, it does at least suggest some of the influences that may come to bear in any given engagement with the song. It is also important to note that the focus here is not on a set of discursive influences that hold sway over the entire audience and the band, but rather on any given audience member's relationship to that particular song as it is performed. Any attempt to theorize a concrete set of values that influence an entire audience at any given moment would by necessity be far too general to be of much use, and as such the following discursive elements need to be understood as possible influences that may or may not be available to any given audience member at any given time.

As we shall see in the following case studies, rock discourse brings with it a valorization of working-class identity that speaks of authenticity, integrity, dignity, community, youth and (often, but not always) masculinity. As such 'Common People' immediately works alongside such values given its disavowal of the voyeuristic and complacent middle classes. Where Skeggs (2004b) suggests that middle-class participants are capable of vicariously appropriating working-class 'authenticity' due to enhanced access to social and cultural mobility, Pulp attack that very mobility through virtue of their medium. Rock discourse and its prioritization of the folk voice allows for such cultural mobility to be seen in inherently inauthentic terms, yet at the same time the invitation made by the mode of address of the song allows for that very vicariousness to exist on the part of the auditor. The use of class as an idiom of authenticity paradoxically allows for a greater level of inauthenticity through its presentation as a performance of class. The Glastonbury audience are being asked to perform a working-class role, exactly what the lyrics of the song are railing against. Is the audience then failing to *perform* the song properly? Or is the level of commitment from the audience to the performance questionable? As suggested in the previous chapter, one way to accommodate such a problem is to understand the role that authenticity plays in rock discourse, that is to reconcile the mass-produced nature of rock music with its more abstract motivation to be perceived as music from the people, to articulate the folk voice. Such aims are often seen as antithetical, yet the strain between the two positions can be felt throughout almost all rock music. The ways in which that strain is reconciled are often wildly different, and the level of concern felt on the part of the auditor is likely to vary considerably too, dependent upon how much of a contradiction the mass/folk opposition is seen to be. However much investment the listener puts in the concept of authenticity when relating to a piece of popular music, the construction of authenticity by rock discourse is only ever *authentic* in that construction, its status as a link between the text and the world is wholly illusory.

Of course rock texts do not always come fully loaded with working-class symbolism to counter the effects of a global media industry. One of the most potent weapons in defining rock as an area of working-class culture, at least in the United Kingdom, is the music press, which has consistently prioritized the music of young working-class males[14] from jazz to rock 'n' roll, rhythm and blues to punk and beyond. It is here that much of the debate around authentic articulations is performed, and it is here that the site of contestation illuminated by Gracyk (1996) in his analysis of US rock is fought over. The liberalism that Gracyk suggests supports notions of authenticity, becomes in the UK canon, a split personality of artistic endeavour on one side (often treated with some suspicion by the British weekly music press because of its affiliation with middle-class bohemia, unless it is offset by other authenticating categories such as ethnicity), and the folk voice (valorized due to its connections with marginalized voices, lack of economic and social power and greater displays of musical integrity) on the other. Both of these forms, even when they are overlapping and indistinct, display a form of authenticity that, to paraphrase Gracyk, separates rock off as music that *matters* (it is not so much relevant what rock matters about, but its concern and relevance are what set it apart from mainstream pop which is perceived by Gracyk to hold less in the way of significant value for consumers, although this is an arguable point). However, priority is given over to articulations of the working-class folk voice as it most powerfully signals the opposition between the form and the medium, between the music and the music industry. Recent examples of such a trend in British popular music are Arctic Monkeys from Sheffield (as are Pulp) and The Streets from Birmingham, both acts that were prioritized by the music press due to their perceived removal from the music industry at their inception,[15] a factor reinforced by geographical removal from the hub of the music industry, London.[16]

As such Pulp's status at the Glastonbury performance relies upon both strands; their 'folk voice' status is reinforced primarily by the song lyrics, their northern origins, and the documentary mode of address employed by Cocker, while the 'artistic' strand is present in Cocker's reputation as a wry social commentator, and his musical and visual style that pilfers from a variety of sources as disparate as loungecore, The Velvet Underground, psychedelic pop and 1960s kitsch. However, the power of the performance of 'Common People' at Glastonbury is the rate of uptake, the success of interpellating over 50,000 festivalgoers into a specific class-oriented drama with quite specific identificatory directions.

Self and subjectivity for a common people

While the initial use of performance theory in an analysis of popular music would tend to suit forms of subcultural expression, its use does not end there. Subcultures suit the idea of performativity as they provide a spectacular, carceral way of articulating identity. It is relatively easy to understand the way in which subcultural agents perform specific forms of identity, governed by discourses that exist outside themselves. The evolution of the gothic subculture, for example, can be understood as a discourse that in the first instance sets itself in relation to dominant discourses of 'mainstream' identity. That very subcultural discourse can be understood historically as an iteration of a variety of influences (Hammer horror, literary Romanticism, eastern-influenced psychedelia, 1950s rockabilly[17]) that form subjectivity primarily through spectacular signification upon the body, both in terms of style and habitus. Yet performativity does not merely operate in highly visible ways, it is always, and often only a psychic process.

The Glastonbury audience watching Pulp does not constitute a subculture. What is significant about Pulp's performance is that they are not playing to a partisan crowd, as they would be at one of their own concerts. In the first instance they were a last minute addition to the bill, therefore the majority of the crowd were not expecting them to appear. Secondly, even if they had been expected it is clear that the audience present in front of the Pyramid stage (the festival's largest) on the Saturday night (the festival's most attended) would not have uniformly conformed to a homogenous crowd of like-minded auditors. However, when listening to the performance of 'Common People' at the close of their set, one is struck by the sheer volume of the audience singing back almost every word to Cocker and the group on stage. 'Common People' was released in April of 1995 and the Glastonbury performance took place a mere two months later; so it seems clear that the song had certainly seeped into the consciousness of a significant proportion of the audience present. Cocker has even been presented with the claim that 'Common People' represents the defining moment of the Britpop phenomenon, precisely because of its engagement with class identity (*Live Forever*, 2003), and the Glastonbury performance would certainly go some way to validating such a claim.[18]

But is it possible to state that singing along to a band at a festival constitutes a form of performative subjectivity? Certainly, in the process of singing along to any artist, audience members are displaying a form of commitment to the performance they are watching/listening to. While it would be clearly incorrect to assume that every person in the Pyramid Field was displaying a similar level and type of commitment, it certainly seems clear that the particular instance of 'Common People' aroused particular reactions. The significance of the song seemed particularly acute following the release a year earlier of Blur's *Parklife* album. Blur had been accused of appropriating working-class Thames Estuary culture for their reinvention, and 'Common People' served as a timely rejoinder to the idea of middle-class Essex boys pretending to be cockneys.[19] Equally, Pulp's place on the bill at Glastonbury seemed ironically appropriate following the cancellation by The Stone Roses. The Roses' guitarist John Squire had been hospitalized following a bicycle accident causing the band to step off the bill; however, the band themselves were struggling following the release of *The Second Coming* (1994), largely seen in the United Kingdom as a disappointing follow-up to their groundbreaking debut. In March of 1995 original drummer Reni left the band and was replaced by Robbie Maddix, a session drummer who had worked with Simply Red, a band renowned for their MOR quasi-soul sound. As such a certain level of cynicism and disappointment was levelled at the band from the music press and fans who felt that *The Second Coming* owed far too much to 1970s blues-rock (references to Led Zeppelin were common), and that the core of the band had been largely replaced by session musicians (an opinion reinforced by the addition to the line-up of Nigel Ippinson, another session player, on keyboards and later Aziz Ibrahim, also from Simply Red and melodic progressive rockers Asia, who replaced Squire when he left the band in 1996). As such the appearance of Pulp in the headlining slot seemed to not only pass comment on the working-class pretensions of certain bands in the Britpop movement, but also to show a band who more clearly articulated the gang mentality of working-class musicians in contrast to The Stone Roses, who were increasingly viewed as out of touch with their audience as they became a more slick, professional outfit.

Of course Pulp themselves were not responsible for either of these developments, and it would be inappropriate to suggest that they deliberately capitalized upon a crisis forming around notions of authenticity, partially articulated along class lines. Yet their performance at Glastonbury provided entirely the right conditions to engage with a crisis of authenticity, and 'Common People' particularly acted as way of dealing with that crisis. Again we must be wary of the assumption that the entire audience felt that certain areas of British rock music were becoming in any way artificial; yet the prevailing sense of disappointment in the music press at The Stone Roses' return and concerns around the level of authenticity displayed by Blur and other Britpop bands supplied those who were interested with a framework against which to read Pulp's performance. As such it is possible to read Pulp's performance as a means of granting authenticity to a musical moment as a whole (Britpop), or at least as a means of laying out some discursive limitations that might be applied subsequently to other acts and musical moments. Erving Goffman (1959), a formative influence on the work of performance theorists, suggests that in moments of crisis, the performed subjectivities between 'teams' or specific social groupings that separate them from each other can become eroded:

At moments of great crisis, a new set of motives may suddenly become effective and the established social distance between the teams may sharply increase or decrease . . . However, in general, when the crisis is past, the previous working consensus is likely to be re-established, albeit bashfully. Similarly, during sudden disruptions of a performance, and especially at times when a misidentification is discovered, a portrayed character can momentarily crumble while the performer behind the character 'forgets himself' and blurts out a relatively un-performed exclamation. (166–7)

If we are to understand Pulp's performance at Glastonbury as effecting a performative strategy to deal with a crisis in authenticity (Blur's 'fakery' and 'The Stone Roses' 'professionalization'), then it is possible not only to understand the erosion of the distinction between Pulp and the audience, fusing them together as *common people*, but also to understand The Stone Roses as a group whose perceived authentic performativity has crumbled and exposed them as professional journeymen musicians (an identity distinctly at odds with their earlier, more influential work and identity).

Goffman also shows how performed identity can be transitory and fluid in the face of crisis. One of the enduring claims made about popular music in general is its disposability. The three-minute pop single, particularly in its seven inch vinyl format, was capable of producing a feeling of intense but transitory satisfaction, reinforced by the rapid rate of turnover of releases every week. It seems likely that this notion of disposability will increase as digitalization allows for non-physical manifestations of the pop song such as the MP3. Yet one of the elements that has historically differentiated rock music from chart pop has been an increased level of commitment to the musical text on the part of the consumer, be it the single, or more probably, the album. While it is not difficult to argue over differing levels of commitment among popular music listeners (from preteens buying singles with their pocket money to the dedicated adult record collector), the popular music text has become a powerful part of popular culture precisely because of its transitory and temporary ability to transform subjectivity in the space of a few minutes. Almost anyone who listens to a piece of pop or rock in any dedicated way (in other words, with some level of attention beyond the music merely being a background noise) is likely to experience some change in mood or behaviour predicated upon the lyrics, the beat or the intensity of the music. Such changes may have the ability to inform subjectivity over a longer period of time than the music takes to play, some may not, yet the popular song often provides the listener with performative elements that may appear attractive or empowering in a very short, intense burst. The recent phenomenon of compilations of rock music oriented around the practice of air guitar seem to explicitly invite the listener to perform the role of the virtuoso guitarist in his or her own home.[20] While the example cited above seems to outline a context for reading Pulp's performance in relation to issues surrounding a crisis of authenticity, it is only ever a transient solution.

Subjectivity and the contradictions of rock

The temporary nature of such reconciliations of the contradictions of rock music, accounting for the relationship between art and commerce by the use of categories of authenticity, is bound to be an open-ended process. The commercialization of popular music may be increasingly visible to audiences (particularly via sponsorship and branding), yet the idea of artists and bands being in some way *tainted* by commerce continues to be an enduring theme through popular music cultures. As Longhurst (1995) states:

> What did open up in a clear way in the late 1960s and early 1970s was a new divide between what was perceived to be the more serious and, somehow more 'authentic' rock music, and 'commercial' pop music. Devotees of rock could be scathing in their attacks on pop and commercialism, and the criticism of groups 'selling out' became exceptionally shrill. This accusation, which continues to this day, was regularly hurled at musicians like Marc Bolan who moved from being a hero of the so-called underground to mass-selling single records. (108–9)

What is at the heart of the idea of 'selling-out' is a process of 'taking away' music. If perceptions of authenticity are often a question of how much the listener can make the musical text their own, then commercialization (often perceived in terms of sound, form and image) is problematic for two reasons. In the first instance the question of musical mediation is highlighted, in other words, how much has the music that I am hearing been compromised by commercial imperatives enforced by the record industry? Secondly, commercialization equates with an attempt to gain larger audiences, thus foregrounding the realization that the music is in fact *not* my own, but that I am simply part of a potentially global network of consumers, all of whom will be attempting to make it their own too. As such the musical text is taken away from me as I recognize its commercialization. That is not to say that if a band gains a wider global audience due to signing to a major label, or refining its sound to a more commercially palatable form, it will be impossible to understand its music as in any way authentic. Nirvana's transition from Sub Pop to DGC Records (an imprint of the Geffen corporation) in 1991 brought their music to a far larger audience than would have been previously possible, yet they still to this day hold a vital place in youth culture, even over a decade after the death of Kurt Cobain. Yet equally that pivotal importance is often situated in terms that foreground Cobain's resistance to commercialization, thus ensuring a dialogue between mass distribution of a cultural text, and the ability, through a discourse of permission centred primarily around Cobain, to make that music personally significant and subjectively performative. The significance of this is not that the reality of record company mediation may have particular effects upon musical texts, but rather the perception that such an effect is possible, therefore potentially compromising the relationship between the text and subjectivity, becomes paramount. If the musical text offers a variety of performative options (not just class related) for the listener, then the problem of selling out becomes an issue of how much the listener's subjectivity itself is compromised by commerce.[21]

As such rock discourse offers up authenticity as a strategy to counter the ever-present relationship between art and commerce, even if that relationship is one that is mythologized rather than materially present. Even bands releasing their music through the smallest independent labels are in some form relating their art to commerce; they are, after all, businesses as much as the majors are. However, the level to which this relationship is specifically visible varies widely.[22] Where the relationship assumes a highly visible aspect, particularly in a context that deems commercialization as problematic, such as punk in Nirvana's case, claims of authenticity provide a way to work against commercialization that will in turn affect the listener's subjectivity:

> Cleaning up the sound of fringe styles for the mass-media seems to be popular among corporate labels these days. The Seattle-based grunge scene has been commodified in the same manner as California pop-core. All one needs to do is listen to Nirvana's first album, *Bleach* (first released on Sub Pop in 1989), and compare the music to that released later on the Geffen labels. Like the material Green Day released on Lookout, Bleach contains a certain amount of noise and discordance that are inherent to grunge music. These culturally significant elements are absent on both *Nevermind* and *In Utero* (with the possible exception of 'Endless, Nameless,' the final track on *Nevermind*), and their absence was fully intentional.
>
> (Theis, 1997)

The result was a wave of popular radio music that swept over international youth culture and became one of DGC's primary moneymaking machines. Indeed, the momentum of the Nirvana phenomenon has maintained a scene of commodified 'grunge'-like music that continues to dominate MTV and popular radio. Kurt Cobain himself, in his suicide note, seems to have understood the degradation of creativity caused by this corporate scene:

> ...the, shall we say, ethics involved with independence and the embracement of your community has been proven to be very true. I haven't felt the excitement of listening to, as well as creating music, along with really writing something for many years now. I feel guilty beyond words about these things...
>
> (Cobain qtd. in Theis, 1997)

A Nirvana fan may choose to prefer their debut album *Bleach* (1989) due to its rawer sound and release via an independent label, or their final album *In Utero* (1993) due to its attempts to subvert the commercialization of its predecessor *Nevermind* (1991), precisely because the commercialization of the band and their sound has implications for the subject's relationship to global commerce. As such this hypothetical fan performs an authentic 'rock fan' identity in relation to criteria relating to commercialization that separates him or her from that very commercialization.

Pulp's performance at Glastonbury makes less visible not only the commercial leap that the band had made with the release of the album *His 'n' Hers* in 1994 after over a decade in indie obscurity, but also the potential distance between the protagonist of a song like 'Common People' and the audience. 'Common People' constructs a performative identity that invites a communal reaction to both class tourism and the relationship between art and commerce. Therefore for a brief period of time a disparate group of festival goers are performing a specific form of authenticity that creates a subjectivity that obscures not only the commercial nature of the performance they are watching, but also their part in that performance. As such authenticity is articulated in such a way that it obscures the very relations of commerce and power that would deem such a performance inauthentic. This process thus creates both an *authentic* band performance and an *authentic* subjectivity that seems to resist the commercial imperatives of the practice that audience is a part of. Further this subjectivity is reinforced by a communal reaction to the song being performed.

Iteration and ambivalence

At this stage a number of points need to be reasserted to account for the peculiarity of rock discourse. Class signification within rock music acts as a method of connection with the audience that reassures the listener of the song's authenticity. Authenticity is required to assert the supremacy of creative expression over commercial imperatives. The supremacy of creative expression is required because as the listener performs class signification in the act of listening, subjectivity and agency are potentially compromised by the impact of commercial imperatives. In other words class representation obscures the status of performed subjectivities as being commercially oriented. Where pop music in a more general sense (i.e. mainstream pop) fails to articulate authenticity, the status of the listener as a consumer, or rather as a specific performative subjectivity formed around consumption, is not questioned.[23] So class signification acts as a strategy to reassure the listener in the act of listening that performed subjectivities (perceived as their own) are not an effect of an industrialized process.

The peculiarity of rock discourse is that it prioritizes working-class identity and subjectivity. As Fraser (1999), Lawler (1999b) and Skeggs (1997) suggest, the ability to perform across class divisions seems to be the prerogative of the middle classes, while working-class identity is '(through representation) continually demonized, pathologized and held responsible for social problems' (Skeggs, 1997, 76). However, within rock discourse representations of working-class identity act as attractive strategies to deal with the contradictions of a form of artistic expression that is inherently tied to commercial considerations. So why should working-class identity be attractive within British popular music when it is 'demonized and pathologized' in most other areas of cultural life? As the later case studies show, the articulation of a folk voice, a performed form of communion and articulation that appears to be more related to the *vox populi* than the commercial considerations of the music industry, has continually haunted popular music in Britain since the Industrial Revolution. Where rock music separated itself from mainstream pop (and where such separations can be made evident), the folk voice acts as a means by which to perform a connection with a people and a tradition that masks the commodification of rock music.

The reiteration of previous idioms is central to the construction of the rock discourse that shapes working-class identity and presents it as desirable and authentic. The destruction of equipment and property by the band Towers of London mentioned in Chapter 3 acts as an iteration of Pete Townshend's demolition of his own equipment, itself an iteration of the auto-destructive art of Gustav Metzger. While this particular strategy affirms authenticity through the iteration of a performative discourse (trashing your equipment means that you mean what you say, so excessive is the passion of performance), it is a performance that masks its own performativity through the immanence of the event. Yet it is unequivocally a performance within a certain discourse. The destruction of equipment is almost wholly particular to rock music as a performance of commitment and passion, and it is an element of performance that develops a discourse of the externalized display of interiorized drives. Of course it is the role of discourse to present such a performance as interiorized and particular to the performer, rather than as a mode of behaviour conferred upon and forming subjectivity externally.

Through the iteration of a working-class identity through a folk voice that in certain ways informs British popular music, working-class identity assumes an ambivalent relationship to more culturally dominant discourses that produce far more negative manifestations of working-class culture. It is this apparent resistance to the dominance and power of other class positions that gives working-class subjectivity its resonance within rock discourse. Again the prioritization of working-class identity in the face of the preferred middle-class subjectivity identified by Lawler, Skeggs and Fraser positions rock discourse itself as being marginal and 'authentic', despite its place within a global entertainment industry concerned with and constructed around the sale of product and the accumulation of profit. Quite why a strain of working-class experience has come to be prioritized by rock discourse is the subject of the next chapter.

5
The Folk Voice

To understand the nature of the performative articulation of class within popular music, it seems appropriate to explore exactly where the valorization of working-class experience has come from. This chapter will explore the development of the British *folk voice* from the English folk tradition, through the urbanized music of the working-class music halls, and ultimately through to the advent of rock 'n' roll and popular music as we are more familiar with it. This folk voice is not, as may be surmised, a style of singing or even a particular style of music (although there may be musical motifs and styles that unite various different styles of music that utilize it), but rather a strain that has run throughout popular music in Britain for the last 200 years. It is a voice that claims to speak in the vernacular, in the everyday, a voice that articulates the concerns of the working man (and sometimes the working woman too) and acts as an authentic arena within which class preoccupations are often evident. The focus of this chapter, as with the book as a whole, is Anglocentric; however, it is not difficult to discern a similar folk voice in the popular music of the United States. Of particular significance here are the activities of archivists such as Alan Lomax and Harry Smith, collectors of American roots music that had a significant impact upon the development of American popular music from the 1960s onwards.[1] Where appropriate I will use the evolution of popular music in the States, particularly the post-depression period, to further outline the implications of the existence of the folk voice within the mass medium of popular music. However, the British strain provides us with ample material to account for the prioritization of working-class experience within popular music discourse, and that will be this chapter's focus.

The very idea of a folk voice at the heart of popular music seems at once both strange and familiar. The importance of folk culture for critics such as Leavis and Adorno, despite their differing political positions, was in its opposition to mass culture. Meanwhile the sense that popular music is inherently tied to the commercial considerations of its production and distribution (both literal and semiotic) might lead one to conclude that popular music has long since shed its claim to articulating the concerns of its audience. As such it might seem difficult to understand popular music as a manifestation of folk culture. However, equally strong is the feeling that popular music does connect with people, at a profound level, through emotion, nostalgia, sentiment, geography, identity and countless other categories. Despite the steady industrialization of popular music over the last 200 years, audiences often still perceive a voice at its heart, a voice that speaks to them as one of their own. The perceived distinction between the music and the industry[2] suggests that there is an 'organic' or 'natural' form beneath the glitter and marketing, a form that has culturally communicative properties. Theodor Adorno's critique of the culture industry, and in particular the music business, articulates the division between music and business, and even explicates the concerns over the impact of the latter upon the former. While subsequent work has been forced to critique Adorno's concept of mass-industrialized popular music in the face of the blatant heterogeneity of pop and rock, his 1941 article 'On Popular Music' still resonates precisely because it strikes at the heart of a relationship that is so often situated as being oppositional. As Jason Toynbee suggests (playing the devil's advocate), 'according to one commonly held approach to the music industry, commerce suppresses creativity, giant corporations squeeze out independent companies, and production for the market replaces music making for the people' (227). While Toynbee goes on to introduce work that often challenges this idea, he is right to suggest that such judgements about the commodification of pop or rock (or indeed other forms of music) continue to be made in Britain and beyond every day. The criticisms of Adorno point to this idea, that there is an organic form that attempts to work, although almost always unsuccessfully, through the music industry, and the coming of rock 'n' roll and everything after has done very little to dispel this concept. More recently Andrew Blake (1997) has pointed to the search for (and invention of) an English musical tradition that works to reconcile the rampant pace of modernity for the middle classes, a vital group in the construction of the folk voice. Blake understands this musical tradition, insofar as it incorporates folk music, to have a role that is precisely designed to offset modernity and capitalism, even as those two conditions allow such a tradition to be constructed:

> So we have a musical Englishness which used both the fetishised version of popular music under the 'folk' label, and the music of English consolidation and expansion; and we have the use of similar sources for the differentiation of the peoples and musics of the Celtic areas of Britain. Through all these sources, the ideology of romantic anti-capitalism was clearly reinscribed, in a repetition of a paradoxical creation of a 'past' within the process of modernisation which had seen the establishing of the classical music canon in the eighteenth century and after. (46)

It is this creation of a past and a tradition that produces the folk voice, a voice that is both a product of the commodified nature of the popular music industries, and a means to manifest meanings that nominally resist commodification. The task of this chapter is to outline the very shape and evolution of this folk voice, and account not only for its historical origins, but also for its presence as a valued concept within modern popular music. For it is within the folk voice that one finds the motivation for the articulation of class signifiers, as a unifying and bonding performative strategy.

The uses of folk

It is ultimately impossible to disentangle the evolution of the folk voice in Britain from its American counterpart. The British folk voice has its own currency, but it is one that has been heavily influenced by American tastes and cultural influences particularly since the Second World War. The nature of this influence will be considered later in this chapter, but first one needs to understand the cultural attitudes towards popular music in the United Kingdom that allowed the American influence to shape what we know as the folk voice today.

The story of the folk voice is inherently tied to the growth of industrialization and urban living in Britain throughout the 1800s. The folk music of the British Isles, rather perversely, does little more than provide a backdrop for the folk voice, as its articulations are almost completely rural. Were one to explore the musical geography of Britain in the mid-1700s, one would discover a range of song and music playing a number of important roles. The work songs, based primarily around agricultural or maritime labour (the sea shanty being perhaps the most famous form in the United Kingdom), articulated the conditions of working men and women lyrically, as well as voicing the stranglehold of class divisions. There are of course parallels here with the plantation work songs of America's south, not least of which is the call-and-response form taken by many sea shanties ('Blow th' Man Down' being a prime example). These work songs might be the very organic[3] music that the folk voice seems to represent. It is music composed by working-class people, performed by working-class people, and free from the trappings, on the whole, of a reproductive industry. Indeed the very notion of reproducing these folk songs in permanent form almost came too late. Samuel Pepys collected over 1800 ballads during the seventeenth century, and he was followed by other archivists such as Joseph Ritson in the eighteenth century and the Reverend John Broadwood and the Reverend Sabine Baring-Gould in the nineteenth century. By 1898 Cecil Sharp had founded the Folk Song Society (later to become the English Folk Dance and Song Society in 1911), an organization dedicated to preserving the oral music and traditional dance of the British Isles, and it is primarily through the efforts of the above that many of the folk songs from pre-industrialized Britain have survived to the present day (Lee, 1982).

Dave Harker (1985) has problematized this process of archiving and documentation by suggesting that the very notion of folk song in Britain has been inherently embourgeoised by the primarily middle and upper-class origins of the collectors themselves. For Harker, the gathering of Britain's folk music has led to a static form, allied too heavily to notions of heritage, therefore detaching it from the experiences and historical/class contexts from which it came. Further, Harker points to the state support for folk music not just in the United Kingdom but also in the Soviet Union, Zimbabwe and South Africa amongst others, as an example of the prioritization of nationalism (through a national concept of the folk song and folk identity) over any form of international working-class solidarity. Here folk music is actively used as a way of reconnecting with a past that never really existed (the middle-class notion of the folk troubadour or the ancient music of the tribe) in order to 'mystify workers' culture in the interests of bourgeois ideology and therefore of capitalism, east and west' (xii). Keightley (2001) makes the point that during the American folk revival of the 1950s, white folk and particularly black blues forms actually provided a stronger sense of the cultures from which they came for the predominantly white, educated middle-class audience. This is a point borne out by the record producer Joe Boyd in relation to the Dixieland jazz revival of the 1930s, motivated primarily by white musicians and archivists. In this way marginalized musics are made more conspicuously visible, but possibly with problematic consequences. Boyd (2006) points out that,

> There are generally two strands to white fascination with African-rooted music. First, dance floors fill with people excited by a new way to shake their behinds. Then as the fashion shifts and the beat changes, the intellectuals and wallflowers who have admired the music's vitality and originality move in to preserve or resurrect the form. (26)

While this may be the case, Harker seems to suggest that the appropriation of these musics out of their context has a profound effect on their use and meaning, an effect that alienates the music from its environment. While Harker's thesis does throw up an enlightening prospect, allowing us to view the processes of the organization of folk forms by subsequent (mis)reading and dissemination through primarily middle-class social and cultural structures, he is candid in his qualification that he is unable to situate folk song in its 'correct' historical context. This is a problem for which he has no answer, at least to date. Were we able to situate folk music within the lived experience of its originators; without the influence of collectors such as Sharp, popular music may have turned out very differently, but this is conjecture. What Harker does provide us with is a model of the organization of class signification (primarily a process of dislocation) by the institutional practices that provide for mass dissemination. Contemporary popular music continues to articulate class signification in a manner that may be informed by, but that is not directly reflexive of, class experience. The difference between folk music and pop music is that this dislocation is happening at the point of origin in the pop world, primarily because the accumulated discourse of rock and pop has arranged a pre-existent lexicon from which class signification can derive, one that is distanced from class relationships in the 'real world'[4] however they are constituted. Further, the presentation of popular music in contemporary society automatically places the listener at a distance from the social sphere, articulating experience as fantasy, thus alienating class signification from any form of lived experience.

Robert Cantwell's analysis of the American folk revival in *When We Were Good: The Folk Revival* (1996) goes some way to reconcile the sense of separation inherent in Harker's work. Cantwell's project is not to historicize the folk revival in the 1950s and 1960s in an objective sense, but rather to understand his own position within it and the revival's own connections to ideas of 'folk'. The most important aspect of Cantwell's work is an understanding of folk as representation, a distanced form that is no less significant for its abstraction. Particularly Cantwell picks up on the role of the middle classes in forming a notion of folk that while it may be nostalgic, does real things in the real world that are of real significance. In this way the mythologized folk become transformed through the ways in which they are objectified. Cantwell uses Mike Seeger (half-brother of folklorists and musicians Pete and Peggy and son of the ethnomusicologist Charles) to exemplify a 'noble' social conscience, born of some privilege, that utilizes folk music and traditions to engage with social problems in the present:

> In this . . . [Seeger] . . . follows the work of the great folklorists from the Grimms to the Lomaxes, who understand that theirs is a work of cultural cathexis, dreaming the felt but untheorized political urgencies of the present into historical memory where they may reanimate the problem of the present with impulses that transcend the inertia and banality of fact. Such is the prerogative of nobility. (43)

Seeger's adoption of folk idioms as a musician himself is understood by Cantwell as a strategy to deal with the a bourgeois self that is diffuse and objectifying, allowing for both a constitution of selfhood and a revolution against the circumstances of that selfhood's formation. Cantwell seems to ally himself with Butler and Skeggs (in essence if not practically) when he sees the ability to appropriate folk forms (or indeed create them in a mythical sense) as part of a privileged bourgeois social position. However, this is not to say that folk forms and the folk voice are necessarily adopted in any cynical or manipulative form by bourgeois citizens.

In the final chapter of his work Cantwell examines the social formations that go some way to creating a folk sensibility that leads to the folk revival of the 1960s in America. Again the idea that the folk sensibility is an effect of mass culture is raised:

> In a sense the folk revival represents a reconciliation of originally antagonistic socio-political developments, temporarily making common cause against what must have been understood, on some level, as the same adversary, mass or commercial culture. The various musics that prefigured or informed it – jazz, blues, calypso, rock-and-roll – were each of them touched with the spirit of protest. (356)

However, this protest is not so much of the people, as it is what certain stratas of society perceive the people to be, and further, what use they make of such objectifications. For Cantwell the folk revival is in many ways a 'compound concept' (373) forged between the 'genteel' and the 'revolutionary'. Here Cantwell's social analysis traces a division in American culture between old money, the aristocracy and new money, the merchant classes and the new bourgeoisie (this is by implication applicable to British and European culture as well, although the European influence on American culture transforms Europe into the old country, and therefore goes some way to confer tradition and status in the States). The genteel nobleman, Cantwell argues, shares more in common with the working classes as he is born from the same class structures and recognizes his obligation to them. In this way gentility is bound to the working classes through its protective and patronizing responsibilities, a bind that is recognized and fulfilled. This is further enforced by the allegiance towards romanticism and an idealization of nature and the pastoral:

> The genteel tradition, then, is complex, ambiguous, sometimes paradoxical, sometimes at odds with itself. It implies the everlasting involvement of class, rank, degree, power, and privilege with the love and idealization of common people. (364)

It both romanticizes the working classes as a more naturalized form of humanity, and equally it seeks acceptance from them, understanding their place within a relationship of obligation and need.

The new bourgeoisie, however, have no such allegiance, placed in their social position by changes in the class structure and social mobility. No such obligation is evident, yet that is not to say that the bourgeoisie are dissociated from folk traditions, rather they are used in different ways. Cantwell identifies two sub-strata of the 'genteel' and 'revolutionary'; the noble and the patron, and the literate patriot and the 'red'. Gentility both promotes and stands guard over the folk sensibility while the revolutionary either finds inspiration in it for social improvement (Cantwell's work is particularly useful in tracing the connections from a folk sensibility through Quakerism and the Temperance movement amongst other socially reformative organizations) or utilizes it to mobilize the masses in a political sense. What is ultimately of importance here is that the notion of 'folk' is predominantly articulated in terms defined by social classes other than 'the folk':

It is a kind of sixth sense, capable of discovering where the arts of the poor, with what is often a curious precision, meet elite standards of taste, momentarily releasing in them what custom and convention have dulled, the emancipatory gleam. (376)

It is this realization that marks the folk revival out as 'good', despite its dubious claims to authenticity and historicity. It marks out a social trend in American culture that engages with ideas rather than actualities, and in so doing it constructs a myth of itself that is performative in nature.

The history of the folk voice

Harker and Cantwell's analyses of the evolution of the folk song are significant for this study, however, one needs to appreciate how the evolution of the folk voice merely starts from regional folk music forms. It is the move from rural to urban settings that British culture starts to articulate as a music that is supposedly 'of the people'. In the first half of the nineteenth century, rural folk music, in all its regional and stylistic diversity, went through a tremendous upheaval as workers moved from the country into the burgeoning cities. The metropolitan musical landscape at the time was made up of street singers (often originally musicians from the country), organ grinders and German waltz bands. The street singers were particularly involved with ballad publishers, such as Jeremy Catnach who worked out of the Charing Cross area of London from 1813 (Lee, 25). Catnach is emblematic of the embryonic music publisher, not a musician by trade, but a lyricist providing words that would be accompanied by a more traditionally well-known tune. Often these ballads would perform an informative function, particularly in relation to gory or salacious topics of the day. Indeed the murder of Maria Marten in 1828 prompted a run of ballads that collectively sold over a million copies. However, the development of mass-circulation newspapers soon meant that the function of the ballad as a means of transmitting events widely was becoming redundant and by 1871 there were only four ballad presses left (29).

However, the decreasing popularity of the ballad form as a means of income for publishers far from sounded the death knell of professional music making at this time. Indeed the professionalization of music already had a strong history in Britain. As early as 1469 Edward IV had given a charter to the Fraternity of Minstrels of England, an organization designed to 'examine the pretensions of all who exercised the minstrel's profession, to regulate, govern and punish' (40). Equally, the position of

Town Wait, a kind of civic minstrel, provided particularly gifted musicians with the chance to be employed in a municipal role, providing music for civil events and festivities during the Tudor and Elizabethan periods. Also many musicians made a living from wandering minstrelsy, despite legal attempts to curb their efforts. The professionalization of music is perhaps not the motivation for the folk voice; indeed the idea of professional musicians does little to undermine the idea of organic music *per se*. Rather the centralization of music becomes the crux upon which the folk voice hangs. Through the 1800s Britain underwent two serious changes to its musical landscape; it embraced classical music and arranged music primarily associated with the working classes into a larger theatre or hall setting. Edward Lee suggests that it is the rise of classical music, and the growing popularity of Italian opera in the seventeenth and eighteenth centuries, that initiates a class divide along musical lines. For Lee the complicated nature of classical works, alongside an often classical or historical lyrical setting, starts to divide audience and performer. The prioritization of interpretive skill on the part of the musician (a paradigm shift encouraged by the reliance on notation at the expense of tunes that had been handed down over generations without transcription) and the attentive experience of listening to classical music in a theatre or concert hall suggest an aura of removal or separation oriented along class lines and professional expertise between those performing the music and those consuming it.

Lee suggests that the professional nature of the classical musician meant that this particular form of music was allowed the space and time to evolve in new directions (in other words the musicians had little else to do other than concentrate on their music). While this seems somewhat simplistic, the attachment of a burgeoning middle class to classical forms was motivated by the increasing embourgeoisment of the cultural sphere for large numbers of the population following the Industrial Revolution:

> While Victorian Street Music was essentially an intensification of a pre-existing cultural form, the appearance of concerts aimed at a broad-based, ticket-buying audience was a new phenomenon. The public 'concert' had, by the late eighteenth century, become dominated, at least in London, by the nobility. The period from the end of the Napoleonic Wars until 1848 witnessed what the premier historian of concert development, William Weber, has described as an 'explosion' in concert life throughout Europe as the middle classes,

anxious for social and cultural respectability, began to attend in large numbers.

(Russell, 76)

This shift provides us with a template for the articulation of middle-class experience within contemporary popular music. Classical music is often perceived as a rarefied form that removes itself from explicit social commentary, a music that for nineteenth century English ears would seem far from the hustle and bustle of metropolitan life. Of course here one needs to make the distinction between the middle-class taste for classical music in the nineteenth century and contemporary tastes for progressive or post-rock, for example, amongst middle-class youth today. The status of classical music has changed rapidly over the last 100 years, and middle-class tastes have come to incorporate more popular styles as middle-class performative identities have evolved. However, the division between class experience and, by extension, class subjectivities, particularly as articulated by Lee, is still evident.

While the middle classes were removing themselves to the concert hall and the drawing room, the working men and women of the cities and large towns were experiencing the rise of the music hall.[5] A natural evolution can be seen from the song and supper rooms behind public houses to larger, dedicated theatre-style venues that would house music hall. Already we can see the establishment reaction to popular music, a reaction that depends on the very division between middle-class and working-class tastes. Lee provides us, for example, with the words of the composer Sir Hubert Parry, who in 1899 commented,

> The modern popular song reminds one of the outer circumference of our terribly overgrown towns... It is for people who live in those unhealthy regions, people who scramble for subsistence, who think that the commonest rowdyism is the highest expression of human emotion; for them this popular music is made, and it is made, with a commercial object, of snippets of slang. (52)

Such sentiments would continue to be heard throughout the following century. The middle classes had a variety of places to experience music whether it was the concert hall, the pleasure garden, the theatre or through family entertainment in the home. For the working classes music similarly moved out of the streets and into the 'song and supper' rooms around 1820, and subsequently the early music halls. The evolution of public house entertainment into the music hall is exemplified by

Charles Morton who, after having promoted performances since 1848 at the Canterbury Arms in Lambeth, extended his premises in 1851 to incorporate a seated hall suitable for around 1500 customers. By the 1880s some estimates suggest that London had around 500 such music halls, spaces orientated around a theatre format after the Certificate of Suitability Act of 1878 which required a stage separate from the auditorium, a ban on alcohol and the provision of a safety curtain. While Morton, commonly acknowledged as the 'Father of Halls', was putting on large-scale music hall concerts in the 1850s, precedents had already been set in other parts of London and particularly in Lancashire and Yorkshire. Through the 1830s and 1840s entrepreneurs such as Thomas Sharples in Bolton were developing their public house concert halls into larger music halls that could hold an audience of a few thousand, although it was figures such as Morton and Richard Preece in Southwark who initiated the move into dedicated music hall theatres. By the turn of the century, a significant network of music halls had established themselves around the country, and would provide much of the foundation for the development of live popular music through the 1900s (Russell, 1997). This form of the music hall survived well into the 1900s and provided space for the working-class family to come for a night of entertainment.

It was clear very early on that the music halls provided an entertainment physically and culturally apart from the more sophisticated tones of the concert hall. As such, working-class experience began to creep into the performances (Albert Chevalier's character of the costermonger boy provides a comical glimpse at an urban working-class life that would be recognized by much of the audience), alongside parodies of upper-class society, such as George Leybourne's rendition of 'Champagne Charlie' or Albert Vance's 'swell' character, a portrait of a newly affluent, socially mobile gentleman (Lee, 1982). Such caricatures served to delineate working-class values and define a sense of community that was not conferred upon from above. As Skeggs (2004a) suggests, 'music-hall entertainment enabled the working class to challenge the moral authority of others, and to value their experience differently from the dominant value systems. This is another important legacy weaved into the contemporary' (40). However, even within music hall, the folk voice could be utilized to ultimately suit the ends of the theatre managers and performers. Appealing to the new urban vernacular could be highly profitable. The performers, if popular enough, could command a substantial income (by 1915 Marie Lloyd was earning £10,000 a year (Lee, 108)), yet the music halls remained a staunchly working-class environment. It was at the point that music was taken off the streets and into the music hall and the concert hall, respectively that class affiliations made their most significant impact on music in England.

The separation between classical music and what we might term the *urban* folk voice has remained with us throughout the twentieth century to the present day. Classical music has taken the folk idiom on board, most notably in the work of Ralph Vaughan-Williams and Percy Grainger in Britain, but rarely has the voice of urban, working-class experience manifested itself in 'serious' music. Rather the ghost of music hall has provided a template for music that speaks of class experience, to an audience who understand the vernacular and the parochial. This ghost may well have had its roots in the connections between working lives and rural folk music, but it is in the music halls that such a connection becomes a commodity, and it is also within the music halls that folk music is relegated in favour of more populist, mass entertainment. Following the Second World War Britain experienced an influx of American music that reawakened the class divisions of the previous century, after a steady output of predominantly light music via the BBC. This focus on light music, often orchestral in nature, again suggests a primary focus on middle-class tastes. As such it is necessary to understand the American fascination with working-class experience in popular music,[6] and only then to examine the implications across the Atlantic.

Rock and the folk voice

The United States follows a pattern replicated by Britain in the first half of the twentieth century in that the dominant styles of music available for consumption, via the radio particularly, are supplanted by music more closely associated with working-class or racially marginalized groups. H F Mooney's 1968 article 'Popular Music Since the 1920s: The Significance of Shifting Taste' gives a useful summation of the drift from 'the blandness, urbanity or introspection of the 1920s and 1930s' (9) in musical terms towards a fascination with working-class experience and in particular Afro-American musical styles. Mooney suggests that the decline of Tin Pan Alley in the late 1930s, followed by the demolition of the ASCAP (American Society of Composers, Authors and Publishers) monopoly on musical production in 1941, led to a rise in nationally diverse music distribution and production across the States, away from the hub of New York, allowing a wider range of voices to be heard. The role of local radio networks in the United States was important for filling the void in programming through more localized musical sounds such as country, bluegrass and the blues. The two primary forces at work were the increasing influence of Afro-American sounds and rhythms within big band music during the 1930s and 1940s and later the vogue for folk-inflected protest music which similarly sought to give a voice to anyone who was not immediately cosmopolitan or socially affluent.[7] The resuscitation of the careers of artists such as Woody Guthrie and Muddy Waters stems from this opportunity afforded by the collapse of the ASCAP monopoly.

Mooney suggests that even where jazz entered significantly into the big band sound, it often followed a safer, more melodic format created for a predominantly white, middle-class audience:

> Duke Ellington himself was influenced by Guy Lombardo's 'sweetest music this side of heaven', and brought something of the sound of the Roosevelt Hotel ballroom to Harlem. Commercial orchestras of the period around 1920–1950 followed more or less the 'safe bet' – the aesthetic aspirations of the middle class market – as did, indeed most of the big Negro bands. (10)[8]

This middle-class market was predominantly an older, affluent sector, one that was of course about to be supplanted by what Mooney describes as,

> [T]he ambivalent generation of 1920–50, which supported ambivalent orchestras like that of Glenn Miller, [who] would have its cake and eat it too. A generation of transition, facing both ways, it compromised between the gentility of the Victorian parlour and the libidinism of the beatnik's pad. (14)

This generation would see the influx of sounds previously ostracized by the ASCAP monopoly gaining influence from regional centres, to fuse Afro-American song forms with country and folk to create exciting new styles such as rockabilly. Mooney suggests that an increasingly affluent post-war America did not feel the need to glamorize the nightlife and penthouse existence exemplified by Sinatra, Como and Bennett.[9] As such younger audiences were becoming increasingly disenfranchised from the light band music that their parents listened to and found solace in the new music coming from across the States. Mooney even suggests that the onset of the Cold War provided a backdrop that prioritized national music (Harker would certainly agree with this conclusion) over light entertainment. What follows, for Mooney, is a section of urban middle-class America becoming anti-bourgeois, coupled with a rise in affluent minority groups sharing space particularly in the Northern cities, who were able to become a significant force in the music audience, thus granting yet more access to primarily Afro–American-influenced styles. Indeed, in 1959 the major market for popular music in the States lay between the ages of nine to eighteen ('Mr Harper's After Hours', 1959), an audience rapidly moving away from the sophistication and nuance of the band sound, towards the rougher hues of rock 'n' roll. Equally, the intellectual fascination with the hard bop jazz sound coming out of the West Coast suggested that an adult audience were also engaging with more visceral forms. Mooney concludes,

> Crosby and Como were passé in a period which sang, 'Here's to the losers.' Perhaps the first indication of the change had been Johnny Ray's 'Cry' in 1951. At any rate, music of the sort young people felt WASP over thirty would sing, compose or listen to, went into a decline. The liner blurbs, intended to sell records at first sight, spoke less of the home and family of the performer than of his 'searchings,' his bitterness, his inability or refusal to accommodate to the Establishment, his mental and/or physical handicaps or deviations, his daemonic immersion in environment-obliterating alcohol, sex or drugs. (20)

The shift from this position to the dominance of rock 'n' roll as a cultural force has been extensively documented elsewhere (Gillett, 1983, for example), but the class affiliations, perceived or otherwise, suggest that popular tastes were already responding to an authenticity closely allied to working class or minority experience.[10] One can see the 'Crosby and Como' sound as white, middle-class America singing to itself. Pop music has, from its inception, had some form of engagement with class experience, but what is fascinating about Mooney's account is that he makes much of a generation of middle-class kids who are estranged from the tastes of their parents, who therefore gravitate towards a new market of folk-inflected music or music that is connected to non-middle class idioms, be it rock and roll, be bop, traditional American folk music or the blues. The gravity that pulls this generation towards music with which they may have no direct relationship can in these terms be seen as the folk voice. In other words, dissatisfaction within middle-class generational communities with the mainstream music market seems to draw the audience to music (once it is widely disseminated) that holds the perceived authenticity and integrity lacking in the 'Crosby and Como' sound, be it rock 'n' roll, rockabilly, or any of the other new forms coming through before and after the Second World War. Were one able to extrapolate Harker's thesis on English folk music to the popularization of previously marginal American music forms in the 1950s, one would have to conclude that this folk voice becomes a mode of performativity, a refraction through middle-class subjectivity of working-class experience, something to be performed through the articulation of the folk voice as an ambivalent relationship to the dominant discourse of pre-war popular music. A case can of course be made that such generic adoption on the part of young (often white) middle-class consumers results in a level of appropriation that renders the origins of provincial music dehistoricized. However, it is not this chapter's intention to plot the embourgeoisment of American popular music *per se*, but rather to understand how that embourgeoisment connected with similar trends in Britain.

The ambivalent voice

As suggested above, the translation of rock 'n' roll across the Atlantic in the late 1950s allowed a similar demographic of teenagers to distance themselves from their parents through the application of a taste that favoured the 'authentic' sounds of rock 'n' roll. As outlined in Chapter 2, the formation of subcultural activity allied to music and fashion at this time has been seen, particularly by the CCCS, as an attempt by working-class youth to provide a social framework that makes sense of the changing nature of working-class experience after the Second World War. If we focus our attention on middle-class youth audiences, who were by no means restricted from rock culture, we can see a similar emphasis emerging. The pop music listener has the option to partake in music that can allow them to perform their way out of their class position, albeit momentarily. For the working-class listener the prioritization of masculinity, authenticity and the social sphere may provide alternatives that hark back to perceived notions of a lost communal experience, one eroded by the social changes that their parents went through. For any other listening position, the class insinuations of rock 'n' roll provide an idealized option contrary to the safety and comfort of suburban British life.

Of prime importance here is the form in which this music is available. The mass distribution of rock 'n' roll, via radio, television and records, means that these forms are not restricted to the cultural groups that we might immediately associate them with. In the States the ASCAP monopoly on music publishing had previously held such musics back, but by the 1950s they had a strong standing in the record market, albeit in an often-bastardized form. The rock 'n' roll making its way to Britain via the pirate radio stations, the American air bases and the import shops therefore was readily available, without necessarily having any real social context within which to place it.[11] As such it provided a readymade totem around which to place the newfound generational independence gained from the taste shift away from the light music of their parents.

It is here that we can identify the resurgence of the folk voice within British pop music culture. The adoption of folk music as a heritage style had long since relegated it to the museum and the classroom (the folk revival was still yet to happen in Britain until the 1960s), and as such the indigenous music of the British Isles could not provide the alternative that middle-class youth sought. Indeed it is telling that English folk music is not an option in the search for authentic, visceral culture on any significant mainstream level primarily for the exact reasons that Harker outlines. Rather, British youth gravitate towards forms that articulate the folk voice without specific reference to British culture. The skiffle craze of the late 1950s in Britain marked a gravitation towards a music that embraced and exemplified the folk voice while not being overtly situated within either British folk culture or the British class system. However, it did represent a form of 'authentic' music that had obvious links not only to contemporary pop forms via a shared historical lineage that had largely bifurcated during the mid-war period in the States, but also to more marginal American forms such as jazz, blues and folk music. In 1958 the novelist Colin MacInnes noted that,

> A few years ago, for reasons that remain mysterious, and coinciding with the eruption of the coffee bars... all over London, skiffle groups appeared and spread like mushrooms till there are today certainly many hundreds of them, several of which have won commercial fame. The movement is, of course, a 'mannerist' one – somewhat similar, in a way, to the revival of English folk-dancing some decades ago. That is to say, the teenagers in the groups are reviving, artificially, a musical style that was once spontaneous... But what's odd is that the ballads the skiffle musicians sing are American, and their singing accent even more so. Songs about transatlantic gals and jails and railroads, intoned in a nasal monotone, seem entirely convincing to Cockney kids from Camberwell and Wood Green, sitting huddled in these Soho basements – and their idol, Lonnie Donegan, has sold some of these back to the Americans with resounding success. (85–6)

There are two elements that are of interest in the above passage in relation to the folk voice. In the first instance MacInnes is right to point to the revivalist nature of skiffle, a musical form that has its roots in the American south at the turn of the century. Even in recorded form skiffle had existed since 1925 with recordings by Jimmy O'Bryant and his Chicago Skifflers. As such skiffle cannot be simply understood as a new musical craze with its roots in the contemporary cultural sphere of the 1950s. Secondly, this is a musical form that not only has its origins some 50 years prior to its success in Britain, but also in another country altogether. Yet the success of skiffle depends both on the recognition of marginalized subjectivities (again emerging and gaining currency through institutional shifts such as the end of the ASCAP monopoly and a buoyant economy in the United States in the post-war period) and the ability to utilize signifiers of authenticity that performed subjectivities in ways that British teenagers could use. Such use can be understood as an ambivalent reaction to more pervasive discourses surrounding class, gender, race and generation. Skiffle's importance lay in its bipartite role both as a scion of authenticity and in its ability to translate authenticity away from ethnic, national and social status. As such it is not so much skiffle's musical heritage that paves the way for rock music in the 1960s, it is its function as a form of music that relocates subjectivity through performativity.

However, it is important to note that skiffle, particularly as popularized in Britain by Lonnie Donegan, did continue its assimilation of disparate styles by incorporating nuances of British cultural life:

> Skiffle, like punk, stripped music to the core. Its quirky combination of acoustic guitars, tea-chest bass, and washboard sent out a clear anyone-can-do-it signal, and as the skiffle explosion proved, anyone could and did...For a nation's youth that had looked so long to America for musical inspiration and instruction, skiffle offered a distinct British 'accent' that would prove an important stepping stone in the development of more Anglo-centric popular music.
>
> (Ellis, 2006)

Ellis particularly sees a comedic vernacular in Donegan's work that sets itself against the British middle-class establishment (and the music associated with by the crooners), and alongside marginalized identities in the United States. As such the adoption of skiffle not only acts as an ambivalent reaction to dominating discourses of national/gender/

class/generational identity, but also as a direct strategy to undermine those discourses.

> For... [Donegan], the music had to be raw and amateur, a reflection of the 'folk', a contrast to the elite. His way of saying 'Roll Over Beethoven' was to exaggerate his cockney accent and sing about topics of the everyday. Skiffle may have been rooted in the American South, but Donegan brought the British streets into the music, and, most significantly, a sense of celebratory humour that had its roots in 19th-century British music-hall comedy.
>
> (Ellis, 2006)

It is no surprise that one of Donegan's biggest hits is the most overt fusion of working-class music hall comic form and southern US roots music, 'My Old Man's a Dustman' (1960); however, this also shows the level to which Donegan had started to appeal to an older mainstream market as well as children by the turn of the decade.

The influence of skiffle as a homegrown form (Ellis points out that many people at the time assumed that skiffle had its origins in the United Kingdom) would have profound ramifications for the evolution of popular music in Britain for decades to come. It would also be an important link between rural folk musics in the United Kingdom and the development of the folk voice in rock discourse. This evolution is the subject of the following case studies.

6
Folk Revival and Folk Rock

To be able to explicate a performance of class within popular music in any meaningful sense, we must first understand its role as an arbiter of authenticity. Displays of class affiliation are most often used as grounding elements that may place a piece of music, an artist or a performance within a social and historical context, and also provide a method by which audiences can form a class allegiance with the performer or the text. However, while class might have its own specific role to play within the pop music experience, it has to be understood as part of a much wider attempt to establish authenticity. The third chapter of this work dealt specifically with the idea of the *authentic* in pop music, and it is not the intention here to interrogate this problematic category too closely. However, when one looks to the role of class in relation to folk rock and the folk revival in Britain from the 1960s onwards, it is difficult to extricate class from more general debates concerning authenticity. Of course, such debates spring primarily from the way in which folk music in Britain was compiled and performed by the archivists, and also the inescapable influence of the English Folk Dance and Song Society. As outlined in the previous chapter, the activity of collecting folk song in Britain often suggested a temporal freeze of the material, an attempt to perform folk song in a pure and undiluted form. It is precisely such an approach that became untenable as the folk rock scene in Britain developed in the late 1960s and early 1970s.

This case study will specifically focus on the impact of artists such as Fairport Convention, Pentangle and The Incredible String Band, as well as solo artists such as Nick Drake, John Martyn and Richard Thompson, many of whom recorded with Chris Blackwell's Island Records through the late 1960s and 1970s. However, it is also significant to note the evolution of folk rock into progressive rock throughout the 1970s. Brocken (2003) suggests that while folk music takes much from rock music, rock music similarly adopts a dewy-eyed pastoralism that forms a connection between Sam Larner or The Sweeney Men and Donovan or Tyrannosaurus Rex. The impact of psychedelia on British rock music, coupled with the electrification of folk music on both sides of the Atlantic, allowed British rock to forge a mythology that it could call its own. While The Byrds and The Band could mine a rich vein of frontier mythology in the States, reconnecting the hippie scene with a supposedly organic American past, British folk music allowed the pop singer to reconnect with a similarly imagined vision of pastoral, pre-industrialized Britain. That such a connection was crucial in the formation of both progressive rock and heavy metal (to differing degrees) suggests that the prioritization of class and authenticity connected to the folk movement had mutated somewhere along its evolution. Indeed the popular music form, particularly as articulated through the emerging prism of rock discourse, caused a significant change in the way in which folk idioms could be understood. This resulted in a shift from a perception of folk music as a socially binding and often class-based set of musical practices that sat exactly within the lives and preoccupations of those who performed it to a facet of rock music that largely refuted class identities in favour of more interiorized and introverted subjectivities that harked back to a pastoral Englishness. That such a transition had an effect not only on perceptions of folk music itself but that it also informed progressive rock, heavy rock and, to an extent, more mainstream forms of pop music, as well American forms at certain points, suggests the level of impact that the shift in the uses of folk music had. It also suggests a significant paradigmatic shift in the way in which Britain engaged with its own folk history in the wake of the development of a discourse of rock music.

To understand how such a change in the articulation of authenticity comes about from the perceived *vox populi* of folk music to the Tolkienisms of Genesis and Led Zeppelin, one must understand that the signs and meanings of authenticity perceived within the folk community at the start of the folk revival in the 1960s underwent a radical transformation in the face of rock 'n' roll. The very process of the collection and preservation of folk music was invariably motivated by a desire to save something that was being lost (at least as far as the archivists saw it) that seemed to easily espouse organic values. The previous chapter has already dealt with the desire to protect folk forms from the indifference of the urban masses and the rural working classes, a desire that led folk music to become intrinsically linked with primarily middle-class purists who sought to keep traditions alive long past their period of cultural relevance. As Brocken points out, folk rock, as a pivotal moment between traditional folk idioms and the rock mutations it would later influence, 'was a cultural transformation of the representative values of [folk] music' (94). The values of preservation and protection were dramatically rebuked in favour of not only musical experimentation and evolution, but also a desire to reconnect with the people that folk music claimed to represent. However, in the face of an increasingly urban and suburban (and generationally specific) folk voice that was better represented by rock music, folk rock's attempt to reconnect to the present ultimately led to its own cultural cul-de-sac. Again folk rock becomes a bastion of student and middle-class tastes, leading, as previously stated, towards progressive rock and elements of heavy rock. Obviously it is not difficult to ascertain folk's cultural currency in the United Kingdom at the present time. It is still primarily a middle-class preserve, championed by BBC Radio Two, enjoyed at the Cambridge Folk Festival and over a hundred subsidiary festivals around the United Kingdom, watched on *Later... with Jools Holland* late at night on BBC2. But it certainly is not the dominant idiom of working-class experience, even in rural communities. The musics that hold the place once claimed by folk music at the heart of working-class life in the United Kingdom are more strictly popular music forms (hip hop, indie and heavy rock, mainstream pop, R 'n' B etc.) that articulate working-class identity in differing ways. While folk music in its current incarnations holds on to its identity as a music of the people, its status is undermined by its lack of centrality to modern life, despite various attempts to reconnect with a broader, less middle-class audience. Whether this means that folk failed in its attempts to reconnect or not is not of primary importance here, but its attempts at rejuvenation from the 1960s onwards have left us with a map of cultural relevance that says much about the issue of class in popular music.

When approaching folk rock two underlying themes seem to be most immediately apparent. In the first instance, there is a desire to escape the emphasis on the musician to recreate accurately the song in question. Revivalism has often insisted on the submission of the performer to the song, requiring fidelity of reproduction (although the question of the *original* has historically been highly problematic) over interpretation. Secondly, the traditions of folk music are held and revalued to allow a scope within which the artist or performer may express themselves. Of course, rock music already allowed this, placing emphasis on both its own conventions and the idiosyncrasies of the performer. Interpretation becomes of utmost importance, particularly during the early 1960s when cover versions were commonplace in the record-buying charts. The aura of the performer was at least as important as the song, and folk music has historically found it difficult to come to terms with this. The very success of artists such as Fairport Convention, and particularly its two best-known alumni Richard Thompson and Sandy Denny, rests as much on the significance of the band or artist as it does its repertoire.

The transition to folk rock

The period of transition that folk rock represents might best be seen by the book ends of the curatorial approach of A L Lloyd in the 1940s and the freeform work of singer/guitarist John Martyn in the 1970s. Here we see a direct revaluation of the folk idiom, from a traditional music with utopian (and often socialist) leanings, to a music that suggests pastoralism almost at the expense of class signification. It is possible to draw a line from Lloyd and Ewan MacColl through the pioneering work of artists such as Bert Jansch and Davey Graham (both gifted and highly influential guitarists), on to John Martyn, Nick Drake and Roy Harper, and the full folk rock fusion as exhibited by Fairport Convention, Pentangle and The Incredible String Band, noting a significant generic evolution without even going on to the progressive and hard rock hybrids that would emerge in its wake. This line shows a change in expectation that dramatically veers away from the desire to protect a vanishing rural and industrial past. Instead the folk idiom becomes a method of evocative performance that never entirely shirks issues of heritage, roots and belonging (since traditional songs are still discovered and performed) yet never wholly remains faithful to them either.

Rather than attempt a chronological progression through the artists mentioned above, particularly as many of them are synchronous, it is more useful to trace prevailing themes that outline their preoccupations. The influence of pop music in the late 1950s had already had a profound effect on the folk scene. Martin Carthy, guitarist and vocalist with Steeleye Span, Waterson Carthy and a successful solo artist in his own right, remembers the first song he learnt to play on the guitar as 'Heartbreak Hotel',[1] while Ashley Hutchings of Fairport Convention cites Johnny and the Hurricanes and Bill Black's Combo as primary influences over The Spinners or the Kingston Trio (Brocken, 2002). However, subsequent influences on Carthy are telling. His first musical purchase was an album of Negro spirituals and folk songs, which included Elizabeth Cotton's rendition of 'Freight Train', while traditional folk songs performed by the Norfolk fisherman Sam Larner had a profound effect on him at an early age. The combination of a fascination with rock 'n' roll, American folk and blues and traditional English folk song was not uncommon. Indeed, looking at the later trajectory of artists such as Carthy, Martyn and Drake it becomes clear that this amalgam of influences is at the heart of a dislocated traditional mode of music making.

Such a complicated collection of influences might well have appalled A L Lloyd, author of *Folk Song in England* (1967). Lloyd's work is still a staple of the folk scene today, but it represents the more purist curatorial attitude towards folk music prior to the folk revival in the 1960s. Lloyd, a member of the English Folk Dance and Song Society, the International Folk Music Council and the International Commission for the Study of Worker's Songs, saw folk music as not only a means of protest but also as a vision of a utopian future via the display and inspiration of a golden past, 'via the industrial ballads, the part of the tradition that seemed most pertinent to the modern world, Lloyd ... attempted to offer ordinary people not only a place in history that had been hitherto denied, but also a role in the production of historical musical knowledge' (Brocken, 2002). Not only had folk music been subsumed within academic circles, but also the people that it belonged to had been alienated from its production and reception (at least as far as Lloyd was concerned). Lloyd was keen to suggest that he was not merely interested in the folk song of the rural peasantry, indeed he took issue with Cecil Sharp for his focus on rural working-class life at the expense of the urban masses, 'an ideology of primitive romanticism with a vengeance' (Lloyd, 14). As such *Folk Song in England* is keen to concentrate as much on the industrial folk song as it is the rural, at least suggesting some form of continuity throughout a period of urbanization and industrialization. However, Lloyd often showed an inability to deal effectively with the incursion of pop music, at this time easily the dominant musical category amongst working-class communities. Brocken highlights the problem of Lloyd's partial and partisan idealization of working-class culture:

To Lloyd, the growth of urbanized and industrialized communities had a tangible, erosive effect upon hundreds of years of oral traditions. The collection and preservation of those traditions, viewed as being close to irrevocable loss, were deemed to be of paramount importance. However, Lloyd's concentration upon class boundaries and industrial landscapes in his definitions of the uses of folksong in both *The Singing Englishman* [1944] and *Folk Song In England* also delivered-up a sub-textual polemic about the retention of any folk song as a representation of political struggle, a 'longing for a better life'. Lloyd was an inveterate Marxist and his enthusiasm was so manifest that in-depth, contextual investigations about folk-popular dichotomies were glossed-over.

(2002)

The dichotomy Brocken is outlining is inevitably made when positioning mass-produced pop music against the supposedly organic forms of folk music. Lloyd perceived the industrialization of music, as Adorno had,[2] as a threat to the political potential of folk music. Indeed one gets the sense in Lloyd's work that folk music itself loses any relevance when stripped of its potential for social change. Such potential, in the industrialized Britain of the 1960s, manifested itself in the construction of a recollection of communal action and organization throughout the pre-industrialized past. However, in the face of the cultural impact of pop music, particularly with its politicization in the late 1960s, many in the folk community found such claims hard to substantiate. Bob Pegg (of folk rock band Mr Fox) suggests that folk music was,

> ...an illusion created unconsciously by the people who talk about it, go out looking for it, make collections of it, write books about it, and announce to an audience that they are going to sing it or play it. It is rather like a mirage which changes according to the social and cultural standpoint of whoever is looking at it.
>
> (qtd. in Brocken, 2002)

While folk may have held some form of socially progressive potential, it was rarely the same kind that Lloyd espoused. Brocken is quick to question the impact of traditional forms of folk music at a political level when he sees the working classes addressed primarily as consumers rather than political individuals after the Second World War. It was becoming increasingly obvious that the standard bearers of folk music were rejecting the kind of music that the majority of the working classes were actually listening to. The implication was that the working man or woman was becoming alienated from an authentic working-class culture as they dallied with Anglo-American pop music. Even at a grass-roots level in the folk clubs, English folk music was often not the most obvious choice for performance material. Norma Waterson, who ran the folk club Folk Union One in Hull from the mid-1950s, recalled the first time that she saw Martin Carthy perform, remarking with surprise at his primarily English repertoire, as opposed to the usual American fare of the other performers at the time.[3]

The conflation of discursive fields

While it is obvious that Sharp, Lloyd and countless others had provided a repertoire of English rural and industrial folk song that many performers (including those in the folk rock movement) had adopted, there was a similar desire felt by a younger generation of performers to adopt popular music idioms from both sides of the Atlantic. Not only was there a dialectic between traditional folk and popular rock discourses, but the multiplicity of forms that were influencing the folk rock movement, and indeed pop music on a grander scale, make for an increasingly complex family tree. If one moves forward chronologically to Led Zeppelin, a band who owe as much to folk rock as they do to the blues, it is possible to see how a variety of influences fuse together, largely denying any attempt to stay fixed in a socio-historical tradition. The August 2004 issue of *Mojo* magazine carried a free CD compilation entitled *The Roots of Led Zeppelin*, compiled specifically by guitarist Jimmy Page to accompany that issue's article on him. Amongst the usual quota of blues artists, many of whom contributed to Zeppelin's song catalogue, such as Robert Johnson, Muddy Waters and Howlin' Wolf, we also find guitarists such as Bert Jansch and John Renbourn. Both Jansch and Renbourn fuse folk, blues and classical styles, while the inclusion of Joan Baez represents the influence of the American folk revival of the late 1950s and 1960s on Page's musical upbringing. As both Carthy and Page demonstrate, it becomes increasingly difficult to locate a pure lineage for the transition of folk through the age of rock 'n' roll. Prior to the acquisition of Dave Swarbrick on fiddle in 1969, Fairport Convention were primarily considered to be a rock (as opposed to folk) act, albeit one influenced by Baez, Dylan and The Byrds. Whether it was primarily Swarbrick's influence (he had previously played with Carthy in a more consciously folk vein), or not, *Liege and Lief* (1969) saw a concentration upon a more traditional folk sound, including traditional songs like 'Matty Groves' and 'Toss the Feathers'. However, even here the urge to incorporate lessons learned from pop music was encouraged. Perhaps the most notable change is the adoption of electric guitar by Richard Thompson, a move also made by Carthy when he joined Steeleye Span in 1970.

While it is tempting to see the adoption of amplified electric instrumentation over traditional instrumentation as a shift in itself, it merely points to a divergence in the perception of what folk music was supposed to be, and of who the *folk* are. Bob Dylan's much documented adoption of electric guitar at the 1965 Newport Folk Festival might have been greeted with a significant level of scorn, but it does serve as a defining moment in the development and integration of rock discourse. The folk rock that followed in Britain was attempting to situate itself as the articulator of a now refined folk voice by connecting to the dominant paradigms of popular culture through the 1960s and 1970s. Although Lloyd and MacColl would not have approved of an 'updating' of traditional music, Fairport Convention, Steeleye Span and Pentangle amongst others, recognized a need for traditional music to become available in contemporary forms, forms that the majority of the record-buying public, not just the folk aficionados, would recognize. As Blake (1997) suggests, traditions tend to be constructed in the face of modernization and progress, and the evolution of folk into folk rock can be understood as an attempt to reorient folk music's relationship to heritage. Instead of preserving folk song in aspic, as a document of a more socially engaged time, folk rock allowed the possibility that folk idioms might once again play a central role in people's everyday culture through the fusion of a *folk voice* and contemporary manifestations of popular music. However, the fact that folk music today is still primarily a fringe activity in the United Kingdom, a sector of a wider arts environment rather than the primary folk voice at the heart of popular music, suggests that attempts to reconnect the populace with a lost heritage through evolved folk forms largely failed.[4]

John Martyn and Nick Drake

Folk rock's failure to provide an updated folk voice that connected with and was relevant to the majority of the population of the United Kingdom, should not, however, be seen as a dead end in the story of folk music.[5] Rather, folk rock had a somewhat different effect on the perception of folk music in Britain from the 1970s onwards. Indeed it could be suggested that folk rock's significance led to two particular paradigms that would have an influence in a wider sense throughout British popular music, pastoralism (Macan, 1997) and medievalism. The pastoral tradition has been perhaps the most significant effect of folk rock and its roots can be traced back to the same spawning ground of the folk rock movement. Two figures that illustrate the difference between folk rock itself and the pastoral idiom are John Martyn and Nick Drake. Both Martyn and Drake were signed to Chris Blackwell's Island Records and were both managed by Joe Boyd, a significant figure in the story of the blend of folk and pop (he also managed Fairport Convention and The Incredible String Band through his Witchseason company, an imprint of Island). As with Richard Thompson and Martin Carthy, Martyn was a renowned folk guitarist, influenced heavily by the folk singer Hamish Imlach. Indeed his first two Island records, *London Conversation* (1968) and *The Tumbler* (1968) are relatively standard folk-inflected acoustic sets, often delving into blues and American folk rock. However, his most significant recordings, *Bless the Weather* (1971) and *Solid Air* (1973) are notable not just for the increasing visibility of blues and jazz influences, but also for the willingness to incorporate technological innovations such as the Echoplex delay unit. While much of Martyn's music in the early 1970s retains a primarily acoustic ambience, supplemented by the double bass of Pentangle's Danny Thompson, by *Solid Air* the acoustic guitar and Martyn's increasingly gruff vocal delivery start to form impressionistic soundscapes, particularly akin to Van Morrison's *Astral Weeks* (1969). On one side the increasing willingness to experiment not only with form but also with the potential advantages afforded by technological innovation led to music less situated inside the folk movement. However, the presence of folk music in Martyn's work is indisputable, yet it is a presence that merges with jazz (particularly improvisatory practice), blues and, later in his career, reggae.

If one compares Martyn's work with his folk contemporaries, it becomes clear that the performative significance of folk underwent an important shift during the late 1960s and early 1970s for both performer and audience. Rather than being an organic music associated with particular class positions that articulates the folk voice, it instead becomes equated with pastoralism, a desire to return to a mythic past, often a specifically English one. This is best articulated in Martyn's work by his early reliance on acoustic instruments (his live line-up during the early 1970s consisted of Martyn himself on guitar and vocals, Thompson on double bass and John Stevens on drums) and a recurring theme of the rural landscape as a frame for his songs.[6] However, Martyn's music refuses the straight tag of the 'folk' sound through the use of the Echoplex unit, hugely expanding the sonic palette of his acoustic guitar, the inclusion of ethnic percussion such as the tabla, and the fusion of styles from both sides of the Atlantic, as well as more global influences. As such it might be increasingly difficult to place Martyn in a folk idiom at all were it not for the sharp delineation provided by his early Island albums and his later work, incorporating a full band (often including Phil Collins, Steve Winwood and Eric Clapton amongst others), providing Martyn with a chance to divert his attentions to the electric guitar. By 1980's *Grace and Danger* album Martyn had moved almost wholly towards a more straightforward MOR rock sound, contrasting with his earlier acoustic incarnation. While Martyn's transition, mirrored in their different ways not only by Bob Dylan in the States, but also by Richard

Thompson amongst others in the United Kingdom, cannot be seen as a refusal of the folk idiom, it does suggest a shift away from the mythical sense of pastoralism invoked in his earlier work. This pastoralism must be understood as a suggestion of folk musical style, and often lyrical content, removed from the supposed communicative social function of traditional folk song espoused by Lloyd and MacColl. Pastoralism here evokes a sense of rural England, particularly one that can be seen to be at odds with the increasing industrialization of the United Kingdom. It is also important to register the level of the fantastic that creeps into the pastoral as it engages with arcadian visions. Tyrannosaurus Rex exhibit this trend towards the fantastical through much of their early, pre-glam work, operating primarily as the acoustic multi-instrumental duo of Marc Bolan and Steve Peregrine Took. The song 'Trelawny Lawn' from their second album *Prophets, Seers and Sages, the Angels of the Ages* (1968) exemplifies this well through its references to unicorns, prophets, scribes and messianic lions.

Perhaps the best example of the pastoral evolution (or perhaps 'regression' is the better term) that folk undertakes is in the music of Nick Drake. Drake, a contemporary of Martyn's and the subject of his song 'Solid Air' (1973), has assumed much more cultural significance since his death in 1974. Through his lifetime, his three albums *Five Leaves Left* (1969), *Bryter Layter* (1970) and *Pink Moon* (1972) received some critical praise but little public attention. However, he has now assumed a central place in British music lore, the epitome of the troubled English singer-songwriter.[7] This status, partly explained by his early death, is perhaps more explicable because of the primarily acoustic and very intimate nature of his work. Taken as a whole, Drake's output again articulates the rural preoccupation of folk music, coupled with sparse musical ornamentation. *Pink Moon*, Drake's final album, consists of only vocals and acoustic guitar, while his debut, *Five Leaves Left*, has a wider sonic palette. Robert Kirby's string arrangements are understated, and other musical textures are primarily acoustic (including Danny Thompson's double bass), with the notable exception of Richard Thompson's electric guitar on 'Time Has Told Me'. Both albums share a fascination with the rural and pastoral, articulating an organic world often, and not exceptionally, equated with desire and self-realization. 'River Man' from *Five Leaves Left*, perhaps his most idyllic and pastoral composition, suggests a desire to return to elemental forces, written particularly in an English idiom. Here the protagonist of the song is seeking communion with the elemental River Man who carries knowledge of the flow of the river and bucolic summer evenings. Drake's *Pink Moon* album again makes use of pastoral imagery, although songs such as 'Pink Moon' and 'Things Behind the Sun' articulate the elemental force of the River Man in darker hues. 'From the Morning', however, again uses natural imagery to articulate a process of becoming through flight and the recurrent use of romantic summer evenings.

While it may seem rather obvious to place Drake in the role of rural troubadour, it is important to consider the tension prevalent throughout his work between the country and the city. The majority of Drake's first album was written at his family home in Tanworth-in-Arden, just outside of the Birmingham sprawl, and on his travels around Europe prior to his move to Cambridge. The majority of *Pink Moon* was equally written at his rural family home. However, his second album, *Bryter Layter*, documents his move to London, a move made to concentrate on his musical career, and a source of frustration and isolation for him at the time. *Bryter Layter* is notable for the articulation of city life in songs such as 'Poor Boy' and 'At the Chime of a City Clock'.[8] However, the prevailing sense is one of dissatisfaction and alienation when compared to the pastoral scenes of his first album. 'Poor Boy', the nearest Drake gets to a soul number, pits a country boy lost in the urban sprawl against a chorus of soulful admonition.[9] The rural idyll of his earlier works becomes the anonymous trap of city life, a trap that swallows the song's protagonist making his agonies and suffering all but invisible to those around him.

While *Bryter Layter* can be viewed as Drake's 'city' album, suggested also by the expanded band sound augmented by Dave Pegg, Richard Thompson and Dave Mattacks from Fairport Convention and John Cale amongst others, it never feels at home in its more cosmopolitan setting. The city is a huge, alienating space where a fragile soul can only fail in his quest for self-fulfilment. Yet it is not only *Bryter Layter* that problematizes the move to the city. Both of Drake's first two albums have photographs on the back sleeve that seem initially distinctly at odds with the acoustic settings of his songs; a blurred man rushing down an urban street watched by a static Drake, and a car speeding along a lamp-lit motorway again watched by the stationary singer. Both pictures place Drake as a voyeur, still and watching at the centre of a metropolitan lifestyle that he can never keep pace with. Matched with songs such as 'Poor Boy', 'At the Chime of a City Clock' or 'Three Hours', Drake's albums evoke a sense of detachment from the natural (and by association, the self) through urban alienation. The invocation of the dualism between the pastoral and the urban taps right into a discourse that has rearticulated the folk voice into a recollection of subjective innocence rather than as a socially communicative apparatus.

If one attempts to make sense of Drake primarily as a folk performer, it becomes increasingly clear that while he may be employing an acoustic style associated with the folk idiom, his resources are more complex than simply attempting to continue a tradition of English music. Obviously the first problem is that he wrote his own songs, rather than relying on traditional material, although Fairport Convention were equally 'guilty' of this. Secondly, Drake is emblematic of the collision of influences that any youth growing up during the 1960s in Britain may have been open to. Certainly, folk-inflected guitarists such as John Renbourn, Bert Jansch and Davy Graham influence his style,[10] but his songwriting was heavily based on the work of Tim Buckley, Leonard Cohen, Tim Hardin and Randy Newman. Indeed Drake's musical tastes extended to West Coast rock (Love in particular) and French chanson, alongside the classical music that he had grown up with. Drake is typical of many artists emerging in the folk rock scene at the time, influenced as much by rock, jazz and blues music as by folk. While John Martyn's music displays this esoteric melange to most startling effect, Drake takes his range of influences and Anglicizes them, painting portraits that seem particularly English in essence, sung in a quintessentially middle-class English accent. Humphries (1997) suggests that 'by the time Nick came to record, there was certainly no shame in sounding English, but few singers in rock history have sounded quite as English as Nick . . . [his] singing voice is more Noel Coward than Robert Plant' (99). The Romantic ideal of the struggling artist, so much a part of the discourse of rock music, is only enhanced by his refusal to adopt an Americanized vocal delivery. While his masculinity is rarely asserted, if at all, his vulnerability and melancholic delivery forms a close connection between his songs and the audiences' perception of his identity, forming its own kind of authentic significance. The singer-songwriter is privileged within rock discourse primarily because of his or her close connection to the material we hear, and the authenticity of artists such as Drake comes as much from this connection as we understand it than any authenticity connoted by folk forms. Again the transition from music used in a communal, public sense to an interiorized, private subjectivity is significant, showing as it does the performative role that music and its associated meanings have in shaping subjectivity for both the performer and any potential listener. The folk voice moves from being a public means of articulation in the real world to a private, psychic strategy of perceived communality, used precisely to offset the effects of modernization and industrialization. Drake's music makes this evident through the conflation of musical moments (lyrics, themes, timbres and tones) and the perceived status of

Drake as an authentic singer-songwriter. However, the relationship that this shift has to class within rock discourse quickly becomes problematic, as will be shown in the later case studies.

Acousticity

Drake, through his articulation of an arcadian vision (one at odds with a troubling urban alternative) and his refusal to subsume his own voice to any form of Americanism, placed himself within a discourse that certainly has its roots in the folk tradition. However, his music is emblematic of the use of the word *folk* to connote acousticity. Peter Narváez (2001) has provided a pertinent account of the myth of acousticity in relation to American blues guitarists, and his observations seem equally relevant when looking at the transition of folk music from a form that pertains to come from the people into an acoustic form of popular music. Narváez suggests that blues revivalists in the 1950s and 1960s 'embraced "country blues" and the cultural "myth of acousticity", an idea cluster that mixed authenticity with ideology' (27). This myth works on the supposedly more authentic and unmediated potential of the traditional wooden guitar. The more direct relationship between musician and audience, via the acoustic instrument, suggests not only a minimum of intervening stages in the transition of the music, but also a certain level of tonal purity, a notion borrowed from the 'legacy of cultural hierarchy' (29) that embedded the guitar within the classical tradition. Further than that Narváez focuses on the use of the acoustic guitar as a democratic vehicle (as opposed to the 'sonic authoritarianism of electric instruments' (29)) utilized particularly by the folk music sectors of the Popular Front, a New York-based socialist collective associated with blues artists such as Leadbelly, Sonny Terry and Brownie McGhee. The famous image of Woody Guthrie with the slogan 'this machine kills fascists' scrawled across his guitar (taken by the photographer Lester Balog (*c.* 1941)) exemplifies the potential of the acoustic guitar to connote a confrontation with centralization and cultural dominance, an attack obviously coupled with lyrical discourse. However, these political associations have become unravelled on both sides of the Atlantic by the adoption of electrification and amplification.

By the late 1960s and early 1970s, acoustic timbres were more commonly associated with pastoralism. Artists such as Tyrannosaurus Rex and The Incredible String Band evoked a sense of quasi-medievalism or pastoral idyll (Moore, 2001, 108–9), largely removed from the social consciousness perceived by Lloyd and MacColl. It is this strain that has come to largely dominate the perception of folk music in Britain since the 1970s, as acoustic music, often with a particularly English enunciation.[11] Even in the case of primarily progressive rock bands such as Genesis or Jethro Tull, acoustic guitars, flutes and accordions provide a softer, 'natural' tone that often offsets heavier electric tones. Macan (1997) suggests the attribution of feminine characteristics to acoustic timbres within progressive rock, and certainly listening to 'For Absent Friends' or 'Harlequin' from Genesis' *Nursery Cryme* album (1971) one gets the sense of acoustic tones producing a sense of whimsy or melancholy, distinctly at odds with the heavier, masculine, more conventionally *rockist* tones of 'Return of the Giant Hogweed' from the same album. Macan understands this opposition between masculine electric tones and feminized acoustic tones as an articulation of the dialectic between differing modes of social organization inherent in the counter-culture from which progressive rock emerged, particularly the tensions between capitalist (masculine) and socialist or communal (feminine) ideologies. Whatever the gender associations[12] of acoustic tones and instrumentation, certainly acousticity suggested an opposition to urban electric music through its articulation of the pastoral. However, it is interesting to note that such an opposition was often suggested through acoustic presence *per se* rather than a specific suggestion of Englishness. That is to say that the inclusion of acoustic sounds from across the globe played a large part in the format of acousticity during and after the folk rock explosion. Moore points to the inclusion of sitar, rebec, tabla and bongos within the mix of the Incredible String Band's *5000 Spirits or the Layers of the Onion* (1967) album 'while the subsequent The Hangman's Beautiful Daughter [1968] adds organs, harpsichords, kazoos and others' (108). That The Incredible String Band should share a label with Fairport Convention, John Martyn and Nick Drake, and also a musical legacy with Tyrannosaurus Rex, Jethro Tull and even the jazz-inflected Pentangle, suggests that the remit of what folk music was and did had broadened considerably by even the late 1960s. In this broadening of scope, class positioning becomes less relevant in an overt way, replaced instead by a concentration on pastoralism that stands in opposition to urbanization and modernity in a much more implicit fashion. As Moore points out,

> The Incredible String Band grew out of the folk circuit, and there was at least a tenuous link with folk music *per se*. The output of Tyrannosaurus Rex, on the other hand, was based solidly on Marc Bolan's very private mythologies – their purely acoustic instrumentation was

perhaps the only 'folk' connotation their style had. The intimacy this
ensured being most strongly a feature of the second folk revival. (109)

It is in such intimacy, afforded by acousticity and the ideological connotations that are contained therein, that the alienation of urban
experience can be resisted, if only temporarily. As such the acoustic
'folk' form within popular music assumes significance in its articulation
of authenticity for the subject not because it has any specific resistance
to commodification, but rather because it suggests a lack of mediation
and therefore gives the impression of organic development. The perception of the folk voice therefore resides in the sound, texture and
instrumentation of the music rather than in any lyrical articulation of
everyday lived experience. The performative experience of being connected to a tradition and heritage through the music, no matter how
elusive and mythological it may be, creates the sense of authenticity
required to place both the music and the subject in an ambivalent relationship to the commodification of popular music. That rock discourse
transforms the folk voice in this way shows exactly how articulations of
the authentic can only ever be performative strategies that actually go a
considerable way to obscure the relationship between art and commerce
in popular music.

The contemporary experience of folk-based music rises out of the conditions that folk rock set in place. Traditional folk music is not only a
marginalized musical form in Britain, but also one that shares space with
a wide variety of other musics. While there may still be an emphasis on
preservation and curation in some quarters, folk music is now regarded,
particularly in Britain, as part of a wider realm of roots music. One need
only pick up a copy of the best-selling folk magazine in the United Kingdom, *Folk Roots*. Alongside what one might call *traditional* British folk
practitioners are a variety of folk rock acts, acoustic artists and a plethora
of roots music from across the globe. Equally, most folk festivals in Britain
have widened their remit to encompass roots music from around the
world, as well as a selective amount of the pop form. As an example, the
Broadstairs Folk Festival in Kent affords not only shanty workshops and
performances of worker's song, but also a noticeable amount of acoustic
(and non-acoustic) music that shares closer ties to the singer-songwriter
traditions of popular music. From personal experience, one performer at
Broadstairs in the early 1990s repeatedly played versions of Pink Floyd
songs during his set (alongside more recognizably folk oriented material)
on an acoustic guitar relayed through a variety of digital processors to a
folk festival audience. Is it possible to integrate such a performance into

a concept of folk music? Was he merely playing the wrong material in such a setting? Given the reaction to his performances it would seem that the audience certainly had no problems with his choice of material. Rather, the Pink Floyd covers seemed to sit perfectly at ease in the context of an audience who had predominantly grown up listening not only to progressive rock but pop music on a broader level. Folk music was simply another facet of popularly enjoyed music that was tied together by a general level of craftsmanship and attitude. It certainly would not be pertinent to suggest that a cover of an S Club Seven song would have been as well received, other than in an ironic way, but at the beginning of the twenty-first century folk music has been easily assimilated within the values of popular music, and indeed provides its own contributions to rock discourse. While working-class music might no longer be necessarily folk music in its generic form, folk and acoustic music has continued to carry associations of authenticity that speak about class positioning. One of the problems for folk rock was that it was significantly associated with an audience made up of students and the middle classes, which made its connections to working-class identity increasingly problematic, particularly in the face of punk in the late 1970s. Punk positioned itself very quickly as the *folk voice* without recourse to acousticity, articulating its authenticity in different ways. However, the return to folk forms from artists coming out of the punk scene says a lot about an attempt to engage with a musical tradition of the folk voice rather than a merely ideological one.

Punk and neo-folk

Folk music has had a flirting if stable relationship with mass audiences throughout the last 40 years. It is not so difficult to find a broad range of artists, either directly from folk backgrounds, or influenced by folk idioms, who have made their way into the national record charts. During the early 1970s, after the departure of both Martin Carthy and Ashley Hutchings (arguably taking the hardcore folk element with them), Steeleye Span had top 20 hits with 'Gaudete' (1973) and 'All Around My Hat' (1975). Equally both The Chieftains and The Dubliners scored a number of chart entries through the 1980s. Perhaps most significantly, the Irish group Clannad made a number of incursions into the national consciousness, primarily through their contributions to television series such as *Harry's Game* and *Robin of Sherwood* in the 1980s. However, there seems a world of difference between the ambient folk tones of Clannad and the more traditionally celtic songs of the Dubliners. But while that difference is evident, neither group presents itself to the consciousness of the pop audience as in any way class affiliated. Rather they appear as paradigms of pastoralism and nostalgia, respectively.

Such presentations have not been the only form through which folk or traditional music has appeared in a mass forum. Perhaps the best example of this is The Pogues, an Anglo-Irish group that came out of the punk boom of the late 1970s. Fronted by Shane McGowan, the Pogues can be seen as an attempt to reclaim traditional Irish music from the archivists. The comparisons between folk and punk are many, and it seems only natural that the two should become fused in a band like The Pogues. McGowan's famously inebriated public persona seemed to portray the classic Irish poet, and indeed much of the band's material, particularly on albums such as *Rum, Sodomy and the Lash* (1985) and *If I Should Fall from Grace with God* (1988) treads a fine line between contemporary urban commentary and pastoral nostalgia. The Pogues operated in the middle ground between the traditionalists and the inno-vators, embracing amplified instrumentation and contemporary settings for their songs, as well as an archive of traditional material such as 'A Pair of Brown Eyes' (1985), 'The Irish Rover' (1987)[13] or 'The Broad Majes-tic Shannon' (1988). Certainly, their ability to play folk music to punk and post-punk audiences suggests a feeling of solidarity, of a national (albeit predominantly Irish) music being reclaimed. Other bands such as The Waterboys, Runrig and The Oyster Band attempted similar fusions of the popular and the traditional, particularly utilizing suggestions of celtic heritage and continuity, articulating a punk ethic through the use of folk music and style that seemed particularly appropriate in the face of Thatcherism during the 1980s. Billy Bragg's early work similarly explores the folk voice and acousticity, even given the fact that he performed on an electric guitar (its hard sound and lack of over-production placing it in a similar context to the acoustic guitar in relation to the slick produc-tions of the New Pop and dance music dominating the charts in the last half of the decade).

What is striking about The Pogues' attempts to reinvigorate folk music and return it to some form of social and cultural context is that it seems largely at odds with folk-inflected music in subsequent years. While other acts, such as The Oyster Band managed to provide a revved-up version of folk music, the prevailing tendency was still towards pastoral-ism over social and cultural connection. Indeed, the very motif of the pastoral has quietly evolved into chill-out music, which does not even need to be primarily acoustic. Artists such as Beth Orton, Pooka and even John Martyn in more recent years, have been adopted as artists whose music is as much a part of urban experience, despite the more relaxed instrumentation and acoustic performance. Orton, despite her links with Martyn's early work and the American folk musician Terry Callier, has as much to do with dance culture and the post-club environment, as she does with pastoralism. Indeed, her first recording was as a vocalist for the William Orbit[14] vehicle Spill in 1992, covering John Martyn's 'I Don't Want to Know About Evil'.[15] That her subsequent solo albums have received as much coverage from *Mix Mag* as they have from *Folk Roots*, suggests that the folk idiom is transforming again into a tone or mood, acousticity returned. However, the notion of acoustic music signifying authenticity is not as important as the implied opposition between itself and harder forms such as heavy rock or dance music. The shadow of singer-songwriters such as Drake is still a significant part of new acoustic music, and currently this can be seen across the Atlantic to great effect in the neo-folk movement. Songwriters such as Devandra Banhart and Joanna Newsom and bands such as Vetiver and Six Organs of Admittance are producing music[16] not only influenced by 1960s folk artists, but also with an eye on developing the use of instruments such as the banjo, harp and dulcimer, that have often been shunned by popular music. However, it is important to note that neo-folk, such as it is, follows on from the American lo-fi movement, again a tradition born from punk roots. The pastoral idioms are certainly at work here; however, the music fails to engage in anything other than a sonic fashion with notions of traditionalism, legacy or folk culture.

While class may be a factor in the perception of folk music in Britain, it seems clear that any pretensions it had towards being a 'voice of the people' have been largely disturbed by an engagement with popular music, at least for a generation growing up since the 1960s. The profusion of styles that have been incorporated (blues, jazz, rock, punk etc.) into the folk sound have increasingly placed more emphasis on its sonic characteristics, as signifiers of the pastoral, at the expense of folk music's culturally communicative function by word and narrative. As such, the idea of folk music as working-class music is as tenuous as it was at the start of the twentieth century. Instead the aura of authenticity, with all its class preoccupation, sits uneasily around the folk movement, particularly in its more recent engagements with popular music. One may look to a band such as The Pogues to see an attempt to reconcile a working-class pop/rock audience with music traditionally seen to be part of that very working-class culture, but in the final instance a purist folk music has been positioned as either a memory of heritage or a signifier of anti-rock calm. In both situations, its portrayal as the folk voice has largely been superseded by more urban strains of popular music.

The implication of the developments outlined above meant that the folk voice as a sign of authenticity needed to move elsewhere. Punk's significance, as we shall see in the next case study, was that it could perform the role of the folk voice whilst also being a form of music at the heart of British popular culture. While punk was never a hugely successful commercial proposition, at least in the 1970s, its cultural impact was highly visible, and it provided a means of articulating authenticity using class as a weapon. Whether punk was co-opted by the music industry (it obviously was) is irrelevant, its role as a voice of the people, even if only illusory, made it a profoundly effective way to mask the commercialization of popular music and therefore confirm the autonomy of those that listened to it.

7
Punk and Hardcore

The relationship that punk rock has with class, especially in Britain, has become ever more complex since the late 1970s. This chapter will explore previous attempts to characterize punk's class affiliations from both sociological and musical directions, and elicit a framework of connections that make up the somewhat contradictory nature of punk experience. Of course 'punk' is a contested term in itself, and this chapter will consider its meanings from the British punk explosion of the late 1970s through the post-punk era of the early 1980s and up to several strands of contemporary punk practice. While the focus will be maintained upon the British forms of punk rock, the American hardcore experience of the 1980s (primarily based around the DC scene of Minor Threat, Black Flag, The Minutemen and others) will provide insights into the stratification of the UK punk scene.

This stratification involves a (sub)cultural prioritization of certain bands and figures within the punk movement based upon class positioning, primarily in relation to the audience and the music industry. Broadly, this prioritization, utilizing and formed by the value system of British rock discourse, situates punk as primarily masculine and working class. Of course punk has its feminine aspects, but the masculine/working-class aspects of punk are exemplified not only in certain bands and artists, but also in certain sub-genres of punk, most notably the 'Oi!' movement. Oi! as a subculture (in affiliation with certain aspects of skinhead culture) reconfigures a working-class masculine identity against not only lived experience, but also perceived failings within the punk movement itself, failings that are in fact primarily about masculinity and class.

Defining punk

When exploring punk one encounters a number of problems, as with most music scenes. Initially seeing punk as a movement or a genre is problematic. One may consider its origins in Britain in the machinations of Malcolm McLaren and Vivienne Westwood, driven by determined (if rather second-hand) motivations and aesthetic principles. However, it is difficult to see such a deliberate strategy making a uniform impact across the country. Certainly, the punk experience in Manchester, Liverpool and Sheffield for instance was radically different to the one experienced in cosmopolitan London (Cope, 1994; Cobley, 1999; Haslam, 1999). These differing experiences become all the clearer when one looks at punk away from the metropolitan centres. Mark Kidel (1977), for example, illustrates the less regimented nature of punk in Plymouth with his review of a Talking Heads and Ramones concert in 1977:

> From a distance it was not easy to tell the punks' closely-cropped hair from the many navel crew-cuts, but closer inspection revealed the dedicated followers of fashion had dressed much more carefully, highly conscious of striking the right stylistic note. The genuine article was in a definite minority, surrounded by demi-punks, left-overs from the denimed Woodstock era, and dreary examples of clerical chic in ill-fitting perms, terylene clothes and passé platform heels. Most of them had come up to watch the freak show, to catch up on the new thing. (506)

Similarly, punk as a musical genre eludes any kind of single definition, at least in its first ten years. There is a desire to escape the elaborate musical trappings of progressive rock and the highly produced adult-oriented rock primarily coming from the States, but otherwise the punk musical template widens within a short period of time. Simply compare some of the most notorious bands of the late 1970s punk scene, say The Damned, The Clash and Siouxsie and the Banshees, and a network of differing musical influences emerge as the bands develop. The Damned perhaps continue the musical project of The Sex Pistols but by the mid-1980s have embraced elements of the growing gothic scene, allowing more musical complexity and a shift away from the guitar as the only primary musical focus. The Clash famously embraced reggae and dub (always a fascination for John Lydon but one that failed to make it into the Pistol's sound to any real extent) while Siouxsie and the Banshees incorporated eastern and European ethnic tones into their later work. The problem is further compounded by the incorporation of latent musical scenes and individual acts into punk. For example, punk afforded the pub rock circuit in Britain a level of exposure that it had previously been unable to attain, giving acts such as Brinsley Schwarz, Doctor Feelgood and Nick Lowe a new platform. Most famously, The Stranglers attached themselves to punk despite having existed since 1974, and even The Police were initially seen as a punk band despite scepticism from the music press and the punk fraternity. As such punk quickly encapsulated a wide sonic spectrum, despite its primitivist musical inclinations. To suggest that punk can be identified as a particular musical genre therefore becomes increasingly difficult. Instead punk becomes a catch-all phrase to encompass an attitude to music style and society in general at the close of the 1970s. This perhaps explains why almost 30 years on punk is still such a contested issue amongst cultural commentators.[1]

Despite these problems in identifying exactly what punk is, it is possible to notice certain trends that unite the artists grouped under the umbrella of punk. The relationship to audience is important, more so to some bands than others, and raises questions about the power relationship between audience and performer (a trend typified by the hardcore movement both in the United Kingdom and the United States). Similarly we can trace an interrogation of the anxiety surrounding notions of locality and place, particularly regarding suburban experience. This particular concern results in an exploration, sometimes implicit, sometimes explicit, of class relationships. This preoccupation with class, particularly in the (at least supposedly) more socio-realist bands, has lead to the perception that punk is primarily working-class music, an extension of the folk voice. While there is certainly evidence to support this viewpoint, closer inspection reveals a musical sphere that is not only at war with social class, but is also at war with itself regarding its relationship to class positioning. Punk, at least in Britain, has staggered between its own artistic pretensions and motivations and its desire to stay connected to everyday lived experience, particularly that of disenfranchised urban youth. Keightley (2001) understands this as a desire by punk to place itself outside of traditional rock structures while remaining inherently tied to those very structures:

> In the 1970s, punk was seen as the antithesis of rock, a mortal enemy intent on destroying rock culture. But punk was simply fulfilling rock's traditional investment in differentiation and authenticity,

distinguishing itself from the rock mainstream. Punk drew on Modernist conceptions of authenticity to attack the dominant Romanticism of 1970s rock. (138)

Perhaps this is best illustrated by the transition from The Sex Pistols to Public Image Limited. PIL afforded John Lydon a chance to explore his preoccupations with world music, dub, *Krautrock* and the avant-garde, a chance that The Sex Pistols would never have given him as the band tied itself too quickly to a garage rock template. This shift in musical focus also suggests a shift in class affiliation, at least in so far as PIL ceases to be directly about urban British youth experience in the direct way that the Pistols arguably were. Indeed PIL's transition to an aesthetic based upon business models highlights the ways in which issues such as class have been utilized by the music industry, demystifying many of the discourses that surrounded punk in the first place. Further this shift of musical focus encompasses an engagement with musical forms traditionally feminized by rock discourse,[2] a discourse that sees working-class experience as traditionally masculinized.[3]

Gendering class

Simon Reynolds and Joy Press (1995) make a comprehensive case for the way in which rock discourse oscillates between a desire to return to a maternal womb-place that neutralizes gender and identity and an attempt to escape the maternal, a more masculinized position that confirms and reinforces identity. Both strains are constantly in operation; however, it is the function of discourse to determine which strains maintain dominance at any one time (although usually the masculine wins out). Reynolds and Press suggest that this embracing of the maternal can be identified in the rural and oceanic imagery of psychedelia, ambient house and dream pop (of which more in the following case study). However, this desire to be subsumed within nature/the ocean/the mother is countered by a tradition of masculinized rock that is primarily about separation and escape from the suffocating confines of the familial environment. Women, in this particular mythology, are often seen as emasculating figures, entrapping and ensnaring. This can be seen most evidently through the lineage that connects blues and rhythm and blues through to mod and garage rock (and of course eventually on to punk). Reynolds and Press use the example of John's Children's 'Just What You Want, Just What You'll Get'[4] (1966) to illustrate this fear of engulfing femininity. Here the female object is depicted as a plotting schemer, whose plans have been identified by the song's protagonist, promoting a vengeful rejection that borders on the spiteful. Seduction by a woman entails a giving-up of one's self and hence becomes inherently threatening. Similar approaches towards women abound throughout the work of the Rolling Stones for example ('Tumbling Dice', 'Sitting On A Fence', 'Let It Loose', 'Out Of Time'), portraying women as either 'dominating, malicious or treacherous...or...used up and discarded' (21). This struggle against the feminine as a shackle is further articulated throughout punk, whether in the body-horror of The Sex Pistols' 'Bodies' or The Clash's pseudo-military posing. The gang/band is consistently articulated as a masculine unit, untamed by the family or femininity in any fashion.[5] The phallic preoccupations of punk are evident in band names alone: The Sex Pistols, The Buzzcocks, The Members, Stiff Little Fingers, Penetration. However, this should not be confused with the blatant sexuality exhibited by American glam rock during the 1980s, but rather as an affirmation of masculinity as identity against a threat of engulfment.

Blake (1997) suggests that the gendering of performance along class lines commences in Britain in the late 1800s as musicianship becomes associated with effeminate artisanship and the private familial sphere. In opposition to this stood the public masculinity of sport, a pursuit that a bourgeois gentleman could follow without being associated with a denigrated leisure activity such as performing music in public. Blake illustrates how,

> The perception of music was clearly that it was out with the norms of acceptable bourgeois masculinity; there was continuing suspicion of the 'effeminacy' of French and Italian music teachers and dancing-masters, even when they had unequivocally indicated one important aspect of their masculinity by seducing their female pupils. (32)

In Blake's example the public performance of music was seen as an activity that threatened bourgeois middle-class respectability and actively hampered upward social mobility. In the case of punk, the familial home is still understood to be the domain of the mother, the wife and the girlfriend and the traces of the artisanship of music making cling to that space. Punk's way of getting around this is to situate *proficient* musical ability as being particularly effeminate, suburban and 'arty'. An analogy can be drawn here between punk's raw, hard, untutored sound, designed to be heard in a live environment and working-class manual labour, as opposed to the technical complexity of progressive rock and synth pop, for example, which fitted the feminized artisanship of the suburban middle-class home.

The sound of [getting out of] the suburbs

While Reynolds and Press make a convincing case for the tensions surrounding gender and identity, they fail to bring the same illumination to issues of class in popular music within the same light. What becomes apparent throughout their work is that when class positions, however they are achieved, are assigned to the musicians and bands within their survey, working-class representation is primarily configured as masculine while middle-class representation is feminized. This is not to suggest that we can look at working-class experience in all social spheres as being inherently masculine, but rather that rock discourse, at least within British culture, has traditionally created such a position. Pink Floyd, as an example of southern, 'middle class' rock music, exemplify the pastoral, oceanic and cosmic imagery of British psychedelia and all that that entails for a gender position within rock discourse, particularly within the arcadian/sci-fi preoccupations of Syd Barrett. Punk has often been seen, arguably, as a reaction to this narcotized, diffuse and feminized approach as typified by psychedelia and progressive rock, a shift away from not only potentially pompous musical complexity and introspection, but also away from the maternal. Punk articulates this shift not only in a rejection of the maternal but also a rejection of domesticity and the family home. Rock discourse continually situates working-class experience and expression on the urban street, whether it be in punk or hip hop, relegating middle-class experience to the suburban home. For here, the mother rules, allowing no space for the phallic individual to blossom. It is the mother who dominates the private space of suburbia (the father is representative of the public sphere through his traditional role as wage earner and representative of social law and discipline).

Suburbia is consistently seen as a site of restraint. This is a theme borrowed most notably from The Kinks in the 1960s, but one that continues through punk into the work of Suede and Blur in the 1990s. The rejection of suburbia, or rather its identification as a site of conformity and stultification, has implications not only for gender positioning but also for class positioning within rock discourse. Indeed, it is this positioning that informs much of the power and significance of working-class subjectivities within British rock discourse. Michael Bracewell (1997) makes a convincing case for suburbia rather than the inner city as the birthplace for punk. He points out that 'around the extreme southeast of London, along the Bromley, Croydon and Sutton belt (a suburban curve, linking the urbanity of Lewisham and New Cross to the quasi-ruralism of Epsom and Leatherhead), the suburbs would become famous as a launch pad for punk rock' (126). Simon Frith (1978) illustrates both the importance of the suburbs to British pop music and its own ambivalent relationship to middle-class identity when he quotes jazz musician George Melly, writing in *New Society* in 1963:

> Scratch the rebel, art student, beatnik, CND supporter, jazz musician, and you'll usually find a lower-middle class background. The suburbs have thrown up most of the young people who are in conscious revolt . . . their only sin, and it's a minor one, is sometimes to lie about their origin. They pretend to be working class. (22)

The Member's 'The Sound of the Suburbs' (1979) situates punk directly as an expression of, rather than as a celebration of, suburbia. Punk exists in this context as an explosive reaction to a stifling lower middle-class environment that needs to be escaped from, rather than tolerated. However, punk constantly defers this escape by its acknowledgement that it is primarily formed by this very setting. British punk has perhaps its closest relation in this sense in John Osborne's *Look Back in Anger* (1956) and the writers of the *angry young men* movement through the 1950s.[6] The play's protagonist Jimmy Porter is trapped within suburban domesticity, fuelled by it but ultimately unable to escape. As Reynolds and Press suggest, 'mired in low-rent domesticity, all he can do is fester in his own bile. Abusing his wife is the only way he can feel like a man, the only terrain left for his class warfare' (7). This antagonism against middle-class domesticity and the matriarchs which are seen to represent it is a mainstay of punk, equally fuelled by a sense of being let down. In Porter's case (and indeed Osborne's) his resentment is based around the absence of a paternal figure, a figure that can provide an active direction for individualization. Punk's anger can in this sense be seen as a railing against middle-class mediocrity and domesticity, but perhaps this anger can never truly transcend its origins. For it is also the environment that provides much of British popular music with its vocabulary, from The Beatles and The Who to Arctic Monkeys and The Kaiser Chiefs.

The feminization of middle-class experience can be seen clearly in the music of The Undertones. Although set in a somewhat comical idiom their 1980 single 'My Perfect Cousin' outlines the class boundaries presented by punk. The song concerns the narrator's frustration with not only his seemingly middle-class relative but also his mother's disappointment at her son's own social failings. The song creates an image of middle-class identity based around financial and social privilege, educational advancement, but ultimately also narcissism and self-obsession. The titular Kevin has expensive clothes and a synthesizer bought for him by his mother, a degree and a dedicated attitude to personal grooming. Not only is the issue of financial independence being articulated here but also the class divide built explicitly within rock discourse. Kevin is accepted into the realms of art rock through his association with synth pop and The Human League. Subsequently, his masculinity is called into question as he becomes increasingly narcissistic and uninterested in heterosexual desire. The last verse sets up a distinction between the narrator of the song and The Undertones themselves against not only Kevin but art rock too, as opposed to the 'social commentary' and 'protest' of punk.[5] The synthesizer, only becoming widely available at the tail end of the 1970s, represents a shift away from the manual labour practices of the traditional rock band format, as utilized by the majority of punk bands of the time. The Musicians Union in the United Kingdom was contemporaneously expressing concerns, through its 'Keep Music Live' campaign, part of which concerned the potential obsolescence of live musicians by synthesizers, a fear never subsequently realized. However, the synthesizer did at the time represent a shift away from the immediacy and humanity of live performance for many. Further, the utilization of synthesizers in this context represents a move towards art rock, as expressed by the reference to The Human League and art school boys. Kevin becomes a sign of indulgence, a primarily middle-class trait within the context of punk. This indulgence goes further to suggest self-absorption in the final lines of the verse as Kevin becomes immune even to sexual attention as his focus is so entirely narcissistic. 'My Perfect Cousin' thus situates the narrator, and by implication The Undertones themselves, as working-class lads whose interests extend to girls (in a rather undefined manner) and the raw immediacy of punk rock itself. There are even intimations of the integrity of working-class experience against a somewhat amoral middle-class stance as exhibited by Kevin's cheating at Subbuteo. The fact that Kevin is a relation goes further to suggest a level of class mobility open to certain members of the family which has resulted in associations of pretension and artificiality. In other words, the narrator of the song has remained true to his class position, whilst Kevin and his side of the family (note that Kevin's move towards art rock is motivated by his mother) have advanced their social positioning and reinforced that position by the acquisition of cultural capital that privileges middle-class subjectivity. The interesting point about 'My Perfect Cousin' is that the song actually privileges working-class subjectivity to be able to critique Kevin, a strategy particularly afforded by punk and the rock discourse from which it comes.

The link between maternal identification and class experience within 'My Perfect Cousin' is marked. The narrator's mother is disappointed with her son as he fails to achieve the social elevation that his cousin enjoys. Kevin meanwhile enjoys the favour of his mother and benefits accordingly. For the narrator the problem is that his mother fails to appreciate the punk ethic. Of course this lack of understanding is an extension of the traditional generation gap that rock music has revelled in since the 1950s, but here it takes on a new dimension, one that exhibits a desire to escape the middle-class domestic home and create a masculine identity that evades the familial environment, literally to be 'your own man'. The implications of not being able to escape are somewhat menacingly articulated within another song by The Undertones, 'Jimmy Jimmy' (1979). While the lyrics are somewhat vague about exactly what happens to Jimmy, there is a clear association between the family environment and Jimmy's failure. Jimmy literally disappears within the home, his identity subsumed by his family. Again the opening lines suggest that his inability to break away from his mother is his downfall, emasculating him and denying him autonomous identity. This is a theme revived some seven years later by The Smiths' 'The Queen is Dead' (1987); however, Morrissey takes on the role occupied by Jimmy and remains forever trapped within maternal domesticity. Stan Hawkins (2002) offers a performative reading of Morrissey's ambiguous sexuality, a sexuality that subverts more conventional forms of pop and rock masculinity. In this sense Morrissey is not so much feminized as opening up a sense of discursive ambivalence around the notion of gendered identity in popular music, something he achieves throughout his career both with The Smiths and as a solo artist. Of course The Undertones are rebelling where Morrissey is acquiescing. This rebellion is at the heart of much punk, not simply a rebellion against social injustice as such but rather a call to resisting the maternal and the familial, a resistance that will allow the autonomy of the punk practitioner and reinforce a working class, masculine subjectivity.

'My Perfect Cousin' does not simply highlight the familial tensions at the heart of punk, it also hints at attendant problems regarding musical form. Much has been made of punk's relationship to progressive rock, certainly legend tells of Lydon's recruitment to The Sex Pistols based purely on his Pink Floyd t-shirt that had 'I Hate' scrawled above the logo. Ironically, Lydon has been candid in his appreciation of Pink Floyd, Can, and Gong, all associated with psychedelic or progressive rock. His fondness for such musical forms has done little to dim the antagonism between punk and progressive rock; indeed cultural history commonly suggests that punk was, in many ways, a direct reaction to the perceived pomposity of bands such as Genesis, Van der Graff Generator and King Crimson, as well as the stadium rock excesses of Led Zeppelin and Deep Purple. While these bands do differ remarkably between themselves in many aspects, they do express musical excess and egomania when placed against the context of punk, both in form or content. The musical blueprint of British punk mirrors attempts by American bands such as The Ramones and The New York Dolls to return to the brevity of the 1950s rock 'n' roll single. Songs are commonly between two and four minutes long, a drastic shift away from a track such as Genesis' 'Supper's Ready' (1972) which lasts over 23 minutes. Similarly, punk sought to reduce musical content down to a bare minimum, relying on a conventional guitar, bass and drums format that kept the sonic palette to a minimum. Again a link to the early incarnations of rock 'n' roll is suggested. Danny Baker, a writer for the seminal punk fanzine *Sniffin' Glue*, suggests, 'musically I think the line carries on. A three-minute single is a three-minute single. "Anarchy in the UK" is not that different from "Doo Wah Diddy" by Manfred Mann' (Perry, 131).

This sense of returning to pop music basics is not so much a desire to be primitivist, as a rejection of the technical sophistication that progressive rock entertained. Again the perception of progressive rock and psychedelia as the preserve of students and hippies, and therefore linked to the middle classes, causes punk to react musically to voice a working-class subjectivity within its sound. Of course there is no reason to suggest that musical complexity and working-class experience are mutually exclusive, but musical discourse at the time equated virtuosity within a musical form with middle-class domesticity or *artiness*. Here education and the student experience are equated with domesticity and a removal away from engagement with the *real world* or *the street*. Such domesticity does not immediately mean that students are expected to stay at home, rather that their perceived disengagement with *the world outside*, through study, drugs and prog rock, is marked as an interiorizing strategy that is analogous to hiding underneath mother's skirts at home. That such a claim can be made says a lot about the state of the political aspirations of the counter-culture at the end of the 1970s. John Lydon goes so far as to claim that clinging on to the hippy ideal in the mid-1970s, articulated primarily through music and style, amounted to a refusal to recognize the reality of British social existence at the time (*The Filth and the Fury*, 2000). As such punk set itself up as being what progressive rock was not. The above analysis may seem overly simplistic, and indeed such a philosophy proved untenable within punk, primarily because of the genre's disparate nature. The approach above outlines the working-class model of punk, intent on musical reductionism to offset the indulgences of progressive rock, all the better to act as a social commentator that has direct access to the folk voice. Upon closer inspection punk is far too multiple to be able to uphold such a position, even if it acted as one of its guiding principles.

Ever since Lydon's infamous exhortation to the audience at the last Pistols show at the Winterland Ballroom in San Francisco in 1978 ('Ever feel like you've been cheated?' (*The Filth and the Fury*, 2000)), there has been a pervading sense that, despite its cultural impact punk was a failed, perhaps doomed, project. The internal tensions, particularly in the insular London scene, were too great a weight to bear. It might be tempting to see the demise of The Sex Pistols as the beginning of the end for punk, but that would suggest that punk was a unified phenomenon in the first place. It is also important to stress that while the transition from The Sex Pistols to PIL might mark an aesthetic leap, not just on the part of Lydon but on the part of punk itself, punk did not suddenly become post-punk in late 1978. As the example of The Undertones proves, the initial reverberations of punk continued well into the next decade, spilling out across the country (and eventually the rest of the world) to create interesting new variations on the theme. These musical variations allow us to explore the initial contradictions of punk as, in a variety of ways, they sought to address those very contradictions.

Perhaps the most obvious of these contradictions is the connection between punk and the music industry itself. The Sex Pistols were never shy about their record deals (three in one year with A&M, EMI and Virgin), and it would seem clear from the discourse around the band that a deal with a major label would be ideal from McLaren's point of view. However, more generally mainstream acceptance of punk was always going to be problematic. As Mark Perry, editor of *Sniffin' Glue* suggests,

> When The Clash signed to CBS I was devastated. It seems like nothing now, but at the time I felt really let down. I believed that the best way forward for punk was to stick to smaller, independent labels. People like Stiff and Chiswick Records had already showed the way but it seemed like the lure of a big record deal was too much for some. (38)

Perry's comments typify the tensions surrounding punk, an ideology under threat from its own success. The growing popularity of punk was proving problematic for some at the same time. By late 1978 punk was being successfully marketed by major record labels like Virgin and Decca, and the growth in its audience allowed a perceived influx of middle-class listeners who alienated sections of the earlier punk community. However, to suggest that punk was initially an exclusively working-class phenomenon is untenable. The Clash's Joe Strummer, for example, was the son of a diplomat, while punk's art school origins are well established, particularly around The Sex Pistols. While the incorporation of the art schools does not preclude students from working-class origins, it does place the roots of punk in the United Kingdom in much the same social and academic circles as the more middle class-oriented progressive rock and art music in a more general sense. However, the incorporation of a perceived folk voice into punk's armoury automatically had implications for its class affiliations, and such middle-class connections were at best ignored or disguised. The increasing popularity and 'dilution' of punk's perceived ethos resulted in a splintering of punk, and it is one of these splinters, the 'Oi!' movement, which will now be explored.

Oi! and street punk

Oi! represents working-class masculinity refracted through punk and reconfigured to compensate for the failings of both working-class masculinity and punk itself. In other words, Oi! is a mythical solution to social and musical problems and contradictory performances of class identity. As Schwarz (1997) puts it, 'one takes over the negative judgement of the social order in order to form an identity at its margins' (102). Schwarz, in his analysis of the German Oi! scene, provides a psychoanalytically inflected picture of working-class males *anxious* at the state of both Germany and their own sense of masculinity, articulated through a fear of flooding or dissolution, both in personal and political terms. While the German experience of Oi! takes its roots from the United Kingdom in the late 1970s and early 1980s, it has its own concerns relating specifically to nationhood and racial identity. However, to see Oi! as a site of anxiety is equally applicable to its British counterpart.

Oi! can be characterized as an offshoot of punk, ostensibly originating with Sham 69 and their vocalist and lyricist Jimmy Pursey. Pursey, a fierce working-class idealist, formed Sham 69 in 1976, and over the next few years gained some national success with the anthemic singles 'If The Kids Are United' (1978), 'Hurry Up Harry' (1978) and 'Hersham Boys' (1979).

Sham 69 promoted a punk ethic built around working-class solidarity; however, the band attracted a sizable contingent of far right skinheads and neo-nazi punks who were attracted to the rabble rousing nature of the music (Laing (1985) refers to Oi! as 'a music for racists, if not a music of racism' (112)). As such Sham 69 suffered seriously from a reputation as a band that brought violence with them wherever they went. Thus a pattern was set for the Oi! bands that used Sham 69, The Cockney Rejects and The Angelic Upstarts amongst others as a template.

Oi! can be characterized as a puritan form of punk that maintains a strict reductionist musical template (it has links to the 1980s hardcore movement both in Britain and the States), an inclusionist relationship to its audience, and commonly a disavowal of mainstream acceptance. Savage (1991) outlines the development of Oi! as an expression of an internal division within the broader punk scene, particularly in London:

> August [1977] saw the start of a vicious class and ideological battle between the opposing tendencies united by the Sex Pistols: the arties and the social realists. The arties had a continued interest in experimentation; the social realists talked about building 'a brick wall' and extolled the virtues of punk's latest sensation, the *ur-punk* Sham 69 [and later Oi! itself]. Punks had focused attention on working class culture, albeit cloaked in art school rags, but somebody was bound to take them literally. (396)

As a movement Oi! is exclusively proletarian in its self-perception; however, politically Oi! encapsulates both far left and far right ideologies, fused as it is with skinhead culture. Its aesthetic is perfectly encapsulated by Sham 69's 'If The Kids Are United'. It is working-class youth united, presumably by punk, against an amorphous and divisive dominant culture. The proletarian theme is echoed by the final few seconds of the song where the chorus refrain becomes a football terrace anthem. This conflation of rock performance and working-class communal experience reinforces the bold, stomping nature of the music, again a template taken up by subsequent Oi! bands.

When compared to bands such as The Sex Pistols, The Damned or The Clash, Oi! becomes an attempt to shore up the inconsistencies of the first wave of UK punk. Class allegiances are made explicit by referencing working-class culture and articulating overt working-class masculine subjectivities. However, ironically Oi! runs into the same paradox of critiquing social problems while attempting to maintain a specific class position. As Reynolds and Press point out, 'Oi bands stayed stuck at a pre-political level, protesting the conditions of their everyday life while maintaining a ferocious pride in working class culture...both left and right were disciplinarian and dogmatic...both were equally contemptuous of effete, middle class, arty decadence' (70–71). This apparent contradiction between social critique and social pride is seemingly circumvented within Oi! by the mechanism of a fantastical reconfiguring of working-class culture within the subculture itself. Oi! allows the listener to place himself (women are noticeable by their absence within Oi! culture) within a masculinized subcultural system, sufficiently outside of the mainstream music industry to avoid the threat of co-option, and sufficiently outside the reality of working-class experience to create a new version bounded by punk as an ethos and class as a structure. The influence of the art schools on the first wave of punk and the potential artistic pretensions that were manifested within the post-punk movement are circumvented by a distinctly anthemic and blunt musical style that allows little room for aesthetic manoeuvre (indeed such flexibility seems to be actively rejected). As such the kind of class problems thrown up by punk are circumvented in favour of a more rigorously controlled and structured subculture. The very notion that Oi! should be anti-progressive rock seems absurd when one realizes that Oi! is primarily anti-fake punk, however that is constituted. Certainly, Oi! can be read as a reaction to the perceived dilution of punk and its appropriation by the culture industry. Such a reaction must, by its very nature, be inherently militant, whichever political stance it takes. Again the authenticity of Oi! is largely constructed in relation to something (punk itself) that is identified as being inauthentic. Commercialization and artistic pretension form the backbone of Oi! in as much as without either concept being perceived within punk at a wider level, Oi! would have no reason to exist.

Oi! as a movement still flourishes at subcultural level, primarily in Britain and Europe, although its influence has touched the States and Canada, particularly. As with skinhead culture, of which it is a part, Oi! has mutated somewhat to incorporate aspects of ska and reggae into its sound, adopting it as a remnant of the punk sound after the fact rather than through any socially motivated reasoning, as with the Two Tone movement. The Oi! ethic prioritizes itself as the 'true voice' of punk, a reimagining of a unified male working-class subjectivity and solidarity directly opposed to the perceived artistic pretensions of not only punk but also popular culture in general. Literally, Oi! prides itself on its straightforward nature and lack of aesthetic complication. The journalist Gary Bushell (a prime motivator in the origins of Oi! through his time as a writer for the weekly music paper *Sounds*) sums up the tensions between the first wave of punk and the development of Oi!:

Punk seemed different. It was raw, brutal and utterly down to earth. Punk sold itself as the voice of the tower blocks. It wasn't. Most of the forerunners were middle class art students. The great Joe Strummer, whose dad was a diplomat, flirted with stale old Stalinism and sang about white riots while living in a white mansion. Malcolm McLaren and Vivienne Westwood tried to intellectualize punk by dressing it up in half-inched Situationist ideas, all the better to flog their overpriced produce to mug punters...The Oi poloi didn't need Punk's proletarian wrapping paper – invented backgrounds and adopted attitudes, accents and aggression – because they really were the cul-de-sac, council estate kids the first punk bands had largely only pretended to be. The forerunners of Oi! were bands like Cock Sparrer, Menace, Slaughter & The Dogs and the UK Subs although none of these bands were as successful as Sham [69] whose raucous brand of football chant punk dented the Top Ten three times.

(2001)

Contemporary Oi! (or street punk as it is otherwise known, incorporating more explicitly aspects of the skinhead subcultures) continues the tradition of working-class music for the working classes. The more commercially successful bands such as The Exploited (note the quasi-Marxist sense of alienation) and The Dropkick Murphys have found acceptance amongst the fertile punk scene that has blossomed primarily out of US hardcore. In Britain bands such as The Anti-Nowhere League, Cock Sparrer (note the articulation of the cockney vernacular and phonetics) and The Business have continued to flourish on a small live circuit and frequently appear on punk bills alongside such disparate acts as The Damned and the reformed Dead Kennedys. However, Oi! has remained a controversial area of punk, attacked most notably by anarcho-punk collective Crass. Their attack on Oi! 'It's the Greatest Working Class Rip Off' (1982) suggests that the movement represents an artistic and political antithesis to punk idealism, one that replaces political idealism and creative innovation with violence and anti-social behaviour. Crass' Penny Rimbaud has made a vociferous attack on what he sees as the idealization of a mythical state of working-class experience that ultimately lacks the utopian values of punk (arguably) and Crass (particularly). For Rimbaud the prioritization of class as an overarching value system is politically problematic as it cements the punk movement within a class ideology, thus allowing no means of escape. When Crass ask if weekend violence is the only option to class subjugation they are suggesting that Oi! is doomed to stay forever mired within its own social positioning. Ultimately, Crass are ideological polar opposites to bands such as The Partisans or The Business within the spectrum of punk ideology.

As suggested earlier in this chapter, such ideological considerations ultimately inform the desire to reconfigure a class-based vision of masculinity. It is easy to suggest that this vision arises primarily out of a number of social tensions at work throughout the 1970s and 1980s in the Britain. Initially one might point to the decline of the UK manufacturing industries under the Thatcher government, leading to record levels of unemployment throughout the 1980s, and therefore a loss of rationale for working-class males. Dramatic cuts in the mining, steel working and ship building industries in particular, contributed to a sharp rise in working-class unemployment, as successive governments shifted the focus towards the service industries (a process that is still ongoing). While the hardest blows were felt in the north and the midlands, the very concept of working-class masculinity across the country suffered a severe blow.

Punk in general sought to address this issue in a number of ways and Oi! in particular responded by celebrating the social aspects of working-class experience that remained. The flipside of such a strategy is that the concept of being middle-class becomes almost anathema to the Oi! brigade, and again middle-class experience is seen as privileged, effete, soft, introverted and oriented towards the suburban home. Such a positioning, when seen within the context of rock discourse, places Oi! as quintessentially within the hardened phallic, individualistic template of British rock in general. When threatened not only by the conflicts at the heart of punk itself, but also by incredible social upheaval, Oi!'s response was to formulate a mythic version of working-class experience that could be participated in not only by the band concerned but also at audience level, a participation made all the more possible by the seeming lack of artifice inherent in Oi! performance.

Hardcore and straight edge

The attempt by Oi! to recast a new version of working-class experience can be best illustrated by focusing not on Oi! itself, but rather by examining the US hardcore scenes during the 1980s. As mentioned previously, Oi! had a strong musical effect on, particularly, the Washington DC hardcore scene, although its cultural relevance was perhaps not so important. As the name suggests hardcore is punk music stripped to the bare essentials, and it shares with Oi!, at least in its early incarnations, a refusal of musical complexity, artistic pretension and separation between audience and performer. During the early 1980s particularly influential bands such as Black Flag, Minor Threat, Bad Brains, The Minutemen and TSOL defined a musical form that shared much with Oi! but differed particularly in its relationship to speed. The very point of hardcore is to play as hard and fast as possible. Steven Blush's *American Hardcore* (2001) outlines the birth of the genre, influenced as much by British bands such as the UK Subs, Sham 69 and The Damned as by The Ramones, The Misfits or Iggy and The Stooges. Indeed it is worth pointing out that The Sex Pistols, who are commonly seen as having an immense influence upon the development of British punk, and popular music beyond, are largely noticeable by their absence within the list of influences cited by American hardcore practitioners. The Sex Pistols and in particular Malcolm McLaren's artistic and political aspirations for the band did not sit easily with the youth of America. Instead the more straightforward musical aspects of punk were incorporated into the hardcore sound throughout the 1980s.

The primary areas of comparison between Oi! and US hardcore relate to performance and audience. Hardcore's relationship to its audience is remarkably egalitarian, resisting the prioritization of the band or performer over the crowd. As with punk in general, the suggestion is implicitly made that there is no reason, technical or otherwise, why an audience member shouldn't be replacing the musician onstage. This is particularly notable when examining Black Flag vocalist Henry Rollins' tour journal *Get in the Van* (1994). Performance photographs constantly lose the band within the audience, the proscenium arch is entirely absent, allowing a singularity of experience between performer and crowd. This trend is continued to this day within the hardcore scenes not only in the States but also in the United Kingdom and across Europe and South America. As with punk, hardcore has been chronicled by a number of fanzines, most successfully *Maximum Rock 'n' Roll* and *Punk Planet*. Both these publications have now become almost mainstream within the hardcore community, continuing to publish for so much longer than the British *Sniffin' Glue*; however, smaller 'zines such as *Fracture* have been quick to fill the more marginal and underground aspects of respective scenes. Again, the notion of community and communal action is prioritized, not only by the democratic nature of such publications' editorial policies, but also by the attaching of political agendas, particularly regarding *Punk Planet* which takes an overtly political stance primarily aligned to the anti-capitalist movement. The networks formed by fanzine culture surrounding hardcore have been further supported by the introduction of the Internet through sites such as Pastepunk, supplying reviews, message boards and links to record and gig information. The arrival of file-sharing applications such as Bit Torrent, Limewire and Soulseek as well as profile and music-sharing sites such as Myspace have similarly opened up a musical genre that has historically prided itself on an ideological opposition to the mainstream music industry.

Perhaps the best example of the DIY ethic epitomized by hardcore is Ian McKaye's Dischord label. McKaye is seen as a primary figure within the DC hardcore movement, playing initially with Minor Threat, perhaps the most influential hardcore band of all, before moving on to Rites of Spring and subsequently Fugazi who have now been in existence for over 19 years. McKaye is notorious for his opposition to the mainstream record industry and despite a policy of low record and ticket prices, has been able to run Dischord as one of America's most successful independent record labels of the last 20 years. Importantly McKaye is cited for being responsible for the straight edge movement within hardcore. The term 'straight edge' comes from the Minor Threat song of the same name, and refers to a particularly ascetic faction within hardcore that refuses the traditional rock 'n' roll diversions of drink, drugs and promiscuous sexuality. The mark of straight edge, a black X across the back of the hand, originates historically from early Minor Threat gigs where the mark was placed on underage audience members to allow the bar staff to distinguish them from those old enough to drink alcohol. McKaye's own aversion to alcohol and narcotics soon developed into an ethos within the hardcore movement that promoted, to varying extents, abstinence from drugs, drinking, sex, smoking, eating meat and caffeine.

While straight edge's attitude to alcohol and other forms of self-abuse/entertainment is remarkably different to that of Oi!, both movements situate themselves as a more focused version of their parent subcultures. Straight edge, a notoriously masculine strata of hardcore, has mutated even further by adopting certain aspects of eastern spirituality in the sub-genre of Krishnacore, originally operating around bands such as Shelter (a primary motivator in Krishnacore, Shelter's Ray Capo, was initiated into Hare Krishna as Raghunatha das) and The Cro-Mags and subsequently with Never Surrender and Abhinanda amongst others. The ascetic aspects of Hare Krishna lend themselves almost perfectly to the idea of a stripped down brotherhood of musicians and subcultural practitioners seeking to remove themselves from the extravagances of rock music culture and Western capitalism. Hardcore has attempted throughout its history to strip itself down to ever more fundamental elements, eschewing melodic lyrical movements, guitar solos, performance theatrics (in the more explicit sense), even attempting to remove the onus of stardom away from the band in an attempt to incorporate the audience within the practice of performance. This reductionist attitude to rock music again articulates certain class concerns, although it is worth pointing out that, at least in its early days, and much like British punk, hardcore attracted a wide variety of adherents. However, it is more problematic to read hardcore's development as a musical reaction to a pre-existent musical form, as is arguably the case with UK punk and Oi! Instead it might be wiser to consider hardcore as a necessary meeting point between hard rock such as Black Sabbath and Led Zeppelin and American and British punk. The antipathy felt in the United Kingdom towards heavy rock by the punk movement is noticeably absent in accounts of US hardcore's development, indeed throughout *Get in the Van* Rollins extols the virtues of both Black Sabbath and ZZ Top, regular Black Flag listening. It would take Motorhead and the 'New Wave of British Heavy Metal' (Iron Maiden, Saxon and to an extent Def Leppard) to reconcile the punk and metal worlds in the United Kingdom.[8] Strangely heavy metal's status in Britain has not tended to foreground any particular class position, although it has been identified as music that is certainly consumed primarily by working-class males. However, the hardcore aesthetic demanded a level of conviction from its participants that did in some ways set it against a perceived hippy or *slacker* agenda. Rollins himself describes the negative reaction he received from Black Flag audiences for growing his hair instead of assuming the requisite skinhead, an action sure to produce an ambivalent response within hardcore discourse.

Punk performance

The examples given by Blush do suggest that in many ways hardcore mirrors the evolution of a youth subculture that seeks to establish itself against working-class social upheaval, primarily the same collapse in manufacturing industry that the United Kingdom had experienced. However, it would be a mistake to suggest that US hardcore is primarily motivated by class factors. Equally it would be wrong to suggest that British punk is completely motivated by class factors, although it plays a more overt role, made explicit within Oi! Further it would be wrong to see even the most mainstream of British punk bands as being innocent of class positioning. Primarily this class positioning is presented in terms of the masculine gang, perhaps best articulated by

The Clash. While The Clash tended to avoid direct lyrical engagement with class problems, they did succeed in creating a position within rock discourse that connected with a number of class-related social reference points. These references are primarily threefold: inner-city London ('London's Burning' (1977), 'The Guns of Brixton' (1979), 'White Man in Hammersmith Palais' (1978)), Afro-Caribbean culture ('Rudie Can't Fail' (1979), 'Lover's Rock' (1979), 'One More Dub' (1980)) and Spanish and Latin American freedom fighters ('Spanish Bombs' (1979), 'English Civil War' (1979), *Sandanista* (1980)). What all these elements share is a connection to working-class struggle, be it in Finsbury, Kingstown or Seville, that is more oriented around a level of solidarity with *the oppressed*, rather than any nationalistic articulation of identity. While such cultural appropriation may initially seem problematic, particularly for a band containing members from middle-class backgrounds, it makes sense when one considers the incorporation of Afro-Caribbean culture into the inner-city urban environment since the 1950s, and the strains of socialist ideology shared not only by aspects of the English working classes but also by revolutionaries during the Spanish Civil War. Within rock discourse the requirement that Mick Jones or Joe Strummer be either Spanish or Jamaican to articulate such concerns is erased by the connections of class, connections that are mythical and heroic in the same way that those employed by Oi! are. As such The Clash succeed in formulating a vision of social(ist) working-class experience that takes place in a fantastical London, albeit a London informed by the reality of urban experience. The next chapter will explore the way in which Manchester is re-imagined into *Madchester* in the late 1980s in a similar way.

While this chapter has explored a number of facets of punk, its aim has not been to excavate all the cultural connections that make up this most contradictory of musical experiences. What it has attempted to do is unravel certain facets of class that appear within punk. The notion that punk articulates class by a preoccupation with masculinized solidarity, as typified by Oi!'s pub machismo or The Clash's reggae militiaria, does obviously leave a question of the positioning of women and the feminine within punk. The logic presented above might suggest that female practitioners automatically contradict rock's preoccupation with the working-class rebel; however, bands such as X-Ray Spex, Siouxsie and the Banshees and The Slits get around this problem by interrogating the very notion of feminization that suggests domesticity and hence middle-class experience. In some ways their project is more adventurous than their male counterparts, tapping in directly to Butler's notion of ambivalent performativity in the face of a discourse that shapes desire, gender and sex. However, the articulation of masculine performative identities that use working-class subjectivities to grant authenticity do little to challenge rock discourse, although they do raise interesting questions in relation to more widespread discourses around class in the Britain outside of pop music culture. That both Oi! and hardcore develop a hyper-masculinized class subjectivity set up in opposition to the more 'arty' preoccupations of early punk shows the way in which music operating in relation to rock discourse continually manifests its authenticity in relation to idioms associated with a middle-class, feminized and suburban form. The final case study shows how this articulation of certain forms of authenticity is replicated in the late 1980s and early 1990s around the UK indie scene, and in particular the role that the British music press had in defining the parameters within which articulations of class (or the lack of them) could be understood.

8
Dream Pop and Madchester

Perhaps one of the most visible examples of the prioritization of class positioning in the last 20 years in the United Kingdom, and certainly an influence on Britpop, has centred on the music press' relationships with two particular genres of music. 'Dream pop' and the 'Madchester' scene (or 'shoegazing' and 'baggy' as they are also respectively known) inadvertently formed a spirited dialectic in the pages of *Melody Maker* and *New Musical Express* at the end of the 1980s. Both umbrella terms cover a surprisingly wide area of British post-punk guitar music yet they came to be seen as mutually oppositional, representative in many ways of Britain's schizophrenic attitude towards class and regionalism in popular music. Under examination both musical genres[1] can be seen to occupy a space of class positioning that depends upon discourses of locality, musical historiography and subject relationships. It is important to note that neither cycle utilizes class imagery explicitly within its lyrics or music *per se*,[2] yet their place within the British independent music scene, and their relationships with their audience as mediated through the music press, insinuate aspects of both collective and individual class-consciousness.

Dream pop

Before an analysis of the portrayal of these two musics can be addressed it is wise to outline precisely what is meant by the terms 'dream pop' and 'Madchester'. Dream pop covers a wide range of predominantly white, guitar-based bands, commonly utilizing musicians of both sexes that blossomed throughout the late 1980s and early 1990s. These bands have also been named 'shoegazing' bands (particularly by the music press at the time) the 'scene with no name' and 'miasma' bands (Felder, 1993). The reasons behind these particular appellations deal specifically with concepts of performance (gazing at your shoes as you play rather than jumping around the stage), location ('the scene with no name' referred particularly to groups such as Lush and Moose who socialized around the Camden area of London and attended each other's gigs) and sound, respectively (the miasmic nature of dream pop's sound will be dealt with below). However, perhaps the first noticeable factor in a study of dream pop is the varying sonic qualities of many of the bands so named. Unlike other genres (death metal, for example) the musical template for such bands seems on first inspection very broad although many of the artists in question do share certain sonic similarities, particularly the utilization of digitally processed guitar sounds and an emphasis on studio production.

It would seem pertinent to suggest that dream pop represents the fruition of a particular sonic tradition in post-punk guitar bands that arguably starts with artists such as Magazine, Public Image Limited and Siouxsie and the Banshees. These artists were noticeably part of the punk tradition (Magazine's Howard Devoto was a member of the Buzzcocks, PIL was John Lydon's post-Sex Pistols project and Siouxsie Sioux was part of the infamous Bromley Contingent) but were eager to move on from the 'year zero' blueprint that the first wave of British punk had created. Indeed it is noticeable that perhaps the godfathers of the dream pop sound, Cocteau Twins, were initially derided in the music press as second rate Banshees copyists. Cocteau Twins, alongside The Jesus and Mary Chain and My Bloody Valentine were instrumental as influences on bands such as Lush, Ride, Catherine Wheel and Slowdive who made up the dream pop roster proper.

As suggested above, these bands had disparate sounds but shared many qualities that can be best outlined in the bands that preceded them. Cocteau Twins in particular set the template for the multi-layered guitar sound that would later characterize dream pop. This was primarily due to guitarist and founder member Robin Guthrie who built and honed a highly textured, effect-laden guitar sound over the course of eight albums recorded between 1982 and 1996. Guthrie relied on banks of compressed, delayed and phased guitar sounds that owed much to John McGeogh's guitar work with PIL and Magazine, but afforded new sonic possibilities by improvements in studio technology. In this way, Guthrie's guitars drone, chime and shimmer over Simon Raymond's foundational bass structures, providing an almost Spectoresque wall of sound to offset Elizabeth Fraser's vocals. Fraser herself utilized a broad vocal range with lyrics created out of cut-up phonetic techniques, child-like babble, glossolalia and imaginary languages, making her almost indecipherable. A typical example is 'Persephone' from the 1984 album *Treasure*. While the lyrics may be words that are easily understood, if their intention is unclear, the vocal performance is significantly abstracted in favour of sonic texture over meaning. Many Cocteau Twins songs also leave the lyrics firmly embedded in the mix with the guitars, position-ing them as another instrumental feature rather than as a prioritized element. David Toop (1995) describes the effect of the Cocteau Twins sound as 'immersion' (273), an immersion in sound that speaks of 'a yearning, to float free in a liquid world of non-linear time, heightened perceptions and infinitely subtle communications, as opposed to the everyday world of divided time, building blocks, sequential language and objectification' (273). Indeed 1990's *Heaven or Las Vegas* album was noticeable for the first truly intelligible lyrics Fraser had written for the band, although by comparison to most pop acts at the time they were still opaque and occluded by the production processes of the album. In addition, Fraser, Guthrie and Raymond were often underpinned by mechanistic programmed drum patterns that provided a strangely inhu-man aspect to their sound that offset the highly idiosyncratic sonic qualities of the rest of the band's sound.

While Cocteau Twins set the template for dream pop, providing ambi-ent, *effected* sonic qualities to indie guitar music, The Jesus and Mary Chain and My Bloody Valentine are often credited for introducing a harder, grittier sound to the bands that followed in their wake. The Jesus and Mary Chain in particular provided an almost primitive take on American guitar pop, recalling a blues-like surf guitar sensibility that had more in common with Jan and Dean and Dick Dale than more contem-porary forms, but their sound was swathed in feedback, a far cry from the pristine orchestration of Cocteau Twins. My Bloody Valentine, in many ways, stood between the two former bands, creating a sound that pro-gressed from their first album *This is Your Bloody Valentine* (1985) through to the critically acclaimed *Loveless* (1991). Vocalist and guitarist Kevin Shields engineered similarly processed and manipulated guitar textures to create a sound that owed as much to Cocteau Twins as it did to the garage ur-punk of MC5 and The Stooges. Perhaps the prime example of the My Bloody Valentine sound is the track 'Soon' from the 1990 *Glider* EP which fuses sampled guitar, drum and flute loops surrounded by phasing guitars, often manipulated after recording to create an effect that sounds like the record is warped, coupled with opaque, breathy vocals from Shields and fellow vocalist/guitarist Bilinda Butcher.

What unifies Cocteau Twins, The Jesus and Mary Chain and My Bloody Valentine is an attempt to experiment with the possibilities of the pop song and its sonic qualities against the post-punk independent context. The bands that came after took this blueprint and expanded and elaborated upon it. To examine each band in detail would be an endless task, but they can be initially grouped by certain sonic characteristics. The archetypal dream pop bands were Slowdive, Ride, Lush and Chapterhouse, predominately pop bands who incorporated the sound of Cocteau Twins with the harder, more dissonant guitar sounds of The Jesus and Mary Chain and My Bloody Valentine. Bands such as Levitation, A R Kane and Dr Phibes and the House of Wax Equations added a more psychedelic twist than the former artists, yet were consistently termed as 'shoegazers' by the music press. Bands such as Catherine Wheel, Moose and Swervedriver owed more to American bands (particularly the nascent grunge scene[3]) such as Dinosaur Jr and Sonic Youth. Despite their harder rock format they still retained some of the more leftfield characteristics of their peers, particularly using layers of guitar to provide the wall of sound required of much dream pop. Bands such as Cranes and Curve added elements from the gothic subculture, particularly the edgy vocal stylings of Siouxsie Sioux and industrial beats. As with all scenes a number of bands clung to the coat tales of the dream pop wave (Midway Still, Chunk, Thousand Yard Stare amongst others) but it is not the intention here to outline these bands. Suffice to say that from 1988 (Cocteau Twins' *Bluebell Knoll* album, released on 4AD Records that year, is perhaps the watershed moment) to 1992 the dream pop phenomenon had a firm foothold in the United Kingdom independent music charts. However, its place was soon to be taken by another musical form that would have very different preoccupations.

Miasmic rock

Two texts stand out as perhaps the best work on dream pop (although there is little competition), Rachel Felder's *Manic Pop Thrill* (1993) and Simon Reynolds *Blissed Out: The Raptures of Rock* (1990). For the purposes of this study both books have their problems (Felder speaks from an American perspective, sometimes missing some of the essential Englishness of the music, while Reynolds' book misses some of the developments in the field made after its publication), but interestingly both Felder and Reynolds highlight the abstract nature of the music, and by extension, visual presentation. Felder, quite rightly, makes much of the connection between the sonic characteristics of dream pop, or 'miasma' as she calls it, and narcotic experiences, in particular hallucinogens such as LSD or Ecstasy. Dream pop 'actualises the blur of drugs, the hazy boundaries between chorus and verse, the almost trapped feeling of layers of insistent, won't-let-up guitars. If punk, ever-pounding and direct, is speed, then the miasmics are hallucinogens – making listeners mellow, trippy, sometimes confused, often inactive' (18). This inactivity is essential to the social aesthetic of dream pop. The ultimate extension of this connection to a narcotized state is a womb-like subservience to the *jouissance* or bliss provided by the music (the record artwork and videos similarly reflect this state). Felder sees her 'miasmics' as articulating a sound that reflects the social, political and cultural confusion of Britain at the end of the 1980s. She cites AIDS, the Gulf War and recession as particular examples of the type of obstacles faced by British youth at this time. Her argument is that the musical response to this is a withdrawal into a purely sonic realm, distancing the listener and performer from the harsh realities of the outside world. Certainly, there is much to be said for this hypothesis but it fails to account fully for this musical withdrawal. Punk is historically acknowledged as being in some way a direct musical and lyrical reaction to the rundown Britain of the 1970s (a problematic idea but one that holds some currency). Similarly, social and political dissent appears overtly in popular music throughout its history (Woody Guthrie, Bob Dylan and The Clash are only random examples) and it is difficult to see, in this light, why withdrawal, rather than confrontation should be the reaction at this particular point in history. That said, Felder's focus on the multi-layered, often discordant nature of dream pop's sonic characteristics does seem to point to some kind of retreat into a blissed out (hence Reynolds's title) state of non-engagement with lived experience, caused directly by, and as a reaction to social problems during the 1980s.

Felder seeks to draw out the strands of dream pop's disengagement with the real world along a number of lines. The importance of The Velvet Underground is prioritized by Felder (19), in particular tracks such as 'Femme Fatale' and 'Heroin' (1967). The Velvet Underground are important for dream pop as the pioneers of a repetitive, narcoleptic sound that places more emphasis on tonal and textural characteristics in the song text, at the expense of conventional song structure. This textural approach is vital here, as the sonic characteristics often become the focus for the listener, at least equal to, if not more important than the lyrics. My Bloody Valentine, Slowdive, Loop and Cocteau Twins are particularly good examples of this. Indeed it is not only the vocals that are relegated, but indeed the very notion of individual voices within the ensemble sound. Slowdive's *Just For a Day* (1991), and more influentially My Bloody Valentine's *Loveless* both seek to mix and process the instrumentation in such a way that picking out particular instrumental voices is almost impossible. Slowdive's guitars on 'Catch The Breeze' sound more like cellos while much of *Loveless* defies any attempts at individual identification. My Bloody Valentine's 'Soon' is a particularly good example of this abstraction of the traditional rock sound. A staccato drum loop segues the listener into the track, before guitar and drums come in tight together. As the track continues the sonic palette becomes cluttered with more guitars, slurring in and out of mix, alongside Kevin Shields' and Bilinda Butcher's cobweb thin, multi-layered vocals, low down in the mix. By the time the vocals start, 'Soon' is a deluge of samples, guitars, treated sounds and ethereal voices. This approach to the sheer physicality of sound, arguably pioneered in popular music by figures such as Phil Spector and Brian Wilson, is integral to dream pop's retreat into an interiorized psychic world, away from the social and political sphere.

Simon Reynolds explores the idea of dream pop's withdrawal in particular reference to the London band Loop. Loop can be characterized by an almost fanatical devotion to the power of the repeated riff (see the single 'Collision' (1988) as a particularly fine example) utilizing a Stooges garage guitar sound but stripping its already primitive musical structure of any loose flesh, leaving often one guitar motif endlessly repeated as Robert Hampson's vocals drift by barely heard in the background. Parallels with hip hop's fascination with the endlessly repeated break beat, or techno's fetishization of beats per minute seem appropriate here as the sonic focal point of the song is removed and becomes the song itself. The riff itself becomes fetishized and overdetermined. This focus on repetition is integral to the concept of withdrawal here, and serves the same purpose as the soft focus sonics of Slowdive or My Bloody Valentine:

> Where apocalypse and repetition join up is that both are different routes to oblivion. Whether your mind is overwhelmed by TOO MUCH, or evacuated by focusing on too little, what happens is a kind of fall, outside linear thought and language. Loop manage to fuse together the sensory overload of apocalypse and the sensory deprivation of the mantra.
>
> (Reynolds, 1990, 137)

Here Reynolds is making the leap that Felder never quite attempts. Reynolds sees the gravitational pull of Loop's repetition as a collapsing in of the self, resisting one's position as autonomous listener, instead forcing you into a 'no-place' (126) that denies language, identity and self. Reynolds (with Joy Press) goes further with this thesis in *The Sex Revolts* (1995) when he understands the narcotic, repetitive nature of dream pop in psychoanalytic terms as a desire to escape subjectivity and return to the semiotic state of blissful unawareness. Dream pop is attempting to overwhelm the listener with the sheer scale of its sonic qualities, to nullify the listener's traditional positioning outside of the musical text. Both Toop and Reynolds utilize a reading of a music, highly influenced by the post-Lacanian work of psychoanalyst Julia Kristeva, to describe a music that is stepping outside of its symbolic positioning in an attempt to return to a semiotic space,[4] a space that confuses subject/object positioning. Indeed, as Reynolds suggests, 'listening to Loop you feel wombed' (1990, 138).

The Holocaust

Such a reading of the sonic qualities of dream pop allows for a withdrawal from the 'real world'; however, it is equally clear when listening to even the most abstract recordings that we are still talking about pop bands who utilize structure, however masked it may be. On first inspection dream pop is still firmly connected to the symbolic realm, to order and composition. This would be a valid criticism of Reynolds' argument were it not for a particular musical motif common to many dream pop bands (but interestingly not Loop), the breakdown. Here, usually midway through the song, often just where one would traditionally expect a guitar solo, the guitars, bass and drums collapse in on themselves to create a wall of noise, atonal, dissonant and arrhythmic. Examples of this breakdown can be found in Lush's 'Sweetness and Light' (1990), Levitation's 'Bedlam' (1991), and perhaps most famously My Bloody Valentine's 'You Made Me Realise' (1988). While this particular motif is by no means characteristic of all of the bands that come under the appellation of 'dream pop', it is a surprisingly recurrent event in many of the records of this period. The breakdown marks the point at which the sonic introspectiveness and self-absorption reaches a point of implosion. Literally the music becomes too intense for itself and the structure of the song is incapable of supporting it spatially or temporally. After moments of discord, atonality, feedback and chaos the song invariably rebuilds itself to its conclusion and normality is restored. The links with Kristeva's semiotic realm are clear. The bliss of the music reaches a climax that is outside of representation and symbolization. Structure, that of Western musical tradition, cannot hold this *jouissance* and the chaos of the semiotic realm is conjured up in the waves of unmediated noise. Nowhere is this annihilation of performer/listener more apparent than My Bloody Valentine's 'You Made Me Realise', its breakdown section is even referred to as the 'Holocaust' by the band and their fan base. The track itself is a fast, angular garage punk track, complete with unintelligible lyrics and walls of guitars merging into one another. Two-thirds of the way through the track it collapses into its breakdown, lasting a minute, before the tune reappears out of the dissonance. Live, the Holocaust would often stretch up to 10 or 15 minutes, creating a wall of noise that subsumes not only the performers but also the audience. Time becomes meaningless as there are no repetitive sonic motifs to measure it by, and the sheer noise obliterates symbolic thought and interpretation as the chaos of the semiotic realm becomes the defining environment, even if only temporarily.

Of course, the suggestion that the breakdown is outside of musical structure completely is problematic, but it is perhaps the clearest indicator of dream pop's mission to lose itself in the sonic qualities of the music. Reynolds' hypothesis that dream pop is seeking to return to the womb seems entirely appropriate, and completes Felder's suggestion that there is a concerted effort to retreat from representations of social reality.

Abstracting rock

This abstraction and removal can also be evidenced in the artwork and imagery surrounding dream pop. The artwork commonly seen on EP and album sleeves relating to dream pop shows a marked desire to *unrepresent*. The absence of any type of representation of the band themselves is perhaps the first thing to notice. If one were to take the records as a separate entity away from media coverage of the bands, one might never know what the band members look like (the videos rarely follow this example, although levels of abstract withdrawal are often at work). In the place of a band portrait or some form of recognizable icon, the viewer is presented with opaque patterns, blurred images of everyday objects taken from unusual positions, collages and treated photographs. While there are many styles to the dream pop covers they are all united by their oblique nature, resisting representation and providing a space for ambiguous interpretation.

There would seem to be a lineage from the artwork of bands like Chapterhouse, Catherine Wheel and Swervedriver that extends most importantly from the cover art created by Vaughan Oliver and his v23 design studio[5] (known as 23 Envelope prior to 1988 when Oliver's partner Nigel

Grierson left to pursue other projects). v23 were responsible for almost all the artwork produced for Ivo Watts Russell's 4AD record label, home to Cocteau Twins, Lush, Pale Saints, Dead Can Dance, The Pixies, Throwing Muses, Heidi Berry and many more. 4AD as a record label were renowned for their commitment to music as art, and reflected this in the exquisite covers created by v23. A particularly good example can be found on Cocteau Twins' *Sunburst and Snowblind EP* (1983). The band logo and EP title sit in the top right hand corner of the sleeve, almost apologetically placed, while the cover itself is a collage, seemingly made up from a flower, perhaps sheets of glass, sticks and water. Similarly, the reverse side of the sleeve seems to consist of water rippling over a textured metallic surface, possibly part of the same structure depicted on the cover. Much use is made in both photographs of blurring and manipulated exposure creating a sense of disorientation and a lack of focus. While v23's covers for 4AD vary in style across the years and across the various artists, they all share a desire to obfuscate and confuse. Lush's *Sweetness and Light EP* (1990) shows multi-coloured abstract (possibly organic) patterns on a black background with no mention of the band or the title of the EP. The reverse does feature the band's logo, but also shows two small treated vintage photographs of young oriental women. There are similarly photos of oriental women on Lush's previous records, *Scar* (1989) and *Mad Love* (1990). There is no explicit suggestion as to why these vintage photographs are used other than as a connection to Miki Berenyi, Lush's singer/guitarist who is of mixed Japanese and Hungarian parentage. However, such a suggestion would be missing the point. These elements of direct representation are almost completely context free. Juxtaposed against abstract shapes and patterns, on a British indie band's record sleeve, they leak meaning, providing little room for any interpretation other than a purely aesthetic one. Instead representation, at least in an iconic sense, is replaced by a concentration on texture and juxtaposition. In this sense, the artwork mirrors the sonic characteristics of the music, concentrating on grain, texture and diegetic phenomena, rather than attempting to create a position within a coherent symbolic structure.

After the influence of 4AD and v23, the artwork of bands such as Ride, My Bloody Valentine and Slowdive continues this desire to obscure representation. The three bands mentioned above all released records for Alan McGee's Creation label throughout the late 1980s and early 1990s, and, particularly following the release of My Bloody Valentine's *Glider EP* Creation became as synonymous as 4AD with the dream pop sound, and similarly these artists adopt the unfocused aesthetic of their predecessors. The two most obvious examples here are My Bloody Valentine and

Slowdive. When My Bloody Valentine moved to Creation from the Lazy label in 1987, they transformed from a rather traditional indie pop sound to the more distorted and dreamlike sound that they became notorious for (this change in direction seems contemporary with vocalist and guitarist Bilinda Butcher joining the band, although the motivational force is credited as being songwriter, vocalist and guitarist Kevin Shields). After the release of their Creation debut album *Isn't Anything* (1988) My Bloody Valentine went on to produce their definitive statements, the *Glider EP* and the subsequent album *Loveless*, a record famous for almost bankrupting Creation during its making. Both *Glider* and *Loveless* define the dream pop ethic, sounding, according to the band themselves, as though 'it was played through a transistor radio' (Larkin, 245). At this point they also partake in the gauzy imagery of v23. *Glider* features a white sleeve with a mess of pink, blue and green lines that eventually reveal themselves as two faces kissing. While there is a level of iconic representation at work here, it is once again filtered and diffused almost to the point of obliteration. Similarly, *Loveless* depicts a photo of a Fender Jazzmaster guitar being played but it is blurred, overexposed and rendered in a garish fuchsia colour, to the extent that it is almost impossible to pick out what the shapes on the cover are. In this way, My Bloody Valentine are attempting to depict visually what the music is doing. The iconography of the blurred guitar, swamped by colour, makes a direct connection to the diffused nature of the music itself. Slowdive similarly follow this aesthetic line. Their 1991 Creation debut *Just For a Day* depicts a woman swinging around, possibly dancing, her skirt flaring out around her. Again this image, in much the same way as *Loveless*, is so treated that it becomes merely a mass of swirling dark oranges, patches of light and shade. Ride follow a somewhat different course, using images of flowers (*Ride EP*, 1990), penguins in a blizzard (*Fall EP*, 1990) or cresting waves (*Nowhere*, 1990). There is little attempt to obscure or confuse these images but again they are resisting direct representation by foregrounding their textural properties. The grain of the image is more important than an attempt at iconic representation (hence no band portraits or images relating to lyrical content).

It is clear to see that there is an attempt to replicate the narcotized withdrawal that the music represents in the bands' artwork (a trait seen occasionally in the bands' videos, My Bloody Valentine's 'Soon' being a particularly good example). Dream pop represents a refusal to depict, to represent, to be iconic. Further, it is a music that attempts to withdraw from any notion of rock music as being socially motivated. Dream pop is organized around individualized desire, and makes little attempt to make any connection to its historical place (other than through implicit connections to rock history through quotation and influence) or its social origins. Of course, this attempt is inherently flawed, given the conventional restrictions placed upon the texts themselves. For example, no matter what oblique approaches My Bloody Valentine may make towards the sonic texture of their music they are still a four-piece guitar band essentially writing pop music within a traditional format. Choruses and versus are evident, lyrics are vaguely distinguishable within the mix, often traditionally composed. For all their sonic experimentation My Bloody Valentine and their contemporaries are effectively pop bands singing love songs, as illustrated by 'Soon', one of their more adventurous sonic experiments. While the lyrics are perhaps sonically indecipherable, they concern an exhortation towards a lover that is common to much popular music (albeit with an undercurrent of physical abuse that the song's protagonist is seeking to make amends for).

While dream pop's music and imagery may tell us very little about class positioning, the heavy focus on these artists' southern, middle-class roots was prioritized by the weekly music press, seeing the miasmic sound as a symptom of a social strata with nothing to say. While the forbearers of the scene, Cocteau Twins, The Jesus and Mary Chain and My Bloody Valentine all came from primarily working-class backgrounds,[6] dream pop proper emerged primarily from North London, Slough, Reading, Oxford and Swindon, marking the bands out as specifically suburban, well educated and presumably financially secure. The relative youth of bands such as Ride and Chapterhouse also carried suggestions of the safety net of the family home or student life. Similarly, the artistic ambitions of dream pop brought accusations of preciousness and decadence, again values defined in class terms (the equally middle-class Pink Floyd would seem to be dream pop's precursors in this respect), which resulted in a short shelf life, at least as far as the music press was concerned. It was not long before the supposedly effete introspection of dream pop would be dethroned by a grittier, northern working-class sound that could articulate class as an assurance of authenticity in ways that were largely impossible within rock discourse for the miasmics.

Madchester

Alongside the British music press' fascination with dream pop, a rival musical movement was flourishing in the northwest, a movement that would later be characterized as 'Madchester'. The sonic, textual and visual orientation of the dream pop bands was distinctly at odds with the scene that ultimately subsumed it. Following the split of The Smiths and a stalled New Order at the end of the 1980s, Manchester had failed to provide a solid cultural insurgence of new musical creativity, at least as far as the music press were concerned. However, new talent was emerging, lead ultimately by The Stone Roses and Happy Mondays. Madchester would make the cultural leap out of the weekly music press and into the national consciousness in a way that dream pop was never able to achieve. It provided extroversion, swagger and an exuberance that was distinctly at odds with dream pop's introversion and self-absorption. Perhaps more importantly, the music press saw the Madchester scene as the next incarnation (since the demise of punk) of the folk voice in British popular music. Here the perception of Madchester as a working-class phenomenon cannot be overstated. The northern 'scally' culture, represented particularly by Happy Mondays, worked almost as a reincarnation of the perception of punk as an expression of working-class disenfranchisement.

Although Happy Mondays had made their debut release (*Squirrel and G Man 24 Hour Party People Plastic Face Carnt Smile (White Out)*) in 1986, the same year as the Cocteau Twins breakthrough *Victorialand*, Madchester broke into the national arena in late 1988 and early 1989, with The Stone Roses eponymous debut (1989) and Happy Mondays *Bummed* (1988). Both records share an appreciation of rock historiography, both are essentially guitar albums, but in a departure from the dream pop obsession with The Velvet Underground and The Stooges, an almost cosmopolitan attitude fuses Hendrix-inspired guitar work with tight Sly and the Family Stone rhythmic work. Dave Haslam (1999) draws attention to the multicultural nature of Manchester throughout its history. For Haslam Manchester's role as an industrial port allowed an influx of ideas and a multiplicity of voices and influences to permeate the city's culture. Certainly, Manchester's geographical position allowed it to become one of the first British cultural centres to embrace not only acid house and Detroit techno but also, and perhaps more importantly, Ecstasy. Haslam points to the central role of Factory Records' Hacienda nightclub[7] as a cultural melting pot in which rock and dance would be fused together. It was no accident that both Happy Mondays and The Stone Roses were Hacienda regulars, resulting in Tony Wilson signing Happy Mondays to Factory Records (The Stone Roses were signed to Silvertone before Wilson could make an offer).

Manchester as a city had been pivotal in the evolution of post-punk, most noticeably with Joy Division/New Order, The Smiths and the flourishing house culture centred on the Hacienda nightclub. Following the demise of The Smiths in 1987, Manchester had failed to make any serious incursions into the national pop consciousness outside of the north west of England; however, Manchester effectively became the cultural capital of the United Kingdom (certainly as far as the music press were concerned) between 1989 and 1992. This was primarily due to the influence of two bands, The Stone Roses and Happy Mondays. The importance of these two bands emerging, or at least getting noticed by the weekly music press, cannot be overestimated in the evolution of Madchester as a cultural phenomenon. Following on from these two bands, a whole musical culture materialized and overtook London as the epicentre for pop culture in Britain.

As with dream pop it is important to realize that Madchester fails to constitute a homogeneous musical genre. Neither does it necessarily indicate a cohesive scene that operates along socially compatible guidelines. The term 'Madchester', as with 'dream pop', 'shoegazing' and 'the scene with no name', appeared as a media construction, primarily created by *New Musical Express* and *Melody Maker*. Not only was it an appellation that was foisted onto a number of particular bands, but it was also a term that further sought to encompass a particular generational moment, orientated around leisure and consumption. Two bands appearing contemporaneously from the same locale is rarely enough to warrant an entire pop culture movement. Haslam is the first to point to the fact that although The Stone Roses and Happy Mondays were the pivotal bands to receive national media attention, leading to other Manchester acts such as Inspiral Carpets, Northside and World of Twist getting similar exposure, the motivating factor in Manchester's cultural rehabilitation was primarily the explosion of club culture initiated by the acid house and techno music flowing into the city at the time. The guitar bands that achieved national recognition were merely made up of club goers playing guitar, rather than club goers who made dance music:

> People were in clubs so much of the time, going out became a lifestyle and a career, and many people who were drawn deep into the culture weren't interested in going home and making records...there was something of a time lag – a year, two years – before the dance floor devotees were turning in records that had a direct relationship to house music, and a direct appeal to the dance floor in any great numbers. It was left, instead, to the city's guitar bands to do most of the music-making...according to Noel Gallagher, 'That's how the whole Roses thing kicked off; guys from guitar bands going to clubs.'
> (Haslam, 175)

The fact that there was a strong musical scene in the city merely provided a pre-existent musical community that the attention afforded to the Roses and the Mondays could tap into to. Haslam provides a detailed account of the relationship between the club culture in Manchester and the guitar bands that became synonymous with Madchester, and it is this fusion between white rock and black dance culture that epitomizes the Madchester ethic. However, it is worth noting that it was primarily the guitar bands that gained the most attention on a national scale, at least initially. Notable exceptions to this were 808 State, centred around Manchester's Eastern Bloc record shop, and affiliated artists such as A Guy Called Gerald and MC Tunes, although none of these artists, despite incredibly favourable coverage on behalf of the national music press, made the same kind of crossover that the Roses and the Mondays achieved.

Placing Madchester

Madchester represents a cultural renaissance centred around the northwest of England, connected to both rock and dance culture, fashion, drug use, social organization and locale. Locale is perhaps the most important sign here; the very name 'Madchester' suggests a particular *place*, albeit an imagined one. Manchester, as a city and cultural centre, is diametrically opposed to London, arguably the centre for pop music culture in Britain ever since the end of Merseybeat boom in the 1960s. It is no coincidence that Madchester was often cited as the antithesis to dream pop, a movement that had close ties to London and the Home Counties. Madchester represented the epitome of youth culture, of the folk voice, of the working-class experience, unfettered by the interruptions and mediations of the London-oriented music industry.

To understand Madchester and its relationship to class representation it is perhaps pertinent to explore the principal players in the musical movement and their connections to the city, a space that is re-imagined and redefined in the popular context. Haslam provides an excellent history of Manchester and its culture, suggesting that the city's role as a major British port has historically allowed a wide range of influences from around the globe to cross-pollinate:

> As in other cities, Manchester communities can feel transient; it's like we're all strangers, rubbing together, making it up as we go along. Unlike London, which was a thriving metropolis three hundred years ago, Manchester is a hybrid town, born all in a rush one

hundred and fifty years ago, when those arriving looking for work in the fast-growing factories, workshops, warehouses and foundries included large numbers of Catholic Irish, as well as Scots, and German and East European Jews. These migrations have been replicated since, with incomers from the Caribbean in the 1950s and from the Asian sub-continent in the 1970s. Then there are the students, appearing every September, many not staying more than three years, but others relocating here permanently. (xi)

Of course, much the same could be said of London, yet Manchester's geographical distance has produced a cultural distance from the capital, a remove made all the greater in terms of popular music culture by the dominance of London over the music industry. Within the terms of rock discourse this distance reinforces the associations of an organic environment from which music can be made, uninhibited by commercial considerations. While such an assumption can be largely impossible to substantiate in any real terms, it is clear that Manchester's separation allowed for a range of particularly distinct musical styles to flourish and develop whilst supported by independent record labels such as Factory and New Hormones (or Zoo in Liverpool, or Warp in Sheffield).

Manchester has historically been a cultural crossroads, constantly open to innovation, mutation and experimentation, relatively removed from the notice of the metropolis, able to create its own idiosyncratic cultural mystique. Both The Stone Roses and Happy Mondays had been able to write material, release singles (and an album in the case of the Mondays) and gig extensively around the North West for some time prior to their breakthrough. 'So Young' the Roses debut single, was released in September 1985, almost four years before the release of their breakthrough single 'Made of Stone' (1989). Similarly Happy Mondays had been releasing singles for Factory since 1985, three years prior to the release of their breakthrough single 'WFL (Wrote For Luck)' (1988). This breathing space had not only allowed the bands to hone their musical style, but it had also created a strong live following, for the Roses in particular, in the north of England. This following, based primarily on word-of-mouth recommendation, only furthered the seemingly organic community surrounding the Roses, denying accusations of media hype, whether at industry level or by the music press. As such they seemed to manifest many of the priorities of the folk voice from the offset. Haslam does, however, point out that the hiring of London-based press officers such as Jeff Barrett and Philip Hall did much for the rise in profile for both bands (182).

The notions of community and locale are intrinsic to the Madchester scene, on a variety of levels. One can look to the individual bands involved to see camaraderie, kinship and a (male) gang mentality consistently articulated. Of course, rock music has consistently used the image of the rebel gang, and often with a strong suggestion of class allegiance, but with Madchester, that class allegiance is prioritized. Interestingly this is done in slightly different ways, particularly when one compares Happy Mondays and The Stone Roses, despite the close connections between both bands. Happy Mondays were consistently portrayed as 'clued-up representatives of the city's scally culture; working-class lads from the football terraces, the casuals, the Perry Boys' (Haslam, 177). The street couture of the fashion label Joe Bloggs, married to a strong Salford vernacular, and a less than discrete relationship with narcotics and petty crime, placed an enormous emphasis on the class allegiances at play. Haslam suggests that the Mondays were 'Salford street-corner society on a stage, carrying their friends around with them, keeping their community close knit' (178). This communal approach (lead singer Shaun Ryder's brother played in the band, his father played a part in their management and his cousins Matt and Pat ran Central Station Design, responsible for much of their sleeve artwork) and 'scally' sensibility automatically places Happy Mondays in an idiom of rock authenticity, school friends ganging together to create an eclectic musical style fostered by an environment that encourages a catholic musical taste, supported by local grass-roots support and seemingly independent of the mainstream music industry.

Here it is worth noting that the role of Factory records is intrinsic to the Mondays' story. Anthony Wilson's Factory Records, alongside Creation, 4AD, Mute and Rough Trade, were arguably one of the most important and successful of the independent record labels in the United Kingdom during the 1980s. Characteristically these labels would have one or two large acts that would be able to achieve national success (Factory had New Order, Mute had Depeche Mode and Erasure, even the rarefied 4AD had achieved a number one single with M.A.R.R.S. 'Pump up the Volume' (1987)) providing financial backing for more esoteric artists such as Durutti Column, A C Marias or His Name is Alive. This trickle-down effect certainly benefited many of Factory's fledgling artists, such as the Mondays, or those with more limited appeal such as A Certain Ratio, who were supported by the money earned from New Order's career. Even the Hacienda nightclub and its attendant Dry Bar were paid for by New Order and run by Factory. It is this financial independence that ensures the authentic appeal of labels such as Factory and Creation, allowing a perceived sense of artistic freedom and autonomy that is understood as being explicitly oppositional to the major record labels (a view carried over from independent labels associated with punk such as Chiswick, Stiff and Rough Trade). Interestingly both Factory and Creation were virtually bankrupted by artists' recording costs spiralling out of control.[8]

Inferring class

As with the dream pop bands, class allegiance in Madchester's music itself is rarely articulated, although a composite image is created through the relationships between signifiers. To look at Happy Mondays in detail one can point to a number of signs that suggest certain cultural class positions. The very notion of a band from Manchester suggests an urban working-class position in itself, an assumption that Haslam, throughout his book, suggests is connected with Manchester's fame as a manufacturing city, particularly in cotton during the nineteenth century, that same manufacturing industry's subsequent decline, and the city's strong links with socialism, in particular with the writings of Friedrich Engels and the Chartist Movement.[9] Rawnsley (2000) equally attempts to understand the relationship between northerness and working-class identities. The impact of industrialization and Irish immigration through the 1800s goes a significant way to shape cultural understandings of northern identity:

> The 'rebellious disposition' of the Irish, and their willingness to challenge authority contributed to fears of a political and social upheaval. When such fears subsided, images of the northern working classes as stubborn, independent and unruly, remained... [Equally] the figure of the handloom weaver was an example in which a declining skill and increasing poverty in the face of new technology led to a fusion of real distress with a mythology of the past to create a version of northern labour. (7)

Again the mythological nature of geography is used to articulate class positions, particularly in relation to the south:

> With the spread of Standard English and Received Pronunciation towards the end of the nineteenth century, language increasingly became associated with regional and class origins and dialect became a sign not just of provincialism but also of a supposedly culturally

inferior people. The dialect map of the country became a guide to a cultural hierarchy, with the South of England and its cultural institutions at its apex. (8)

This suggestion of an automatic class position related to place for Happy Mondays is reinforced by band interviews revealing a past of petty burglary, car crime and drug abuse. Such negative associations with class-based identities says a lot about the prioritization of working-class experience in Britain at the time, although it equally says much about the music press' attendant attitudes to the same social class that these qualities become attractive through rock discourse. The band's fashion sense also suggests street wear, particularly the choice of Joe Bloggs, a Manchester designer label famed for pioneering the return of flared trousers (hence the Madchester scene gaining the nickname *baggy*). Jon Savage (1997) sums up the Madchester aesthetic as articulated by the Mondays:

> In the boutiques of Affleck's Palace and the Royal Exchange, the predominant look is a mix of terrace fashion and psychedelia: the Mersey beat fringe, the cagoule and 24-inch baggies of the Northern Soul fan, are put together with wild Day-glo and ethnic styles. Op-Art fashions, which would not have looked out of place on the King's Road in 1966, jostle with Brazilian shirts and old trainers: as House music blares from 20 different nooks and crannies, crowds flick through football shirts with the slogan, 'No Alla Violenza'. (266)

The reference to football is pertinent as Madchester as a scene managed to recreate a sense of terrace community in the context of a rock show. Since Madchester's first impression on the national consciousness there have been a number of pivotal concerts that attempted to fuse the audience with performers at the height of their success. The most famous of these, and a pivotal point in Madchester's evolution, is The Stone Roses performance at Spike Island, Cheshire on May 27, 1990. An estimated audience of 30,000 people travelled to a polluted island in the middle of the Mersey Estuary to experience a performance that was seen by the music press and fans alike as a consolidation of not only the Roses' achievements but also the cultural impact that Madchester was having across the globe. Reviews of the event highlight the coming together of fans from across the United Kingdom to experience an act at the height of their powers, and despite mixed reviews regarding the musical performance itself, the very presence of so many people at a concert, in possibly one of the most unglamorous settings imaginable (the chemical pollution from nearby plants induced asthmatic reactions in many at the gig and produced a heart attack in one case) confirmed the communal euphoria at the heart of the Madchester scene, a euphoria more akin to the football terrace throng than a traditional rock concert. The music journalist John Robb suggests that,

> The significance of Spike Island wasn't so much in the event itself, but that it was the zeitgeist. It was the first time in years that fans were out in force dressed the same way as the band, with the Reni hats and the flared trousers, like a streetsy, harder version of the American West Coast hippy thing.
>
> (1997)

Whether consciously or not, Spike Island was merely the first in a line of significant live performances designed to be homecoming shows for bands at the height of their success (all based in the north of England). Both Happy Mondays and James performed definitive shows at Manchester's GMEX arena, Oasis at Maine Road in 1996 (the football connection being no accident, both the Gallagher brothers being Manchester City supporters) and The Verve at Haigh Hall in Wigan in May 1998. All of these bands share a strong connection to the north of England, and the location of these events seeks to not only create a strong sense of occasion and communal solidarity, but also a connection to place, a connection that ensures the continuation of the folk voice, articulated by the band and through the audience, at a time when such artists are making increasingly strong commercial statements within mainstream popular music. As such these large-scale events affirm not only the relationship between the bands and an 'organic' form of popular music with ambiguous ties to the London music industry, but they also affirm the classed subjectivities of the audience in performance. Correlation can be drawn easily between an event like Spike Island and Pulp's performance at Glastonbury in 1995.[10] Savage sums up the atmosphere of such events, and the ambivalent nature of Madchester in general in his review of the Spike Island concert:

> 'Time! Time! Time! The time is now!' Ian Brown shouts as the Stone Roses come out on to the massive stage at Spike Island. And, despite the extremely laid-back appearance of the concert crowd, there is a palpable sense of urgency in the air. The Manchester groups have succeeded in capturing and stimulating an ambience which is delicately balanced between radicalism and conservatism, between hedonism

and idealism, between androgyny and laddishness, between gentleness and violence. (267)

It is this position at a fulcrum of values significant to rock discourse that explains Madchester's importance in the story of British popular music, and also why dream pop never achieved the same status.

Imagining Madchester

The communal sense that encompasses Madchester seems at odds with the majority of guitar-based rock, indeed perhaps only Seattle has had the same effect on the grunge audience within the last 20 years. As has already been suggested, the musical culture in Manchester had more to do with the emerging rave and club culture than any wave of neo-psychedelicists with guitars. Indeed, club culture was breaking nationally as the 1980s turned into the 1990s, and the club ethos, communal delirium and euphoria fuelled by Ecstasy and Italian house, was leaking over into rock culture. Dave Haslam, in his role as Hacienda DJ, played sets at the Spike Island event, Happy Mondays used DJ Paul Oakenfold to support them and James and Primal Scream similarly incorporated DJs into their live shows. The rhythm-heavy nature of the Madchester bands lent itself to the rave crowd perfectly, and there seems a shared desire to be subsumed by the music and rhythm, not, as with dream pop, in an individual sense, but in the communal collective. Events such as Spike Island are perfect examples of this coming together of band, DJ, audience.

As I have suggested, the media's interest at the time in the music and culture coming out of Manchester cannot be overestimated. Indeed it is here that we start to discern the difference between Manchester and *Madchester*. The key to Madchester's popularity, and both national and global success is its status as rock mythology. The music press in Britain were instrumental in creating a fictional day-glo city of baggy jeans, 'cool as f***' t-shirts, scallies and Ecstasy. While these are elements that have certainly emerged from Manchester's varied cultural heart, the image of Manchester perpetuated at the start of the 1990s was almost totally mediated by the weekly music press. There was certainly enough coverage, *New Musical Express* ran 15 cover stories on Manchester in 1990 alone (Haslam, 184), organizing the chaos of the city into a pop culture experience. It is important to recognize that the wider cultural significance of Madchester was a mediated construction, organized between

the bands, the record labels, the music press and the audience themselves. Madchester becomes a fictional place, but for Haslam it is one
that has definitive cultural value:

> 'Madchester' was a media and marketing version of reality. It's nearest
> equivalent in the real world – Manchester – has all the contradictions
> of every modern urban settlement: areas of poverty, leafy suburbs,
> posh department stores, boarded-up high streets and showcase build-
> ings. 'Madchester', on the other hand, was a primary-coloured city full
> of seventeen-year-olds scurrying about in flares and ecstasy-inspired
> rock groups making a fortune putting out dance records. (185–6)

Haslam does, however, suggest that the fictional world of Madchester
allowed a certain utopian mood to permeate youth culture outside of
the clubs and raves. It is this sense of utopia that turned Manchester into
a city capable of drawing thousands of people each weekend to its clubs
and venues, and boosted applications to its universities and colleges.
As with previous examples of the folk voice, Madchester came to stand
for a cultural form outside of the mainstream music industry, even as it
became a massively successful financial phenomenon, both within the
city and without. Many of the people involved in the local music scene
saw the increasing commodification of Madchester as problematic. The
Fall's Mark E Smith, in particular, felt uneasy with the portrayal of his
hometown and the attendant publicity it created:

> It's absurd now, you can't go into town for a drink. Big coaches from
> Wales – people camping outside the Hacienda. It's like San Francisco.
> It's worse now than it ever was. Like, Friday or Saturday night forget
> about going into town. Racks of people from all over the country,
> all trying to be part of a scene. It's fuckin' terrible. I find it fuckin'
> objectionable.
>
> (qtd. in Haslam, 186)

808 State's Graham Massey recalls baggy jeans and smiley T-shirts on
club goers in Tokyo, while Haslam recounts the uniformity of style that
started to swamp Manchester's nightlife. Madchester was everything that
the modern music press had always adored; it was working class, stylish,
suffused with black rhythm and white edge, communal, raw and uncon-
fined. It is no surprise that Oxford, Reading and the Home Counties
failed to similarly mythologize themselves after dream pop. Indeed the
Slough Festival in 1991, featuring Ride and Slowdive amongst others,

has slipped between the cracks of rock history in a way that Spike Island or Happy Mondays at GMEX have avoided.

Andy Bennett (2000) suggests that the local space in popular music consumption is often a 'series of discourses... a contested space as a place that is both real and... *fictionalized*' (63). Bennett here is discussing primarily music production at a local level, but his model of *fictionalized* spaces, in this case Madchester, seems appropriate. There was obviously a sense of belonging and community that existed outside of lived class positions or geographical location for the audience at Spike Island. Similarly on a global scale, and nearer to home, the appeal of Madchester bands to southern middle-class audiences suggests a renegotiation of the Manchester music scene by the industry that supports it and further a renegotiation by the audience itself. Were this not the case, the locality of the music scene might be inconsequential. Locale is obviously important to the Madchester story, but it is an imaginary city, created around discourses of class, leisure, consumption and pop history that grant it a level of authenticity (even as it is imagined) that the narcotized introspection of dream pop could never hope to capture. It is this failure to capitalize on class sensibilities that ultimately led to the downfall of the dream pop scene in Britain.

Conclusion – A Different Class

In the introduction to this work, the music journalist Anthony Thornton was quoted as saying that in British pop music culture 'no one likes a smart-arse' (2004). Certainly, contemporary British rock bands have had a difficult time when trying to be 'clever' about their music making. Radiohead, despite their propensity for less than conventional arrangements, have tended to receive more praise for their rock/guitar-based work at the expense of the electronica of their later albums, particularly the albums *Kid A* (2000) and *Amnesiac* (2001).[1] Even Oasis' decline can be linked to the album *Be Here Now* (1997),[2] an album that has often been criticized for being overly long and sonically self-indulgent.

However, Thornton's claim requires some qualification. Exactly what he means by 'smart-arse' seems to stand in relation to a vision of contemporary guitar-based rock music that is often structurally conventional, lyrically straightforward and oriented towards live performance (one is tempted to use the term 'easy listening' were it not for its associations with other musical forms). The examples that he gives (Stereophonics, Coldplay) can certainly be seen as a relatively conventional take on British guitar music, and there may be an argument to suggest that what those two bands represent, as well as more contemporary arrivals such as The Zutons, Razorlight and Snow Patrol, has been a dominant idiom within British popular music since the mid-1990s. However, this claim goes only so far. In the first instance, Thornton is very much concentrating his attention on relatively mainstream, guitar-based musics. His implicit assertion that Oasis brought with them a dumbed down version of British popular music fails to take into account the startling electronica (and glitchtronica) released through record labels such as Warp and Ninja Tune, the avant metal of bands such as Sikth or

Queen Adreena, or the post-rock of Mogwai or iLiKETRAiNS. Obviously this is music that sells in far fewer quantities than Oasis, Stereophonics or Coldplay; however, it is clear that Thornton's claim fails to tell the whole story.

That said, Thornton is clearly touching on a theme that resurfaces throughout the history of British popular music culture. As this work has shown, music that comes under the umbrella of rock discourse is capable of being understood in class terms. When it is, 'cleverness' becomes cast as a preoccupation of middle-class artfulness, pretension, introspection and feminization. Of course, not all of the bands mentioned above will be seen in such a light. The work of artists such as Autechre and Mira Calix carries its own values that tend not to intersect with rock discourse in the main, while a band such as Sikth validate their musical complexity by engagement with particularly complex forms of hardcore coming out of America (Dillinger Escape Plan, Converge) that articulate progressive complexity as being expressions of masculine mastery and power. However, at the time of writing British rock and pop seems more fascinated than ever with articulating representations of everyday working-class life, from The Streets and Plan B to Lily Allen and Arctic Monkeys, all of whom engage with the folk voice through their representations of British urban life often performed in a vernacular language that speaks as much of class as place, despite their disparate styles. Of course, the irony is that the folk voice here is almost entirely urban in nature.

Superficially such strategies are an attempt to articulate a popular music that nominally resists the commercial sheen of mainstream pop and American musical styles (such an approach clearly does not preclude the adoption of musical influences from other parts of the globe, although they tend to be oriented around ethnicities that are relatively integrated into British communal life). However, the motivations behind the folk voice go much deeper to the significance of the form of popular music itself. Popular music is almost predominantly music that is made to be sold. It is marketed, promoted, distributed and listened to via an industrial apparatus that has largely been in place for over a century, and contemporary marketing strategies that push large numbers of sales of a relatively small number of releases (Wall, 78–80), often through outlets such as supermarkets, garages and Internet retailers such as Amazon or Play, provide a musical environment that not only narrows the options of consumers (if a record is already successful it will receive more attention than one that is not) but also provides a style of popular music that becomes increasingly reductive. Of course, not all artists will choose to ape the style or genre of another artist who is already successful, the diversity of musical styles around the country, at both local and national levels is testament to this. But the dominant form of production and distribution open to popular music artists remains via the music industry.[3] For listeners of popular music, the implication that in consuming popular music they are in fact *consumers* has profound implications for what rock music might mean.

The argument of this work, and the explanation for the articulation of the folk voice in class terms may be summarized thus; popular music can be understood as a musical form that has its origins within a specific industrial framework that primarily shapes musical form along economic lines. The folk voice arises as a concept precisely because of the engagement with folk forms by middle-class archivists keen to protect a culture vanishing in the face of urbanization and industrialization (this is largely true on both sides of the Atlantic). In the United Kingdom, the particular emphasis on the socially progressive implications of a *folk* music in the face of industrialization and the development of global capitalism carried with it a notion of the people prior to capitalism (even if such a vision was quasi-feudal), a music untainted by commercial imperatives. While this 'rescue' (or invention) of the folk tradition was taking place, the newly urbanized working classes were partaking of musical forms directly provided for by the emergent entertainment industry, music hall in particular. As such the organic folk voice is largely removed from any engagement with working-class culture, as it becomes the domain of the folk associations, schools and museums. Instead the music that the working classes are actually listening to is the emergent pop music of the music halls.

The role of rock music in the story of the folk voice is the rearticulating of the aims of the folk archivists. Rock 'n' roll becomes a form that stands in opposition to the balladeering of Crosby and Sinatra, not only a folk voice but also a generationally specific one. Its 'authenticity' lies in its origins in the hills of the Appalachians, in the fields of Mississippi and the swamps of Louisiana rather than the urbane music of New York and Los Angeles. The impact in Britain of rock 'n' roll is as much an example of the lure of the exotic as it is working-class connectivity, yet when framed against their parents' record collections, music forged by American roots traditions[4] provided an alternative to popular music that did little to hide its status as commercially driven light entertainment. The three snapshots of British musical culture afforded by the case studies above show differing ways in which the tensions between commercialization and the folk voice are practiced; however, they show a clear and important point. The folk voice is not the voice of the people, it is the perception of a cohesive articulation of identity through cultural texts, popular music in particular. That the folk voice as a concept can be understood as a phantasm created by those who sought to save indigenous British musics from commercial and international forms says much about the way in which the music industry has subsequently utilized it. It also explains the class orientation of the folk voice in Britain.

Class is clearly never the only significant factor in understanding a piece of popular music; indeed it might only have a very small role to play, if at all. Yet the academic study of popular music has often used class identities to again call forth the folk voice as an assurance of agency and resistance in the face of global capitalism and consumer culture. Yet it must be understood that, whether deliberately or not, the articulation of working-class identity provides a performative subjectivity that occludes the commercial nature of popular music. Further, the listener's position as a consumer is occluded as a subjectivity that refutes the identity of consumer is brought into being. Of course, this is not a strategy that is going to be employed by all popular music, hence the focus on rock discourse as a mechanism by which class-based performative subjectivities are forged. Mainstream pop, particularly that aimed at the early teenage market, engages with performative subjectivities that are more closely tied to issues of gender, desire and emotive pleasure. However, even a British pop act such as Girls Aloud connect with the folk voice through an engagement with urban musics (hip hop, R 'n' B). Their first single, 'Sound of the Underground' (2002) stayed at the top of the UK singles chart for four weeks following their formation and exposure through the television show *Popstars: The Rivals*. As such it seems difficult to reconcile their exposure and success with their claim that 'it's the sound of the underground' (i.e. not mainstream or highly mediated by the record industry, both claims which were blatantly untrue even to the most casual observer). Yet the claim does go some way to differentiating them from other pop acts, perhaps most notably their predecessors from *Popstars*, Hear'Say, whose mid-tempo debut single, 'Pure and Simple' (2001) was anything but underground. The claims to underground authenticity are coupled by a historically contextualizing pseudo-Duane Eddy guitar riff (placing Girls Aloud both in a tradition of rock 'n' roll and in a contemporary rephrasing of that tradition), a skipping, two-step garage beat and the inclusion of a rock band performing behind them in the video. Rock 'n' roll, urban dance music and hard rock are all invoked to provide a performed/performative identity for a pop group put together by a television talent show, and given the continued success of the band, it seems in retrospect to have been an appropriate strategy (although their claims at authenticity defined in the terms above have been largely left behind, the acquisition of such values has continued to inform their work even as such signification has been suppressed).

The role of class in the above account is significant but not the whole story. The class bias of rock 'n' roll is not so much the issue, rather the authority of tradition, and the band's (not the producers' or songwriters') ability to recontextualize that tradition, remaining both historically faithful and contemporarily relevant in much the same way as folk rock, sought to reinvent a tradition of folk music. The recuperation of rock 'n' roll in 'Sound of the Underground' works in as mythical a sense as folk rock's invocation of arcadian pastoralism as it integrates itself with psychedelia. Similarly, the adoption of a garage beat for the verses says as much about ethnicity (the familiarity with and use of forms associated primarily with black musicians by a group of white girls) as it does about class. However, it is worth noting that black musical identity is often imbued with inflections of working-class identity, particularly around urban music such as hip hop, jungle or R 'n' B, and garage would be understood in these terms as well. The use of a rock band in the video is more difficult to decode. There are a number of signifiers that suggest a link to contemporary hard rock forms (the guitarist's long hair, the stacks of Marshall amplifiers, the black clothing) yet the backing band is only specifically focused upon when the twanging guitar riff is heard (played on a Burns guitar, most commonly associated with The Shadows and more recently Supergrass) or when a rapid glissando down the neck of a black fender Stratocaster is played at the start of the chorus (specifically reminiscent of Dick Dale's 'Miserlou' (1962), made famous by its inclusion in the *Pulp Fiction* (1994) soundtrack. The Stratocaster was Dale's guitar of choice after Leo Fender provided him with an early model). Such iconography provides strategies of authentication that work for younger pop listeners who may be familiar with American hard rock, even if it is not to their taste, as well as older listeners who may be able to decode the more specific musical quotations.

All of the above forms that contribute to 'Sound of the Underground' have class identities although their meaning goes beyond class in a variety of ways. What does unite them is the desire to represent marginal musics in a popularized form, to disavow the extremely overt commercial nature of Girls Aloud through a performative identity that speaks of non-commercialization. All of the strategies employed only make sense in terms of rock discourse, and the conflation of such a discourse into a mainstream pop form says much about attempts to legitimate pop in the face of decreasing singles sales in the United Kingdom at the start of the century. What Girls Aloud (or rather their producers and songwriters who are of course responsible for the inclusion of these motifs) attempt here might be understood as a form of postmodern pastiche of pre-existing musical forms, and indeed the assertion that authenticity within popular music is only ever a myth of authenticity might equally be understood as a postmodern strategy. Yet the use of the folk voice as an assurance of authenticity predates postmodernity, if anything it is the effect of modernity as the industrial face of Britain emerges in the latter half of the eighteenth century. As subjects become consumers the role of the folk voice becomes more imperative. The performative nature of class identity in popular music goes a significant way to mask the listener's status as consumer, reinforcing a subjective perception of self as *subject*, as an autonomous individual who is capable of interweaving popular music texts into their own webs of meaning and value, both on a personal and a collective level. This performativity does not require that the listener be of a particular class position as defined in socio-economic terms, the text as read in relation to rock discourse will provide a classed subjectivity that assures the listener of the authenticity of the text as it is listened to. As such subjectivity itself is assured in the face of global capital.

This work should not be understood as a critique of the industrialization of popular music, but it does outline the way in which authenticity, commonly understood to be a relation between text and lived experience, is constructed in a feedback loop. This loop both creates authenticity out of commercialization and masks that commercialization, denying its origins and foregrounding an 'authentic' organic voice. Articulations of class in British popular music work to connect popular music texts with a wider social and political environment, and the case studies show how the British folk rock, punk and indie scenes have wrestled with class identities to affirm their own authentic legitimacy. That issues of authenticity and articulations of class continue to proliferate throughout the British musical landscape suggests that in an environment where class identities are rapidly changing, rock discourse will continue to use archetypes of class to assure us of its (and our) own subjectivity and authority.

Notes

1 Introduction

1. A problematic assertion as class representation is not specific to music aligned with particular subcultures. However, it often acts, as with the punk subculture, to be a unifying factor that can be used to achieve a level of homology and communion.
2. The differentiation between 'popular' and 'rock' here is significant. Rock discourse operates as a subsection of a broader discourse that relates to all popular music in more general ways. Most of the examples used in this work can be understood as rock music, and often the way in which that claim is made is precisely because of specific attempts to authenticate made in opposition to more obviously commercially oriented pop. Where the term 'popular music' is used it can be understood as an umbrella term within which 'rock' and 'pop' reside with their own stylistic concerns.
3. For discussions of gender pertinent to this work, see Solie (1993), Koskoff (1987), Whiteley (1998, 2000), McClary (1991), Padel (2000), Fast (1999) and Gottlieb and Wald (1994).

2 Class and popular music theory

1. Obviously class is never the only determining factor in a listener's engagement with the sphere of music, an infinite number of variables are constantly in play. For the purposes of this chapter, however, class and its role in musical interaction is the focus.
2. Although such claims assume a level of generalization that makes them almost wholly unusable.
3. The starting point here is often considered to be the CCCS publication *Resistance Through Rituals* (1993) originally published in 1975 as *Working Papers in Cultural Studies no. 7/8*, edited by Stuart Hall and Tony Jefferson. Contributors such as Dick Hebdige, Paul Willis, Iain Chambers and Angela McRobbie forged a template that allowed an understanding of youth culture, and particularly subculture, that was highly determined by class affiliation. While the inclusion of popular music is not always present in such works, the connection between youth subcultures and popular music allows for one of the first engagements between pop music and social class.
4. A somewhat problematic term in that it embraces a huge variety of musical and visual styles. However, Simon Reynolds (2005) sees it as music influenced both by punk and the fallout of punk from approximately 1978 to 1984. Its stylistic variety becomes a primary facet of post-punk's significance.
5. A closer examination of punk and Oi! can be found in Chapter 7.
6. What Laughey describes as 'the neo-Marxist resistance frame' (25).
7. Although Weber's 'status groups' do provide a way of understanding class in terms other than economic determinism (1924).

8. One's perception and articulation of one's own class position rather than Marx's use of the term which stresses a coming to terms with the contradictory nature of capitalism and a removal of such contradictions within class to fulfil revolutionary ends.
9. The ways in which such strategies may occur will be treated within the case studies in subsequent chapters.
10. Beverley Skeggs expands her discussion of the appropriation of working-class imagery in *Class, Self, Culture* (2004a).
11. Rebranding in Skeggs' analysis is not to be confused with social mobility in an economic sense.
12. My use of the term *myth* here needs to be understood as a modification of Barthes (1973). Barthes sees myth as ideologically inflected practices and bodies of ideas. My own use of the term takes the ideological implications asserted by Barthes, but adds a level of the fantastic, in other words the need to replicate reality mimetically through cultural forms is made fantastic through the discourses surrounding popular music. As such ideology can be perpetuated in a form that might seem 'overblown' or 'stereotypical' in other spheres of cultural or social life. That is not to say that my use of myth is pertinent only to popular music (much the same could be said of Hollywood cinema or British soap operas), but the discourses potentially engaged with when listening to popular music allow a level of disengagement from lived experience while performing a *mythical* engagement that stands in for that lived experience. More will be said on this when the subject of rock discourse is dealt with later in this work.
13. For a fuller analysis of the discourse surrounding 'Common People', see Chapter 4.
14. In this particular case there is the further option of identification with the object of the song from a male perspective.
15. See Chapter 5.
16. The same is likely to be true even for a small audience engaging with a performer in a live context, but it is the specific mechanisms that allow for this prismatic effect on a large scale that I wish to engage with here.
17. Although they will no doubt be an influencing factor.
18. As supported by ancillary media operating alongside the artists themselves, such as television, the music press, radio, biography and so on.

3 The problem of authenticity

1. As Dyer points out, the division between grass roots and professional music making is complicated by the acknowledgement that most popular music production, in Britain and America at least, is predicated on professional models and standards even where it is made at an amateur level. 'Any notion that rock emanates from "the people" is soon confounded by the recognition that what "the people" are doing is trying to be as much like professionals as possible' (412).
2. An idea made explicit in the reception and resurrection of folk music in Britain in the twentieth century. See Chapter 6.
3. Keightley (2001) does identify strands of documentary authenticity in rock music that evolve historically from early soul and electric blues artists, which he describes as 'performed autobiography' (119).

4. Authenticity, while prioritized within rock music, can often be an issue within what might be understood as mainstream pop.

5. A move mirrored by the success in the United Kingdom of the MVC chain of record stores, designed again to appeal to this very market.

6. As we shall see later, such associations of authenticity in Young's case may be tempered or complicated by his middle-class southern upbringing against Gates' working-class northern origins. However, within the mainstream pop idiom such class signification is often less valued than a relationship to historically validated pop music forms and predecessors.

7. A point that rearticulates Dyer's assertion of the professional template of popular music.

8. Rage Against the Machine's self-titled debut album (1992) makes similar claims to show that guitarist Tom Morello's innovative guitar sounds were not created through any *inauthentic* means such as a sampler or a synthesizer.

9. Robert Cantwell (1996) recognizes this liberal strand in relation to the American folk revival:

> This libertarian spirit, the spirit of the patriot, has often been characteristic of the folklorist in America, especially where mistrust of central authority, as in the post-Reconstruction south, has been particularly strong. Here one thinks of the Texas folklorist L. Frank Dobie, John Lomax, Jimmy Driftwood, the Ozark folklorist Vance Randolph – the person in love with her locality, the regionalist, often associated, after the invention of the rotary press, with a newspaper, the novelist who draws on the characters and stories of her place for her material, but with a sense that her audience lies in distant parts, who shares with her forbears a distrust of outsiders, especially if they represent urban sophistication, book learning, or central government. (367)

10. For more on the influence of this, see the subsequent chapters on the folk voice and folk rock.

11. His analysis of Blur and Oasis shows how both traditions inform both artists, although they are diametrically opposed in terms of class and aims.

12. Even regarding the influence of art schools on glam and punk, where working-class students came into contact with avant garde and pop art. See Frith and Horne (1989).

13. From the 1989 album *Thunder and Consolation*.

14. Interestingly, Cromwell himself resisted Leveller tendencies within his army and was even responsible for the deaths of three of his own soldiers with Leveller sympathies at a failed uprising in Berkshire in 1649. The name was again taken up by the band The Levellers who supported New Model Army through their early career and shared much of their audience, although they went on to become significantly more successful.

15. In the late 1980s New Model Army had a significant following in north Essex, a relatively affluent area at the time, and by no means northern in a national sense.

16. And the concurrent values associated with that term (see above).

17. Prior to his disappearance in 1995.

18. John Harris (2003) shows how Frischmann was actually at the heart of the London mid-1990s pop scene, exposing her image as a Johnny-come-lately parasite as somewhat erroneous.

4 Performing class

1. While Frith is talking about performance art, it is a category that he allies with music hall and vaudeville, comedy and popular song.
2. A repetition that Butler relates to Derrida's concepts of iterability and citation.
3. 'Text of Pentagon's New Policy Guidelines on Homosexuals in the Military', *New York Times* (22 July 1993) qtd. in Parker and Kosofsky Sedgwick (1995).
4. See Chapter 3.
5. Mark Liechty's analysis (2002) of the development of a new middle-class performative identity in Kathmandu understands class as a practice adopted by practitioners to form subjectivity in a changing economic environment.
6. A somewhat simplistic statement but it provides a nexus for the economic-determinist models of class analysis in relation to popular music.
7. A role that is heavily connected to the experience of Pulp's singer and song-writer Jarvis Cocker, who has talked repeatedly about his experiences at St Martin's College as the inspiration for the content of the song, thus rein-forcing the song's authentic status through biographical suture. Cocker has been equally candid about certain elements of poetic license applied to the narrative of the song, however (*The Story of . . . Pulp's Common People*, 2006).
8. Pulp's headlining slot on the Saturday night of the festival is still considered to be one of the classic Glastonbury performances, and acts as the finale to Julien Temple's documentary *Glastonbury* (2006). 'Pulp's set was rapturously received, launching the band into superstar status in England' ('Pulp Artist Biography', 2006).
9. Even if we treat Cocker's performance as ironic, the authenticity of his own class position within the song becomes undermined by an implicit complicity with the girl in question.
10. Of course, this presupposes a subjectivity that can bring something to bear prior to the textual experience. Given that Butler is at pains to illustrate the way in which subjectivity is constituted by discourse, it should be pointed out that any subject that comes to a textual moment are themselves already constituted in one fashion or another by other discursive fields already in operation.
11. The borough of Camden in London is home to a number of markets and stores that cater to subcultural groups, particularly the metal and gothic scenes. On most Sundays (the borough's busiest day) it has one of the highest densities of subcultural agents anywhere in the United Kingdom, browsing alternative clothing shops such as Black Rose and Cyber Dog.
12. For the sake of this work, read 'rock discourse' as 'British rock discourse', although that is not to suggest that American, or indeed any other form of rock music, is not going to have an effect on British examples.
13. 'Common People' reached number two in the UK singles chart in 1995, held off the number one position by a nostalgic reading of The Righteous Brothers' 'Unchained Melody' performed by two television actors, Robson Green and Jerome Flynn.
14. For more on this, see Chapter 8.
15. Arctic Monkeys famously gained a sizeable following through fan sites and file sharing on the Internet while Mike Skinner of The Streets gained a significant amount of critical kudos due to his debut album's origins in his bedroom recording studio.

16. Although Skinner did move from Birmingham to Brixton in London soon after the release of his debut album.
17. These elements are by no means exhaustive, they are here merely as examples of the range of influences that inform gothic style and behaviour at certain historical moments.
18. Although *New Musical Express* (5 August 2006) celebrated the tenth anniversary of Oasis' two concerts at Knebworth, making similar claims. 'With the band supported by [The Charlatans, Manic Street Preachers and The Prodigy] ... in front of 250,000 people, over two historic nights, the event was one of the defining moments of the Britpop years' ('Oasis Mark Knebworth Anniversary' 2006).
19. Of course, Blur are another example of the iteration of performative identities in much the same way as Pulp; however, Pulp's origins provide a level of validation for their group identity that was never as easily available to Blur.
20. *The Best Air Guitar Album in the World ... Ever* series is now in its third volume with a box set available collecting all three together (2005). It is by no means alone in the market with *Air Guitar Anthems* (2002) and *Air Guitar Heaven* (2002) fulfilling a similar function. A female-oriented version is also available in the *Hairbrush Divas* series.
21. The 'New Pop' of the 1980s addresses this very problem. Bands such as ABC, Scritti Polliti (following their incarnation as post-punk deconstructionists) and Frankie Goes to Hollywood make attempts to disrupt more *rockist* notions of authenticity by embracing the pop mainstream, both in terms of marketing, image and sonics. This subject is explored in greater depth by Reynolds (2005).
22. Nirvana's attempts to make this relationship more explicitly visible for the follow-up to *Nevermind* (1991) included proposed album titles such as *Verse Chorus Verse* and *Radio Friendly Unit Shifter* (which did make it on to the album as a song title), before settling on *In Utero* (1993).
23. That is not to say that listening to Kylie Minogue (for example) allows a form of subjectivity that capitulates to the demands of a consumerist performativity. If such an identity is a problem, strategies other than authenticity may be employed. However, such strategies are not the focus of this work.

5 The folk voice

1. Harry Smith's collection, *Anthology of American Folk Music*, is seen as a particularly vital compilation:

> This six-volume set, originally released in 1952, was arguably the most important single influence on the music of the 1960s, shaping not only the folk revival but rock and roll, as well. As the liner notes to the edition released in 1997 by Smithsonian Folkways Recordings proudly advertise, several generations of musicians on the road to Damascus have been struck down by the Harry Smith *Anthology*, including Bob Dylan and Elvis Costello, and virtually every track on the set, with the exception of some of the more obscure religious and Cajun numbers, have been covered by acts ranging from Peggy Seeger to Nick Cave and the Bad Seeds to Taj Mahal to Huey Lewis and the News.
>
> (Mancini, 2002)

2. As above, see Simon Frith's 'The Industrialisation of Music' (1988) for a particularly compelling critique of this position.
3. The use of the word 'organic' here suggests *natural*, a usage outlined by Raymond Williams (1976). 'An organic society was one that has "grown" rather than been "made". This acquired early relevance in criticism of revolutionary societies or proposals as *artificial* and against the "natural order" of things' (228). One might then suggest a conservative and perhaps reactionary undercurrent to the term; however, that is not this work's project. Rather, Williams does point to the use of the term to suggest interrelatedness, in this case between the music and the culture from which it comes. While such a connection may at times seem fragile, this aspect of connection is the primary focus of the term as used here.
4. This would suggest that there is a *real* that can be experienced through signification in some way, which in itself is a problematic idea. Butler's performance theory is quick to counter this assumption by understanding performativity as constitutive of subjectivity in and of itself, rather than as being representational.
5. It is important to note that the class division between the concert and the music hall was less than exclusive. Russell (1997) makes particular note of the working-class audiences at concerts, most of whom could barely afford the ticket prices (78–9), while later he shows how the music halls not only attracted middle-class audiences (although they were by far in the minority) but also served as a vital form of advertising for local businessmen, and also as a means of constraining anti-social behaviour. He quotes the Chief Magistrate of Bow Street Police Court in London, who in 1866 suggested that 'I know there is scarcely ever a case of drunkenness from any of the music halls' (89) as he believed that they provided a restraint on excessive drinking. The use of music halls by prostitutes was also tolerated in London as it was considered to at least be relatively visible and centralized rather than a problem that had been chased underground. However, the two forms of congregation still existed ostensibly in differing social strata.
6. As is continually stated throughout oral accounts and critical analyses of American popular music, class does not play as significant a role in American culture as it appears to in the United Kingdom. Racial tensions have had a much more significant impact upon the American musical landscape, but it is important to note that racial identity in the United States often carries with it assumptions of socio-economic class positioning.
7. This shift also marks a point at which class becomes an issue in its negation, and adopts a generational perspective in the articulation of its discourse.
8. The less commercially oriented music of the rent parties and juke joints in New York, Chicago and New Orleans remained centred primarily around black performers and audiences.
9. Indeed, Sinatra's resurrection in the 1950s seems to rely on a shift away from the boyish, lyrical romanticism and lush arrangements of Axel Stordhal towards his subtler work with Nelson Riddle and later Quincy Jones. Of course, Sinatra remains an urban(e) figure, but his persona acquires a grittier manifestation, even on the melancholic *In the Wee Small Hours of the Morning* (1955), perhaps still his best work.
10. One might also see the category of youth as a minority experience in this light.
11. The same can perhaps be said of the white middle-class urban and suburban kids in the States.

6   Folk revival and folk rock

1. 'Martin Carthy: English Roots', 2004.
2. Although Adorno's focus was on the intellectualism of modernist composition rather than folk music.
3. 'Martin Carthy: English Roots', 2004.
4. Even the resurgence of interest in folk music, and the wider category of roots music since the mid-1980s, has largely been the preserve of a relatively small audience in comparison to mainstream popular music, and holds little in the way of currency as a class oriented folk voice, even for the largely well-educated and financially stable audience that enjoys it.
5. Assuming of course that this was the intention of the artists concerned. There is little evidence that folk rock was seen explicitly as a strategy to place folk music back in a popular arena with any kind of social agenda, but the attempts to fuse folk forms with more contemporary sounds implicitly held the promise of making folk music relevant again and reconnecting popular music in the United Kingdom with a tradition of British music making that stretched back before the mass industrialization of the entertainment industries.
6. For examples see 'Bless the Weather', 'Just Now', 'Glistening Glyndeborne' (*Bless the Weather*, 1971) and 'Over the Hill' (*Solid Air*, 1973).
7. Drake took his own life in 1974 after battling with depression.
8. Despite the fact that it also contains one of his best hymns to the pastoral, 'Northern Sky'.
9. Supplied by backing singers Pat Arnold and Doris Troy, the only other voices heard on any of Drake's albums.
10. Themselves an amalgam of disparate influences outside of English folk forms.
11. Often with quite specific regional tones. Drake and Genesis' Peter Gabriel both use a very clean enunciation that calls to mind the plaintive singing of a choir boy, an implicit nod to the role of the hymn form in Anglican services experienced by many middle-class English school children at the time.
12. Simon Reynolds and Joy Press also explore the connections between sound and gender in *The Sex Revolts* (1995), an issue that will be returned to in Chapter 7.
13. A collaboration with The Dubliners.
14. Known primarily for his dance projects such as Strange Cargo and Bassomatic, as well as his production work for Madonna, All Saints and Melanie C.
15. Originally appearing on Martyn's *Solid Air* album.
16. Bastet Records' *Golden Apples of the Sun* sampler (2004) is a particularly good repository of such artists, as is the particularly eclectic compilation *Folk Off* (2006).

7   Punk and hardcore

1. Roger Sabin's collection *Punk Rock: So What?* (1999) provides some evidence of continued attempts to account for punk after the event, while John Robb's *Punk Rock: An Oral History* (2006) does an equally good job of showing quite how disparate punk was at the time through the recollections of practitioners in the scene. That many of those interviewed by Robb fail to agree on punk and

the events surrounding it says a lot about attempts to define it as a homologous entity.

2. As with the feminization associated with acoustic and pastoral idioms in progressive rock (see the previous case study on folk rock).

3. The associations between working-class experience and masculinity have been critiqued by Angela McRobbie, most notably in 'Girls and Subcultures' (with Jenny Garber, 1976), 'Settling Accounts with Subcultures: A Feminist Critique' (1980) and *Feminism and Youth Culture* (1990a).

4. Interestingly, John's Children were Marc Bolan's band prior to Tyrannosaurus Rex. The shift to pastoralism marked by the latter band suggests a significant shift in orientation for Bolan, from a hard-edged aggressive masculinity to the cosmic/rural idealization of the maternal.

5. Indeed one strategy open to the gang is to co-opt femininity visually, as The Rolling Stones and The New York Dolls do (although The Dolls' visual identity says as much about *queerness* as it does about a refusal of the feminine) as well as the subsequent genres of glam rock and glam metal.

6. Other writers associated with this suburban angst are John Braine and Alan Sillitoe and the playwrights Bernard Kops and Arnold Wesker.

7. Despite punk's links to art rock (Bowie, The Velvet Underground, Can) by the early 1980s the discourse of punk as working-class music was firmly established. Mark Perry even goes so far as to disparage practitioners within the London punk scene who are considered too arty:

> But [The Sex Pistols'] audience was so naff in those days, just a bunch of fashion victims standing around like the Bromley Contingent. They were all sort of Bowie fans. They all had dyed hair, all sorts of pretentious nonsense. We just had a laugh. We were working class kids from Deptford. We weren't middle-class ponces from Bromley or Chelsea. So in a way we knew what was going on in the terraces, on the streets, more than anyone else.
>
> (qtd. in Robb, 205)

8. And consequently anarcho-punk bands such as Crass and Discharge would spawn the grindcore genre resulting in the punk/metal hybrid of Napalm Death, The Electro Hippies and Extreme Noise Terror (Mudrian, 2004).

8 Dream pop and Madchester

1. 'Style' and 'movement' are both inadequate terms due to the lack of any cohesive musical or socio-political identity in either case.

2. Although Slowdive's cover of Syd Barrett's 'Golden Hair' on the *Catch The Breeze* (2004) compilation, itself a setting of James Joyce's 'Poem V' from *Chamber Music* (1907), might suggest a bourgeois sensibility refracted through British psychedelia.

3. Or 'arsequake' as *Melody Maker* termed it prior to Nirvana's mainstreaming of grunge.

4. Kristeva's development of Lacanian psychoanalysis (1984) understands the symbolic realm as the development of a gendered subjectivity that is constructed through the acquisition of language. Prior to this, the infant resides

in the semiotic realm, a state where desire is expressed without any structural formula such as language. As such the distinction between subject and object is partially formed and the infants sense of its own self is abstract and fluid at best. For Kristeva the semiotic realm never leaves us, manifesting itself in slips of language that express unconscious desires that language cannot account for. The relationship between music and noise can be understood in a similar way to the relationship between the symbolic and the semiotic.

5. For a collection v23's work, see Rick Poynor's *Vaughan Oliver: Visceral Pleasures* (2000).
6. Both Cocteau Twins and The Jesus and Mary Chain came from Scotland whilst My Bloody Valentine originated in Dublin.
7. The Hacienda was given its own Factory Records catalogue number, FAC51.
8. For Factory, Happy Mondays' . . . *Yes Please!* (1992) and for Creation, My Bloody Valentine's *Loveless*, both perhaps highlighting the potential cost of artistic freedom (or in the Mondays' case, expensive studios in the Bahamas and too many narcotics).
9. This relationship between geography, class and popular music is explored by Katie Milestone (1998) in relation to northern soul. She cites Joanne Hollows who claims that, 'the urban sites associated with northern soul, reaffirm and celebrate what Shields (1991) calls the "place image" of "the North" as "The Land of the Working Class" and the industrial slum. Northern soul appropriates a vision of "the North" in which, in Shield's words, "The past hangs . . . like factory smoke must once have"' (Milestone, 143).
10. Although the significance of Pulp's performance was not oriented around place in the way that The Stone Roses at Spike Island was, or indeed around a subcultural audience who had specifically come to see them.

Conclusion – A different class

1. It is interesting that these two albums receive more critical attention in Joseph Tate's collection of essays *The Music and Art of Radiohead* (2005) than either of the band's first two albums, *Pablo Honey* (1993) or *The Bends* (1995), although this says as much about musical depth, experimentation and complexity as it does about the preoccupations of academic approaches to popular music.
2. Despite being the fastest-selling album of all time in the United Kingdom, *Be Here Now* sold around eight million copies, a significant reduction on its predecessor *(What's the Story) Morning Glory* which sold over 19 million copies worldwide.
3. The effect of self-distribution via the Internet remains to be seen at the time of writing as regards musical form. Certainly, the Internet has allowed for artists on the leftfield of musical practice to find an outlet, yet the effect of a century of music industry influenced popular music has left a seemingly indelible mark on the form and style of the majority of music available, despite the lifting of artistic restrictions afforded by home recording and self-distribution and promotion. That one is still able to assert that the average popular song takes about four minutes to listen to says much about the after effects of a form constrained by the amount of music one can fit on to a 45rpm vinyl single, despite the format's relative obsolescence.
4. Itself a problematic idea, much as the concept of British folk music is.

Bibliography

Abbott, Andrew. *Chaos of Disciplines*. Chicago: University of Chicago Press, 2001.

Abercrombie, Nicholas and Brian Longhurst. *Audiences*. London: Sage Publications, 1998.

Abrams, Mark, Richard Rose and Rita Hinden. *Must Labour Lose?* Harmondsworth: Penguin, 1960.

Adorno, Theodor. 'On Popular Music'. 1941. *On Record: Rock, Pop and the Written Word*. eds. Simon Frith and Andrew Goodwin. London: Routledge, 1990: 301–14.

——. *The Culture Industry*. London: Routledge, 1991.

Aitken, Jonathan. *The Young Meteors*. London: Secker and Warburg, 1967.

Alexander, Jeffrey. *Contemporary Social Theory*. London: Verso, 1994.

Arnold, Matthew. *Culture and Anarchy*. London: Smith, Elder and Co., 1869.

Auslander, Philip. *Liveness*. London: Routledge, 1999.

Austin, J. L. *How to Do Things with Words*. Massachusetts: Harvard University Press, 1962.

Barthes, Roland. *Mythologies*. London: Paladin, 1973.

——. 'Listening'. *The Responsibility of Forms: Critical Essays on Music, Art and Representation*. Trans. Richard Howard. New York: Hill and Wang, 1985: 245–60.

Bell, Colin and Howard Newby. 'The Sources of Variation in Agricultural Workers' Images of Society'. *Sociological Review* 21.2 (1973): 229–53.

Benjamin, Walter. *Illuminations*. Trans. Harry Zohn. London: Fontana, 1973.

Bennett, Andy. 'Subcultures or Neo-tribes? Rethinking the Relationship between Youth, Style and Musical Taste'. *Sociology* 33.3 (1999): 599–617.

——. *Popular Music and Youth Culture: Music, Identity and Place*. Basingstoke: Palgrave, 2000.

Blake, Andrew. *The Land Without Music: Music, Culture and Society in Twentieth-Century Britain*. Manchester: Manchester University Press, 1997.

Blush, Steven. *American Hardcore: A Tribal History*. Los Angeles: Feral House, 2001.

Bourdieu, Pierre. *Distinction: A Social Critique of the Judgement of Taste*. Trans. Richard Nice. London: Routledge, 1984.

Boyd, Joe. *White Bicycles: Making Music in the 1960s*. London: Serpent's Tail, 2006.

Bracewell, Michael. *England Is Mine: Pop Life in Albion from Wilde to Goldie*. London: Flamingo, 1997.

Brackett, David. *Interpreting Popular Music*. Cambridge: Cambridge University Press, 1995.

Brocken, Michael. 'The British Folk Revival'. 2002. 27 June 2004 <http://www.mustrad.u_net.com/broc_ndx.htm>.

——. *The British Folk Revival: 1944–2002*. Aldershot: Ashgate, 2003.

Bulmer, Martin, ed. *Working Class Images of Society*. London: Routledge and Kegan Paul, 1975.

Bushell, Gary. *Oi! – The Truth. Uncensored Gary Bushell*. 2001. 3 August 2006 <http://www.garry-bushell.co.uk/oi/index.asp>.

Butler, Judith. *Gender Trouble: Feminism and the Subversion of Identity*. London: Routledge, 1990a.

———. 'Imitation and Gender Insubordination'. 1990b. *Cultural Theory and Popular Culture: A Reader*. ed. John Storey. 3rd edn. Harlow: Pearson Prentice Hall, 2006: 255–70.

———. *Bodies That Matter: On The Discursive Limits of Sex*. London: Routledge, 1993.

———. *Excitable Speech: A Politics of the Performative*. London: Routledge, 1997.

———. *Giving an Account of Oneself*. New York: Fordham University Press, 2005.

Callon, Michel, ed. *The Laws of the Market*. Oxford: Blackwell Publishers, 1998.

Cantwell, Robert. *When We Were Good: The Folk Revival*. Cambridge MS: Harvard University Press, 1996.

Chaney, David. *The Cultural Turn*. London: Routledge, 1994.

Clarke, Gary. 'Defending Ski-jumpers: A Critique of Theories of Youth Subcultures'. 1981. *On Record: Rock, Pop and the Written Word*. eds. Simon Frith and Andrew Goodwin. London: Routledge, 1990: 81–96.

Cobley, Paul. 'Leave the Capitol'. *Punk Rock: So What?* ed. Roger Sabin. London: Routledge, 1999: 170–85.

Cohen, Albert. *Delinquent Boys: The Culture of the Gang*. London: Collier-Macmillan, 1955.

Cohen, Phil. 'Subcultural Conflict and Working class Community'. 1972. *Culture, Media, Language: Working Papers in Cultural Studies, 1972–1979*. London: Routledge, 1992: 78–87.

Conquergood, Dwight. 'Performance Studies: Interventions and Radical Research'. *The Drama Review* 46 (2002): 145–56.

Cope, Julian. *Head-On: Memories of the Liverpool Punk-Scene and the Story of the Teardrop Explodes 1976–1982*. London: Magog, 1994.

'The Darkness'. *The South Bank Show*. ITV. 21 November 2004.

Deleuze, Gilles and Felix Guattari. *What is Philosophy?* New York: Columbia University Press, 1994.

Derrida, Jacques. *Limited Inc*. Trans. Samuel Weber. Evanston: Chicago University Press, 1988.

Devine, Fiona, Mike Savage, John Scott and Rosemary Crompton, eds. *Rethinking Class: Culture, Identities and Lifestyle*. Basingstoke: Palgrave Macmillan, 2005.

Diamond, Elin, ed. *Performance and Cultural Politics*. London: Routledge, 1996.

Diawara, Manthia. 'Homeboy Cosmopolitan: Manthia Diawara Interviewed by Silvia Kolbowski'. *October* 83 (1998): 51–70.

Dyer, Richard. 'In Defense of Disco'. 1979. *On Record: Rock, Pop and the Written Word*. eds. Simon Frith and Andrew Goodwin. London: Routledge, 1990: 410–18.

Edgell, Stephen. *Class*. London: Routledge, 1993.

Eisen, Jonathan, ed. *The Age of Rock: Sounds of the American Cultural Revolution*. New York: Vintage Books, 1969.

Ellis, Iain. 'Alternative Rock Cultures: Lonnie Donegan and the Birth of British Rock'. *Pop Matters*. 2006. 6 July 2006 <http://www.popmatters.com/music/columns/ellis/060511.shtml>.

Fast, Susan. *In the Houses of the Holy: Led Zeppelin and the Power of Rock Music*. Oxford: Oxford University Press, 2001.

——. 'Rethinking Issues of Gender and Sexuality in Led Zeppelin: A Woman's View of Pleasure and Power in Hard Rock'. 1999. *The Popular Music Studies Reader.* eds. Andy Bennett, Barry Shank and Jason Toynbee. London: Routledge, 2006: 355–61.

Featherstone, Mike. *Consumer Culture and Postmodernism.* London: Sage, 1991.

Felder, Rachel. *Manic Pop Thrill.* Hopewell: Ecco Press, 1993.

The Filth and the Fury. Dir. Julien Temple. Film Four, 2000.

Fiske, John. *Introduction to Communication Studies.* 2nd edn. London: Routledge, 1990.

Foucault, Michel. *Discipline and Punish.* Harmondsworth: Penguin, 1977.

——. *The History of Sexuality.* Harmondsworth: Penguin, 1981.

Fox, Aaron A. *Real Country: Music and Language in Working Class Culture.* Durham: Duke University Press, 2004.

Fraser, Mariam. 'Classing Queer: Politics in Competition'. *Performativity and Belonging.* ed. Vikki Bell. London: Sage, 1999: 107–32.

Frith, Simon. *The Sociology of Rock.* London: Constable, 1978.

——. 'What Good is Music?' *Canadian Music Review* 10 (1990): 99–100.

——. *Performing Rites: On the Value of Popular Music.* Oxford: Open University Press, 1996.

——. 'The Good, the Bad and the Indifferent: Defending Popular Culture from the Populists'. 1991. *Cultural Theory and Popular Culture: A Reader.* ed. John Storey. 3rd edn. Harlow: Pearson Prentice Hall, 2006a: 586–601.

——. 'The Industrialisation of Music'. 1988. *The Popular Music Studies Reader.* eds. Andy Bennett, Barry Shank and Jason Toynbee. London: Routledge, 2006b: 231–8.

Frith, Simon and Howard Horne. *Art Into Pop.* London: Routledge, 1989.

Gillett, Charlie. *The Sound of the City.* 2nd edn. London: Souvenir Press, 1983.

Glastonbury. Dir. Julien Temple. Twentieth Century Fox, 2006.

Goffman, Irving. *The Presentation of Self in Everyday Life.* 1959. Harmondsworth: Penguin, 1990.

Goldthorpe, John H., Catriona Llewellyn and Clive Payne. *Social Mobility and Class Structure in Modern Britain.* Oxford: Clarendon Press, 1987.

Goodwin, Andrew. 'Popular Music and Postmodern Theory'. 1991. *Cultural Theory and Popular Culture: A Reader.* ed. John Storey. Harlow: Pearson Education, 2006: 440–53.

Gottlieb, Joanne and Gayle Wald. 'Smells Like Teen Spirit: Riot Grrrls, Revolution, and Women in Independent Rock'. 1994. *The Popular Music Studies Reader.* eds. Andy Bennett, Barry Shank and Jason Toynbee. London: Routledge, 2006: 355–61.

Gracyk, Theodore. *Rhythm and Noise: An Aesthetics of Rock.* London: I. B. Tauras, 1996.

Hall, Stuart. 'Encoding/Decoding'. *Culture, Media, Language.* eds. Stuart Hall, Dorothy Hobson, Andrew Lowe and Paul Willis. London: Hutchinson, 1980: 128–38.

Hall, Stuart and Tony Jefferson, eds. *Resistance Through Rituals: Youth Subcultures in Post War Britain.* London: Routledge, 1993.

Harker, Dave. *Fakesong: The Manufacture of British 'Folksong', 1700 to the Present Day.* Milton Keynes: Open University Press, 1985.

Harris, John. *The Last Party: Britpop, Blair and the Demise of English Rock*. London: Fourth Estate, 2003.

Haslam, Dave. *Manchester England: The Story of the Pop Cult City*. London: Fourth Estate, 1999.

Hawkins, Stan. *Settling the Pop Score: Pop Texts and Identity Politics*. Aldershot: Ashgate, 2002.

Hebdige, Dick. *Subculture: The Meaning of Style*. London: Methuen, 1979.

Hennessey, Rosemary. 'Queer Visibility in Commodity Culture'. *Social Postmodernism: Beyond Identity Politics*. eds. Linda Nicholson and Steven Seidman. Cambridge: Cambridge University Press, 1995: 142–83.

Hodkinson, Paul. *Goth: Identity, Style and Subculture*. Oxford: Berg, 2002.

Hodkinson, Paul and Wolfgang Deicke, eds. *Youth Cultures: Scenes, Subcultures and Tribes*. London: Routledge, 2007.

Hollows, Joanne and Katie Milestone. 'Intercity Soul'. Paper presented at the BSA conference *Contested Cities*. Leicester University 1995.

Humphries, Patrick. *Nick Drake: The Biography*. London: Bloomsbury, 1997.

Iser, Wolfgang. *The Implied Reader: Patterns in Communication in Prose Fiction from Bunyan to Beckett*. Baltimore: John Hopkins University Press, 1974.

Jameson, Fredric. 'Postmodernism, or the Cultural Logic of Late Capitalism'. 1991. *Postmodernism: A Reader*. ed. Thomas Docherty. Harlow: Harvester Wheatsheaf, 1993: 62–92.

Joyce, James. *Chamber Music*. London: Elkin Matthews, 1907.

Keightley, Keir. 'Reconsidering Rock'. *The Cambridge Companion to Pop and Rock*. eds. Simon Frith, Will Straw and John Street. Cambridge: Cambridge University Press, 2001: 109–42.

Kidel, Mark. 'Plymouth Punk'. 1977. *The Faber Book of Pop*. eds. Hanif Kureishi and Jon Savage. London: Faber and Faber, 1995: 506–8.

Koskoff, Ellen. 'An Introduction to Women, Music and Culture'. *Women and Music in Cross-Cultural Perspectives*. ed. Ellen Koskoff. New York: Greenwood Press, 1987: 1–23.

Kristeva, Julia. *Revolution in Poetic Language*. Trans. Leon S. Roudiez. New York: Columbia University Press, 1984.

Laing, Dave. *One Chord Wonders*. Milton Keynes: Open University Press, 1985.

Larkin, Colin, ed. *The Guinness Who's Who of Indie and New Wave*. London: Guinness, 1995.

Laughey, Dan. *Music and Youth Culture*. Edinburgh: Edinburgh University Press, 2006.

Lawler, Steph. 'Getting Out and Getting Away: Women's Narratives of Class Mobility'. *Feminist Review* 63 (1999a): 3–24.

——. *Mothering the Self: Mothers, Daughters, Subjects*. London: Routledge, 1999b.

Leavis, F. R. *Mass Civilisation and Minority Culture*. Cambridge: Minority Press, 1933.

Lee, Edward. *Folksong and Music Hall*. London: Routledge, 1982.

Liechty, Mark. *Suitably Modern: Making Middle Class Culture in a New Consumer Society*. Princeton, Princeton University Press, 2002.

Live Forever: The Rise and Fall of Brit Pop. Dir. John Dower. Passion Pictures, 2003.

Lloyd, A. L. *The Singing Englishman: An Introduction to Folk Song*. London: Workers' Music Association, 1944.

——. *Folk Song in England*. London: Lawrence and Wishart, 1967.

Longhurst, Brian. *Popular Music & Society*. Cambridge: Polity Press, 1995.

Loxley, James. *Performativity*. London: Routledge, 2007.

Macan, Edward. *Rocking the Classics: English Progressive Rock and the Counterculture*. Oxford: Oxford University Press, 1997.

MacInnes, Colin. 'Pop Songs and Teenagers'. 1958. *The Faber Book of Pop*. eds. Hanif Kureishi and Jon Savage. London: Faber and Faber, 1995: 81–91.

Malbon, Ben. *Clubbing: Dancing, Ecstasy and Vitality*. London: Routledge, 1999.

Malone, Bill C. *Don't Get Above Your Raisin': Country Music and the Southern Working Class*. Chicago: University of Illinois Press, 2002.

Mancini, Joanne. 'Vox Pop: Reviving the Folk Revival'. *Common-Place* 3:1 (2002). 15 July 2006 <http://www.common-place.org/vox-pop/200301.shtml>.

Marcuse, Herbert. *Eros and Civilisation: A Philosophical Inquiry into Freud*. Boston: Beacon Press, 1955.

——. *One Dimensional Man*. London: Sphere, 1968.

Marshall, Gordon. 'Some Remarks on the Study of Working Class Consciousness'. *Social Stratification and Economic Change*. ed. David Rose. London: Hutchinson, 1988: 98–126.

'Martin Carthy: English Roots'. *Originals*. BBC Four. 18 June 2004.

Marx, Karl. *Capital*. 1867. Trans. Ben Fowkes. Harmondsworth: Penguin, 1976.

Marx, Karl and Friedrich Engels. *The Communist Manifesto*. 1888. Trans. Samuel Moore. Harmondsworth: Penguin Classics, 1985.

McClary, Susan. *Feminine Endings*. Minnesota, University of Minnesota Press, 1991.

McClary, Susan and Robert Walser. 'Start Making Sense! Musicology Wrestles with Rock'. 1988. *On Record: Rock, Pop and the Written Word*. eds. Simon Frith and Andrew Goodwin. London: Routledge, 1990: 277–92.

McRobbie, Angela. *Feminism and Youth Culture: From Jackie to Just 17*. London: Palgrave Macmillan, 1990a.

——. 'Settling Accounts with Subcultures: A Feminist Critique'. 1980. *On Record: Rock, Pop and the Written Word*. eds. Simon Frith and Andrew Goodwin. London: Routledge, 1990b: 66–80.

McRobbie, Angela and Jenny Garber. 'Girls and Subcultures: An Exploration'. 1976. *Resistance Through Rituals: Youth Subcultures in Post-War Britain*. eds. Stuart Hall and Tony Jefferson. London: Routledge, 1993: 209–22.

Merleau-Ponty, Maurice. *The Phenomenology of Perception*. 1945. Trans. Colin Smith. London: Routledge and Kegan Paul, 1962.

Middleton, Richard. *Studying Popular Music*. Milton Keynes: Open University Press, 1990.

Milestone, Katie. 'The Love Factory: The Sites, Practices and Media Relationships of Northern Soul'. *The Clubcultures Reader: Readings in Popular Cultural Studies*. eds. Steve Redhead, Derek Wynne and Justin O'Connor. Oxford: Blackwell, 1998: 134–49.

Mooney, H. F. 'Popular Music Since the 1920s: The Significance of Shifting Taste'. 1968. *The Age of Rock: Sounds of the American Cultural Revolution*. ed. Jonathan Eisen. New York: Vintage Books, 1969: 9–29.

Moore, Allan F. *Rock: The Primary Text*. Aldershot: Ashgate, 2001.

Moore, Robert S. 'Religion as a Source of Variation in Working Class Images of Society'. *Working Class Images of Society*. ed. Martin Bulmer. London: Routledge and Kegan Paul, 1975: 35–55.

Morley, David. 'Texts, Readers, Subjects'. *Culture, Media, Language*. eds. Stuart Hall, Dorothy Hobson, Andrew Lowe and Paul Willis. London: Hutchinson, 1980: 163–73.

'Mr Harper's After Hours'. *Harper's*. May 1959: 82.

Mudrian, Albert. *Choosing Death: The Improbable History of Death Metal and Grindcore*. Los Angeles: Feral House, 2004.

Muggleton, David. 'The Post-Subculturalist'. *The Club-Cultures Reader: Readings in Popular Cultural Studies*. ed. Steve Redhead. Oxford: Blackwell, 1997: 167–85.

Narváez, Peter. 'Unplugged: Blues Guitarists and the Myth of Acousticity'. *Guitar Cultures*. eds. Andy Bennett and Kevin Dawe. Oxford: Berg, 2001: 27–44.

Newman, Robert. 'Two Thumbs Down'. *Guardian: G2*. 27 July 2006: 21.

Nuttall, Jeff. 'Pop and Protest'. 1968. *The Faber Book of Pop*. eds. Hanif Kureishi and Jon Savage. London: Faber and Faber, 1995: 138–41.

'Oasis Mark Knebworth Anniversary'. *NME.COM*. 2006. 5 August 2006 <http://www.nme.com/news/oasis/23794>.

Osborne, John. *Look Back in Anger*. 1956. London: Faber and Faber, 1978.

Padel, Ruth. *I'm a Man: Sex, Gods and Rock 'n' Roll*. London: Faber and Faber, 2000.

Pakulski, Jan and Malcolm Waters. *The Death of Class*. London: Sage Publications, 1996.

Parker, Andrew and Eve Kosofsky Sedgwick, eds. *Performativity and Performance*. London: Routledge, 1995.

Pastepunk. 2006. 1 August 2006 <http://www.pastepunk.com>.

Pattie, David. '4 Real: Authenticity, Performance and Rock Music'. *Enculturation* 2:2 (1999). 3 May 2006 <http://enculturation.gmu.edu/2_2/pattie.html>.

Perry, Mark. *Sniffin' Glue: The Essential Punk Accessory*. London: Sanctuary Publishing, 2000.

Petersen, Richard A. *Creating Country Music: Fabricating Authenticity*. Chicago: University of Chicago Press, 1997.

Phelan, Peggy. *Unmarked: The Politics of Performance*. New York: Routledge, 1993.

Pickering, Andrew. 'After Representation: Science Studies in the Performative Idiom'. *PSA: Proceedings of the Biennial Meeting of the Philosophy of Science Association, 1994. Volume Two: Symposia and Invited Papers*. (1994): 413–19.

Poynor, Rick. *Vaughan Oliver: Visceral Pleasures*. London: Booth-Clibborn, 2000.

'Pulp Artist Biography'. *VH1.com*. 20 June 2006 <http://www.vh1.com/artists/az/pulp/bio.jhtml>.

Rawnsley, Stuart. 'Constructing "The North": Space, and a Sense of Place'. *Northern Identities: Historical Interpretations of 'The North' and 'Northerness'*. ed. Neville Kirk. Aldershot: Ashgate, 2000: 3–22.

Reay, Diane. *Class Work: Mothers' Involvement in their Children's Primary Schooling*. London: Routledge, 1998.

Reynolds, Simon. *Blissed Out: The Raptures of Rock*. London: Serpent's Tail, 1990.

———. *Rip it Up and Start Again: Post-punk 1978–1984*. London: Faber and Faber, 2005.

Reynolds, Simon and Joy Press. *The Sex Revolts: Gender, Rebellion and Rock 'n' Roll*. London: Serpent's Tail, 1995.

Robb, John. 'Look Back at Spike Island'. 1997. 3 February 2005 <odell.connect-2.co.uk/media/qspike.html>.

——. *Punk Rock: An Oral History*. London: Ebury, 2006.

Rojek, Chris. *Leisure and Culture*. New York: St Martin's Press, 2000.

Rollins, Henry. *Get in the Van*. Los Angeles: 2.13.61 Publishing, 1994.

Ross, Stephen. 'Introduction: Working Class Fictions'. *Modern Fiction Studies* 47:1 (2001): 1–11.

Rubin, Rachel Lee. 'Working Man's Ph.D: The Music of Working Class Studies'. *New Working Class Studies*. eds. John Russo and Sherry Lee Linkon. New York: Cornell University Press, 2005: 166–85.

Russell, Dave. *Popular Music in England 1840–1914*. Manchester: Manchester University Press, 1997.

Sabin, Roger, ed. *Punk Rock: So What?* London: Routledge, 1999.

Savage, Jon. *England's Dreaming: Sex Pistols and Punk Rock*. London: Faber and Faber, 1991.

——. *Time Travel*. London: Vintage, 1997.

Schaeffer, Pierre. 'Acousmatics'. 1966. *Audio Culture: Reading in Modern Music*. eds. Christoph Cox and Daniel Warner. London: Continuum, 2004: 76–81.

Schechner, Richard. *Performance Theory*. 2nd edn. London: Routledge, 1994.

——. *Performance Studies: An Introduction*. London: Routledge, 2002.

Schwarz, David. *Listening Subjects: Music, Psychoanalysis, Culture*. Durham: Duke University Press, 1997.

Searle, John. *Speech Acts: An Essay in the Philosophy of Language*. Cambridge: Cambridge University Press, 1969.

Shields, Rob. *Places on the Margin: Alternative Geographies of Modernity*. London: Routledge, 1991.

Skeggs, Beverley. *Formations of Class and Gender*. London: Sage, 1997.

——. *Class, Self, Culture*. London: Routledge, 2004a.

——. 'The Re-branding of Class: Propertising Culture'. 2004b. *Rethinking Class: Culture, Identities and Lifestyle*. eds. Fiona Devine, Mike Savage, John Scott and Rosemary Crompton. Basingstoke: Palgrave Macmillan, 2005: 46–68.

Solie, Ruth A., ed. *Musicology and Difference: Gender and Sexuality in Music Scholarship*. London: University of California, 1993.

Stefani, Gino. 'Melody: A Popular Perspective'. *Popular Music* 6 (1987): 21–35.

The Story of ... Pulp's Common People. BBC Three. 15 January 2006.

Tate, Joseph, ed. *The Music and Art of Radiohead*. Aldershot: Ashgate, 2005.

Theis, Ryan. 'Popular Music and the Corporate Machine'. 1997. *Perfect Sound Forever*. 21 July 2006 <http://www.furious.com/Perfect/sellout.html>.

Thornton, Anthony. 'Franz Ferdinand: *Franz Ferdinand*'. *NME.COM*. 2004. 4 August 2006 <http://www.nme.com/reviews/franz-ferdinand/7307>.

Thornton, Sarah. 'Understanding Hipness: "Subcultural Capital" as Feminist Tool'. 1995. *The Popular Music Studies Reader*. eds. Andy Bennett, Barry Shank and Jason Toynbee. London: Routledge, 2006: 99–105.

Toop, David. *Ocean of Sound: Aether Talk, Ambient Sound and Imaginary Worlds*. London: Serpent's Tail, 1995.

'Townies Suck, Innit' T-shirt. Advertisement. 29 June 2006 <http://www.smelly-ourmum.com/catalog/product_info.php?products_id=329>.

Toynbee, Jason. 'Introduction to Part Six'. *The Popular Music Studies Reader*. eds. Andy Bennett, Barry Shank and Jason Toynbee. London: Routledge, 2006: 227–30.

Waksman, Steve. *Instruments of Desire: The Electric Guitar and the Shaping of Musical Experience*. Cambridge MS: Harvard University Press, 1999.

Wall, Tim. *Studying Popular Music Culture*. London: Arnold, 2003.

Walser, Robert. *Running with the Devil: Power, Gender and Madness in Heavy Metal Music*. Hanover, NH: Wesleyan University Press, 1993.

'WARNING Townies Give You AIDS' T-shirt. Advertisement. 29 June 2006 <http://www.smellyourmum.com/catalog/product_info.php?cPath=56& products_id=408>.

Warwick, Jacqueline. *Girl Groups, Girl Culture: Popular Music and Identity in the 1960s*. London: Routledge, 2007.

Weber, Max. 'Class, Status and Party'. 1924. *From Max Weber: Essays in Sociology*. eds. Hans H. Gerth and C. Wright Mills. New York: Oxford University Press, 1958: 180–95.

Weedon, Chris. 'Feminism and the Principles of Poststructuralism'. 1987. *Cultural Theory and Popular Culture: A Reader*. ed. John Storey. Harlow: Pearson Education, 2006: 354–66.

'White Punks on Bordiga'. *Uncarved*.org. 1995. 21 June 2006. <http://www.uncarved.org/music/apunk/wpob.html>.

Whiteley, Sheila. 'Repressive Representations: Patriarchy and Femininities in Rock Music of the Counterculture'. *Mapping the Beat: Popular Music and Contemporary Theory*. eds. Thom Swiss, John M. Sloop and Andrew Herman. Oxford: Blackwell, 1998: 153–70.

———. *Women and Popular Music: Sexuality, Identity and Subjectivity*. London: Routledge, 2000.

Williams, Raymond. *Keywords*. London: HarperCollins, 1976.

Wilson, Elizabeth. 'Fashion and Postmodernism'. 1990. *Cultural Theory and Popular Culture: A Reader*. ed. John Storey. 3rd edn. Harlow: Pearson Prentice Hall, 2006: 430–9.

Wright, Erik Olin. *Classes*. London: Verso, 1985.

Zanes, R. J. Warren. 'Too Much Mead? Under the Influence (of Participant-Observation)'. *Reading Rock and Roll: Authenticity, Appropriation, Aesthetics*. eds. Kevin J. H. Dettmar and William Richey. New York: Columbia University Press, 1999: 37–72.

Zweig, Connie. 'The Death of the Self in the Postmodern World'. 1995. *The Fontana Postmodernism Reader*. ed. Walter Truett Anderson. London: Fontana, 1996: 141–6.

Zweig, Ferdynand. *The Worker in an Affluent Society*. London: Heinemann, 1961.

Discography

Blur. *Parklife*. Food Records, 1994.
——. 'Country House'. Food Records, 1995.
——. *The Great Escape*. Food Records, 1995.
The Clash. 'London's Burning'. *The Clash*. Columbia, 1977.
——. 'White Man in Hammersmith Palais'. Columbia, 1978.
——. 'English Civil War'. Columbia, 1979.
——. 'Guns of Brixton'. *London Calling*. Columbia, 1979.
——. 'Lover's Rock'. *London Calling*. Columbia, 1979.
——. 'Rudie Can't Fail'. *London Calling*. Columbia, 1979.
——. 'Spanish Bombs'. *London Calling*. Columbia, 1979.
——. 'One More Dub'. *Sandanista*. Columbia, 1980.
——. *Sandanista*. Columbia, 1980.
Cocteau Twins. *Sunburst and Snowblind EP*. 4AD Records, 1983.
——. 'Persephone'. *Treasure*. 4AD Records, 1984.
——. *Victorialand*. 4AD Records, 1986.
——. *Bluebell Knoll*. 4AD Records, 1988.
——. *Heaven or Las Vegas*. 4AD Records, 1990.
Crass. 'It's the Greatest Working Class Rip Off'. *Christ: The Album*. Crass Records, 1982.
Dale, Dick. 'Miserlou'. Deltone Records, 1962.
Donegan, Lonnie. 'My Old Man's a Dustman'. Pye Records, 1960.
Drake, Nick. *Five Leaves Left*. Island Records, 1969.
——. *Bryter Layter*. Island Records, 1970.
——. *Pink Moon*. Island Records, 1972.
Elastica. 'Connection'. Deceptive Records, 1994.
Fairport Convention. *Liege and Leaf*. Island Records, 1969.
Franz Ferdinand. *Franz Ferdinand*. Domino Records, 2004.
Genesis. *Nursery Cryme*. Charisma Records, 1971.
——. 'Supper's Ready'. *Foxtrot*. Charisma Records, 1972.
Girls Aloud. 'The Sound of the Underground'. Polydor Records, 2002.
Happy Mondays. *Squirrel and G Man 24 Hour Party People Plastic Face Carnt Smile (White Out)*. Factory Records, 1987.
——. *Bummed*. Factory Records, 1988.
——. 'WFL (Wrote for Luck)'. Factory Records, 1988.
——. *Yes Please!* Factory Records, 1992.
Hear'Say. 'Pure and Simple'. Polydor Records, 2001.
The Incredible String Band. *5000 Spirits or the Layers of the Onion*. Island Records, 1967.
——. *The Hangman's Beautiful Daughter*. Island Records, 1968.
John's Children. 'Just What You Want – Just What You'll Get'. Columbia Records, 1967.
Lavigne, Avril. 'Girlfriend'. Columbia Records, 2007.

Levitation. 'Bedlam'. *Firefly EP*. Ultimate, 1991.
Loop. 'Collision'. Chapter 22, 1988.
Lush. *Mad Love EP*. 4AD Records, 1989.
———. *Scar*. 4AD Records, 1989.
———. 'Sweetness and Light'. *Sweetness and Light EP*. 4AD Records, 1990.
M.A.R.R.S. 'Pump up the Volume'. 4AD Records, 1987.
Martyn, John. *London Conversation*. Island Records, 1968.
———. *The Tumbler*. Island Records, 1968.
———. *Bless the Weather*. Island Records, 1971.
———. *Solid Air*. Island Records, 1973.
———. *Grace and Danger*. Island Records, 1980.
The Members. 'The Sound of the Suburbs'. Virgin Records, 1979.
Morrison, Van. *Astral Weeks*. Warners, 1969.
My Bloody Valentine. *This is Your Bloody Valentine*. Tycoon Records, 1985.
———. 'You Made Me Realise'. Creation Records, 1988.
———. 'Soon'. *Glider EP*. Creation Records, 1990.
———. *Loveless*. Creation Records, 1991.
New Model Army. 'Green and Grey'. *Thunder and Consolation*. EMI, 1989.
———. 'Vagabonds'. *Thunder and Consolation*. EMI, 1989.
Nirvana. *Bleach*. Sub Pop Records, 1989.
———. *Nevermind*. DGC Records, 1991.
———. *In Utero*. DGC Records, 1993.
Oasis. 'Cigarettes and Alcohol'. Creation Records, 1994.
———. *Definitely Maybe*. Creation Records, 1994.
———. 'Roll With It'. Creation Records, 1995.
———. *(What's the Story) Morning Glory*. Creation Records, 1995.
———. *Be Here Now*. Creation Records, 1997.
The Pogues. *Rum, Sodomy and the Lash*. Warners, 1985.
———. *If I Should Fall from Grace with God*. Warners, 1988.
The Pogues and The Dubliners. 'The Irish Rover'. Stiff Records, 1987.
Prince. 'I Feel 4 U'. *Prince*. Warners, 1979.
———. 'I Would Die 4 U'. Warners, 1984.
———. 'Money Don't Matter 2 Night'. Paisley Park, 1991.
Pulp. *His 'n' Hers*. Polygram Records, 1994.
———. 'Common People'. Polygram Records, 1995.
Radiohead. *Pablo Honey*. Parlophone, 1993.
———. *The Bends*. Parlophone, 1995.
———. *Kid A*. Parlophone, 2000.
———. *Amnesiac*. Parlophone, 2001.
Rage Against the Machine. *Rage Against the Machine*. Epic Records, 1992.
Ride. *Ride EP*. Creation Records, 1990.
———. *Fall EP*. Creation Records, 1990.
———. *Nowhere*. Creation Records, 1990.
The Rolling Stones. 'Out of Time'. *Aftermath*. Decca Records, 1966.
———. 'Sitting on a Fence'. *Flowers*. Decca, 1967.
———. 'Let it Loose'. *Exile on Main Street*. Decca Records, 1972.
———. 'Tumbling Dice'. Decca Records, 1972.
The Sex Pistols. 'Bodies'. *Never Mind the Bollocks, Here's the Sex Pistols*. Virgin Records, 1977.

Sham 69. 'Hurry up Harry'. Polydor Records, 1978.

———. 'If the Kids are United'. Polydor Records, 1978.

———. 'Hersham Boys'. Polydor Records, 1979.

Sinatra, Frank. *In the Wee Small Hours of the Morning*. Capitol Records, 1955.

Slowdive. 'Catch the Breeze'. *Just for a Day*. Creation Records, 1991.

———. 'Golden Hair'. *Catch the Breeze*. Sanctuary Records, 2004.

The Smiths. 'Hand in Glove'. Rough Trade Records, 1983.

———. 'How Soon is Now?' Rough Trade Records, 1985.

———. 'The Queen is Dead'. *The Queen is Dead*. Rough Trade Records, 1986.

Steeleye Span. 'Gaudete'. Chrysalis Records, 1973.

———. 'All Around My Hat'. Chrysalis Records, 1975.

The Stone Roses. 'So Young'. Thin Line Records, 1985.

———. *The Stone Roses*. Silvertone Records, 1989.

———. 'Made of Stone'. Silvertone Records, 1989.

———. *The Second Coming*. Geffen Records, 1994.

Tyrannosaurus Rex. 'Trelawny Lawn'. *Prophets, Seers and Sages, the Angels of the Ages*. A&M Records, 1968.

The Undertones. 'Jimmy Jimmy'. Sire Records, 1979.

———. 'My Perfect Cousin'. Sire Records, 1979.

Various Artists. *An Anthology of American Folk Music*. Smithsonian Folkways, 1952.

———. *Air Guitar Anthems*. EMI Gold, 2002.

———. *Air Guitar Heaven*. Sony Budget, 2002.

———. *Hairbrush Divas Vol. 1: Music You Just Have to Sing Along to*. WSM, 2003.

———. *Golden Apples of the Sun*. Bastet Records, 2004.

———. *The Roots of Led Zeppelin*. CD Compilation. *Mojo*, August 2004.

———. *The Best of the Best Air Guitar Albums in the World . . . Ever* [Box set]. Virgin TV, 2005.

———. *Folk Off*. Sunday Best Records, 2006.

The Velvet Underground. 'Femme Fatale'. *The Velvet Underground and Nico*. Polydor Records, 1967.

———. 'Heroin'. *The Velvet Underground and Nico*. Polydor Records, 1967.

Westerberg, Paul. 'World Class Fad'. *14 Songs*. Warners, 1993.

Wire. 'Three Girl Rhumba'. *Pink Flag*. Harvest Records, 1977.

Index